A.D. 500

A.D. 500

A Journey Through the Dark Isles
of Britain and Ireland

SIMON YOUNG

Weidenfeld & Nicolson

LONDON

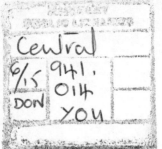

First published in 2005 by Weidenfeld & Nicolson

3 5 7 9 10 8 6 4 2

A CIP catalogue record for this book is available from the British Library.

ISBN 0 297 84805 4

Typeset, printed and bound in Great Britain by Butler and Tanner Ltd, Frome and London

Weidenfeld & Nicolson

The Orion Publishing Group Ltd
Orion House
5 Upper Saint Martin's Lane
London WC2H 9EA

www.orionbooks.co.uk

'And this also has been one of the dark places of the earth.'

Marlow waves his hand across the Thames
Estuary in *Heart of Darkness*

Illustrated by Lawrie Robertson

CONTENTS

PREFACE

AD 500 is concerned with the British and Irish Dark Ages and includes in its pages: massacres; nipple-sucking; saintly ayatollahs; herbal remedies; human sacrifice; bears; wolves; flying ships; boat burials; peculiar haircuts; bizarre forms of Christianity; purple-suited poetry competitions; riddling; tattooed samurai; the siege of Celtic London; and many, many other glimpses of a fascinating but wholly unfamiliar version of these islands. To do full justice to the exuberance of wilder and less orderly times it has been written not as narrative history, but as fictionalised history. This is *not* to say that it is a historical novel, a genre where the author dresses up his characters and ciphers in fancy dress – pirate costumes, Roman togas, Elizabethan drag, what have you – and then allows these to act out a love story or a murder mystery. Here, instead, a series of personalities and episodes have become themselves a way of presenting the British and Irish Dark Ages, in an easily digestible form. The story is a (made-up) sixth-century Byzantine travelogue describing a journey undertaken by several 'civilised' Greeks to the two 'barbaric' islands. But for all that the details and findings of these explorers are placed in a fictional setting, they are 'true' being, in fact, based on the studies of modern linguists, archaeologists and historians; and the reader can, should he or she wish, check these references and the criteria for using them in a series of notes at the end of the book.

Why do this? Why use any form of fiction when pure history is at hand? The simple answer is that there is no straightforward history of sixth-century Britain and Ireland. One cannot write a narrative of the period as one can of the nineteenth century or, indeed, the seventh or the eleventh century over the same territory – not enough evidence survives. And what evidence we do have is buried in texts of incredible

difficulty in languages that almost no one can read; while sup-
plementary material belongs to the even more uncertain fields of
archaeology and linguistics. Though the following pages may not satisfy
professorial standards of history, it is far more gratifying for reader and
author alike to place the little beads of sixth-century knowledge on a
fictional string, than don rubber gloves and forensically isolate them,
putting each in its own sterile museum box.

The fiction, masquerading as Greek travelogue, naturally had to
have sixth-century features. It was an age where pomposity and self-
satisfaction were at an absolute premium and the traveller (that is, the
present author) has tried to convey this in his prose. By our standards
it was a profoundly sexist age; and, for this reason, the explorer –
though not the reader – is always referred to as 'he'. Likewise, though
we are taught not to judge our ancestors, sixth-century Greek writers
thrived on judging, hence the frequent offensive epithets loaded on the
'barbarian' inhabitants of Britain and Ireland. There are also some
changes in terminology. Place names are given in their ancient form:
not least because this allows us to understand what these names originally meant. (Along with other contemporary terms, these are found
in a glossary at the back of the present work.) The ancient English or
Anglo-Saxons – who had just invaded Britain from the Continent in
this period – are described as 'the Saxons' because that was the term
used by their Celtic neighbours and enemies to the west. The ancient
Britons, the ancestors of the Welsh and Cornish are, meanwhile,
referred to as the 'British Celts' to emphasise that they are not the same
as the modern British and that they have a separate identity from the
Irish Celts or Gaels. This is anachronistic in a way that 'Saxon' is not,
but it proves convenient.

The story of a Greek embassy travelling around Britain is based on
a sixth-century fact, though a rather small and uncertain one. Procopius, a Byzantine historian writing in the time of Justinian (527–565),
refers offhandedly to gifts sent to the kings of Britain. Whether or not
the embassy that brought these gifts or other now forgotten Byzantine
messengers ever took seriously the possibility of re-conquering
Britain – as our Greek geographer does – is unknowable. But this was
an age of extraordinary campaigns, as Byzantine armies took back huge
portions of the Roman Empire that had been lost to them, including

the eternal city itself. And that the Byzantines would have viewed Britain as being rightfully theirs need not be doubted: they claimed it in as much as they were the successors of Rome, and, on one occasion, even tried to swap their Britain for Sicily in negotiations with the barbarian! Nor can we wish away the surprisingly large quantities of eastern material that have been found in Britain and Ireland from this period, showing that the two regions were certainly in contact.

The Greeks have been chosen as narrators for two simple reasons. First, because the readership of this text, in never having visited Britain and Ireland, usefully mimic our own armchair curiosity for a distant, unreachable world. And second, because the superior bearing of the Byzantines faced with a series of civilisations that they believed beneath contempt could be twenty-first-century man or woman placed in one of those two islands, c. AD 500. This second point is an uncomfortable one but I hope that even the most passionate relativists would not care or need to contest it after reading through the material amassed here.

The present work would never have been completed without the help of numerous friends, relations and colleagues. I am *extremely* grateful to Ben Buchan, Cristiano Cosentino, Salvatore Costanza, Licia De Benedictis, Danielle Devine, Jon Jackson, Andrew Lownie, Edward and Iris Mullin, Emma Parker, Droo Ray, Lawrie Robertson, Judith and Philip Round, Stuart Spencer, Stephen and Anne Young and, most importantly, my beloved wife Valentina. Noel Burnell first interested me in Britain's Heroic Age almost twenty years ago; I dedicate these pages to his memory: 'My mind to me a kingdom...'.

Santa Brigida, 29 August 2004

INTRODUCTION:
THE DARK ISLES

The Dark Isles, the Pretanic Isles, the Islands of the Earth's End, the Tinny Isles, *Britannia et Hibernia*, Albion and Ierne, the Sacred Isles, the Cannibals' Isles, even, laughingly, the Blessed Isles... For we Byzantines, who dwell in the gentle Mediterranean, Britain and Ireland have proved, by whichever name they travel, a gathering place of wonder, the imagination and, yes, nightmares. And though it is true that contacts between our civilised world and their barbaric archipelago have, through the generations, lapped in and out like the tides that plague the Atlantic coast, it must also be said that we in the court here in Constantinople, even in this the sixth century after our Lord's crucifixion, have never entirely forgotten or lost touch with the last shore of Europe. Indeed, only recently the present writer was honoured to accompany the Imperial household on a rebel-quelling trip in deep Anatolia when these places were called most eloquently to mind. The royal party were standing tensely in a frozen clearing in the late evening while bodyguards were posted – savage ambushes are often worked in the forests there; the wolves gambolled howling in neighbouring valleys and the autumn moon shone so hard and brightly upon us that it seemed to gloat at our exhaustion and cold. It was then that the Emperor of the many-pillared palace in Constantinople turned to the author, whose interests He knows, and heartily said: 'It could almost be Britain!'

1. *Translator's note:* The text is taken from the Greek of Manuscrit Bibliothèque Nationale 12202. To the best of the present writer's knowledge this sixth-century Byzantine work has never before been translated into a modern European language.

It may have been this conversation that led my Royal Master to His most recent project and indirectly to the present work. A month later, back once more in the tallest tower of Constantinople, where I and my assistants work for the Empire's good among the archives and maps, I heard that He of the Holy Face wished me to visit Him. Such an honour – an express invitation to the Emperor's study – had only been granted to me once previously, when I had been asked twenty years before to help plan an embassy to the Dark Isles, a matter to which I will shortly return. And I confess that it was with trepidation that I approached those veiled and guarded quarters in the thousand-roomed palace. But in His presence I was put quickly at my ease. He had called me, He said, not only as His Chief Geographer and Map Maker, but also as the single most renowned Britain and Ireland expert within the bounds of Byzantium. I demurred at this modesty – demanded a few negatives. But I am honoured to say that He insisted on my knowledge. We then talked of the potential wealth of those islands: metals, seabirds, not to mention alcoholic beverages. Of their natives, the four British peoples: the Saxons, the British Celts, the Picts and the Irish. Of their climes: lightning on the Rocks of St Michael, the currents that lead to the north and the short summer nights. Of the sea paths and land paths that can be taken to reach them: the road from Marseilles, the bribes to be paid in the Alps and, of course, the terrifying crossing of Biscay. And I must admit that, after several minutes of such conversation, I began to feel that I was perhaps only the second most learned expert in the Empire.

The question the Emperor insisted upon, in this most interesting interview, was our own rights to these distant lands. Here I removed from my satchel the full dossier that I and my department had prepared many years before on just this theme and read passages to him – I had brought it hoping against hope that this would be the purpose of our interview. For there, in the tangle of my words, was to be found a full description of our contention, nay demand, that Britain and Ireland were rightfully part of our own Empire and would have to be reintegrated as quickly as our resources allowed.

The basis of our claim is as steady as the tower in which I now sit writing. More than half a millennium ago Julius Caesar landed on the island of Britain [55 and 54 BC] and, conquering with his Roman legions, received the submission of the natives; though these soon forgot their humiliation. A century after his time Claudius the Stutterer returned to renew Rome's claim [AD 43], and this time the lesson stuck. Roman proconsuls and administrators occupied the island and began the impossible task of civilising the uncivilisable: one might as well beat moonbeams into horseshoes as domesticate the races who live in those far places. Four hundred years after Claudius had come to the island, and a hundred years or so before the present time, crises on the Continent meant that Britain had to be evacuated by the Romans [c. 410]. Then, a generation later, Gaul and Italy – yes, even sacred Rome – disappeared in a swell of barbarian invasions and rebellions the like of which the world had never known. The only spots of sanity left were our own dear Greece, the Levant and parts of northern Africa. All the territories once held by Rome were now subject to the Byzantine state, the New Rome, and it was not only our right, but our duty, to reassert our rule in the lands that had been ripped from the older empire.[1]

At this the Emperor nodded, but His voice betrayed doubts: doubts that I must say do him credit and give heavy proof of that intelligence for which He is famed. How was it, He sternly asked, that we could lay claim not only to the old Roman province of Britannia, but also to the north of that island, not to mention Ireland where Rome had never ruled? The argument was more complex, I admitted, but nevertheless impossible to gainsay. When our glorious Empire had taken up the Cross as its religion and thrown down the dirty gods and *lares* of our ancestors, we had also taken on the responsibility of protecting those Christians who lived outside our borders. Well, reports have long since proved that the Gospels have reached even Ireland: I described here an Italian acquaintance who, in his youth, had worked in the Irish missions, baptising the unclean Gael. At this the Emperor nodded enthusiastically: Ireland would be ours. But there were still some Imperial questions. Had, He asked searchingly, Christianity even reached the most barbarous of the barbarous world-enders in the far north of

1. *Translator's note:* The Byzantines, in fact, referred to themselves as the *Romanoi*, identifying totally with the Roman Empire out of which they had grown. And in the early sixth century Byzantine armies pulled back many of the lost lands of the older empire in Spain, northern Africa and Italy.

Britain and in the Orcades [the Orkneys]? This I granted was not the case. But there our rule would be based not on a desire to protect Christians. No. It would be built on our desire to create them and, of course, to wipe out forever the filthy heathen deities from the north as they were wiped away in our own homelands, to the greater glory of God.

For many a minute I had talked with the enthusiasm known only to the willing servant. But now it was my Master's turn. He began to discourse on the future: of the dangers of travel to Britain; of the difficulty of bringing the right number of troops there to effect a conquest; of the need first to extend our recent victories in Spain; and many other things that showed His statecraft. Finally, He set out how He intended to send, under the cover of diplomacy, various spies to the two islands to assess potential allies and to prepare – if the fortunes of war should shine further to the south – an invasion.

A powerful sadness spread inside me on listening to these words as I knew that, because of my age, I would never be allowed to join such a mission, much though I wanted to, for, after a lifetime studying these islands at a distance, I had always hoped to visit them. But I also knew that I could assist in other ways and as the Emperor continued to talk of Britain and Ireland and our general ignorance of the conditions ruling in both, I, carelessly, He, by design, came simultaneously to the same word: 'a guide'. A guide! It would be a fitting culmination to almost sixty years in the Imperial map room and a lifetime's reading among the itineraries and descriptions of an earlier age. I would set out in practical terms – and with Imperial funding – a lantern made of words that the traveller would swing before him in the dark of the Dark Isles!

My voice trembling, I told His Royal Eminence that I had long since been asked to write, by one of His mediocre predecessors, an almost identical work for another Byzantine group that had visited Britain and Ireland. Twenty years ago that embassy had similarly been sent off with the aim of testing the loyalty of the world-enders to our Imperial cause and of spying out the terrain over which any invasion would be made. But in that case there had been no time to finish the work and I had had to give what advice I could in a series of lessons to the chosen party. In fact, my only material contribution had been a small codex that I myself had carefully made for them to write their observations in, a kind of log.

'And what happened to this ill-prepared embassy?'

'Your Majesty, that particular group – there were twelve in the party – was never heard of again. They disappeared into the innards of Britain like sheep being sucked down into a bog. Nothing was left of them, not a sign, not a mark, not a name.'

But how wonderful to be corrected by royal sentence, to be made foolish by His wisdom! Smiling mischievously, this Lord of forty million, the regal head of the reborn and eternal Rome produced out of the litter on His desk a warped and small book, a little larger than a Parthian's hand.

'But it is strange, Geographer, surely, that nothing was found. After all this party of twelve took with them a book, a log that they were ordered to fill in every day, one that you yourself had made. This same log, or was I told wrongly, had an instruction written in Greek, Latin and Syriac, promising that if it were to be brought back to the royal court here in Constantinople, then its weight in gold would be given in exchange. Did you really think that this codex would have disappeared into the night of history?'

I confess that I could hardly keep my eyes from the small book in front of me: a book that looked suspiciously like the one that, twenty years previously, I had bound together for those twelve men and their dangerous mission to Britain and Ireland. But I had to reply.

'Your Most Royal Majesty, I have often thought of the log you described and have hoped that somehow... But so many are illiterate there among the barbarians that I suspected that it had been thrown away or burnt by an ignorant bandit or slaver.'

The Emperor handed the small volume over to me.

'It came on a ship from Sardinia: an eastern merchant who has concerns in Tours somehow turned it up there. Use it extensively, Geographer. Lessons were learnt in this voyage – I have flicked through its pages myself – and, though much needs to be cut away, and some is illegible, it is an important resource. Unless I am very much mistaken this will be your key in writing the guide that will serve for the reconquest of the Dark Isles.'

Our work done, I bowed low and began to remove myself with care from His Highness's presence as one might a lash from the eye. But I was smiling. The codex had come home to its maker.

It has taken me almost five months to write the guide that I promised that day and I dedicate it not, as others who have helped me suggested that I should, to the conquest of Britain and Ireland. (That I believe is inevitable and can be found in the very grain of our national history: a manifest destiny that dwarfs and contains us.)[1] I dedicate it rather to my High Imperial Majesty who, in His greatness, governs these lands with wisdom and who ordered fifty-five copies of this work to be made on manuscript and one copy for His private quarters, divided into three papyrus rolls. And, as a tribute to Him, my guide is split into fifteen chapters, to represent the fifteen years that He has ruled over us: the first a general description, the remaining fourteen accounts of the different parts of the two islands, using, as He insisted, the record of the embassy as our principal source. We have made these divisions, for, if there is one lesson to be learnt from the twelve's harrowing trip – and my reading in their log has been extensive – it is that there is not one version of the Dark Isles. Instead, there are many Britains and Irelands and moving twenty leagues to the north, thirty miles to the west, or even a mere valley to the south the explorer will find different tribes, different customs and different languages.

(II) BACKGROUND

What have the books of the ancients and more recent informants such as the scrawled pages of the log to tell us of those distant worlds of Ireland and Britain? There is little that is sure, nothing that is certain. But some facts, at least, we have been able to gather together and collect in one place for future travellers. We know, for example, that observed from the heavens Britain, the larger of the Dark Isles, would appear as a colossal isosceles triangle in the blue of the sea, with the short edge being its broad southern coast. From this wide line of rock and sand to

---

1. *Translator's note:* Clearly, our author was over-confident here. Even the Byzantine conquests in Italy and Spain proved transitory. Greek armies certainly never reached Britain and Ireland.

the northern tip there are almost eight hundred miles of contoured, packed and for the most part wooded earth. We know that its sister Ireland, meanwhile, runs alongside the length of Britain, and though smaller in size stretches so far to the south that it comes almost level with Spain.[1] We know too that the islands are not entirely bereft of wealth. In fact, these insular twins gorge themselves on sea riches. Their fish – especially British salmon – are well known for their succulence; and seals, dolphins and even whales are cut up on their shorelines. Pearl fishing is undertaken and green, red, violet, purple but mostly white spheres prised from out of shells – the voyager could do worse than fill his packs and pockets with these. The whelk that produces a reddish dye can be found in rockpools and is used to colour the rough textiles that the inhabitants make. Then even in the dangerous, forested interiors beyond cloud-capped mountains and swampy plains treasures, it is said, can still be teased out by the cautious explorer. Precious metals, above all tin, are mined in the south-west, though the increasing number of Mediterranean trading ships that visit these places makes bargains difficult. Dogs in Ireland and horses in Britain are bred with success; slaves are regularly exported from the southern markets of the smaller island. And the locals have produced some needlework that has gone beyond their borders to win an almost European fame, including the *birrus* or British woven coat.[2]

Most travellers get to grips easily enough with the geographical basics of life among the world-enders. But they then confess themselves lost when it comes to the races that live there. We have some sympathy here, for certainly the larger island is a mad mosaic of different cultures and strains of barbarism. It was not always so. In ancient days there was only one people that lived in Britain: the Britons or British Celts, first enemies and finally friends of the Roman. However, these proved to be weak in war not only against the legions, but also against their more warlike neighbours. Already in Roman times, but like a plague after the legions had been withdrawn from this island a century and

1. *Translator's note:* Britain's triangular shape and Ireland's southern position close to Spain are ancient fallacies that had evidently still not been dismissed by the sixth century.
2. *Translator's note:* Unfortunately no example of this quintessential item of early British clothing survives, but it seems to have resembled a duffel coat.

more ago, three enemies appeared on the horizon. In the west, the Irish, who had long since held their own island, attacked and captured portions of the west coast of Britain. In the upper part of the island, the Picts came out of the Arctic mists to take much of the north. And then, in the east, the Saxons, a Germanic people, sailed over the Atlantic waves laying claim to much of the eastern coast and even parts of the rich interior. The British Celts, proving unable to stand and fight, fled, meanwhile, to mountain fastnesses, which they used in their desperation, while others of this people took to the seas and, sailing from their enemies, disembarked in distant lands including Gaul and Spain where they set up colonies that still thrive today.[1] These invasions and confusions took place over a hundred years ago and a more stable situation now prevails in the north and west. The Picts have made their peace with the British Celts. And the Irish too have come to a distrusting truce with their old enemies: this after they had been driven out of much of Britain. However, the Saxons still despise the British Celts and continue to conquer and rout the natives from their settlements in the centre of the island, while the British Celts reciprocate this hatred, relishing it with ambushes and raids. [See map of Ireland and Britain divided into four peoples.]

We have heard from many authorities that there are five languages that are spoken by these four peoples: their respective native tongues and Latin. The reader may think that Latin has survived as a language of state among the British Celts from Roman times. And in some very few cases this is so, especially in the British-Celtic enclaves in the valley of the Thames. But for the most part Latin is spoken in the west only as the language of the Church. However, be warned before wading in with a *salve* here and a *rara avis* there. The Saxons and Picts are not only ignorant of the tongue, but they even affect a hatred of it and of all who speak 'the Roman'. As far as the vernaculars are concerned

---

1. *Translator's note:* It is worth here reminding the reader that the Irish or Gael are the distant descendants of the modern inhabitants of Scotland (which in this period did not exist) and Ireland. The Picts disappeared from history in the ninth and tenth centuries. The British Celts are the ancestors of the Welsh, Cornish and Bretons. Then, finally, the Saxons are the first English. The use of 'Saxon' by our Greek writer, instead of 'Angles' or the even more familiar 'Anglo-Saxons' is interesting. He had clearly got the term from the Celts who have always referred to the Germanic invaders from the east in this way: see, for example, modern Welsh *Sais* (Englishman).

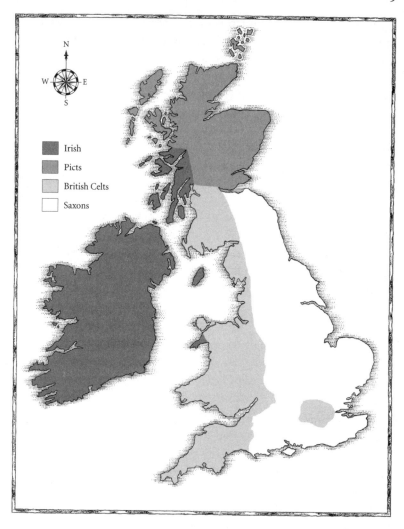

Saxon, meanwhile, is something of an amalgam of various Germanic languages from the north-west of Europe: any traveller who has had experience negotiating with the Emperor's German mercenaries should have no problem in learning one of its dialects. The two Celtic tongues – British-Celtic and Irish – are also close to each other, so much so that the speaker of one can understand many of the words of the other. Then Pictish, spoken in the northern tip of that isosceles of Britain, defies definition. And, though we will describe some of its mysteries later and speculate too on its origins, we assert here that it will prove impossible to learn and that a translator (and a heavy bodyguard) is necessary for any travel in the bereft regions where the woaded ones live.

Finally, the traveller will find only two religions in the Dark Isles: Christianity and the various deformations of heathenism. The British Celts were originally converted to the Cross in the times of the Empire. And even as they were being attacked by the Irish in the west, they undertook the conversion of that people, while some of their missionaries slipped out and banged gospels over the Picts' hard heads. The result is that today almost all British Celts and Gaels and, in the south of their realm, a respectable quantity of Picts profess the Christian faith – though, as we will soon see, with frequent misunderstandings and stupidities. However, a fraction of the Irish and British Celts, not to mention the bulk of the Picts and almost every man, woman and child of the Saxons, follow instead the older traditions and sacrifice in blood to devils.

(III) AUTHORITY, LAW AND HARASSMENT

If a visitor from, for example, India were to arrive in our Empire today and say 'take me to your leader' to a citizen in the eastern provinces, there would be no difficulty. He would be shunted up the Imperial hierarchy, taken first to the local military commander, then to the provincial governor and then by swift transport down the roads that lead to the palaces of Constantinople. There, after a suitable wait, he would be presented to His Imperial Highness, the Emperor, in the sacred bounds of the mechanised throne room.[1] However, go to Britain and ask the same question – granted, that is, that you can communicate with one of the natives – and you will have a shock. For the peasant who in this instant takes you on the first step of your journey will take you himself to the insular equivalent of our glorious reception hall,

---

1. *Translator's note:* The Byzantine Emperor in this period sat on a mechanised throne that would rise in front of any barbarian embassies that came to visit him.

that is to the ditches and mud walls that surround the local chief's home. We say 'chief'. Most of these 'chiefs' would, in fact, call themselves kings. And, though this will be a surprise to the Byzantine citizen, there is no single ruler in Britain or Ireland. There are not even four great kings that represent the four peoples. Instead, there is a multitude of smaller regional lords who rule over a few valleys, a mountain range and, these being islands, a stretch of beach. It is for this reason that the embassy of twenty years ago spent so long in the Dark Isles, for they had to visit most of the two hundred or so kingdoms there and often traipsed uselessly back and forth across mountains and hills.

The first task in legitimising your presence in a territory should always be to find that territory's king. But how do you go about doing that? Travellers to the southern half of Britain make one mistake again and again while looking for royal courts. They fatally search out the most impressive Roman remains in the area and start walking towards mortared walls. However, the explorer needs to remember that Roman rule in the island ended over a hundred years ago and that, with the lonely exception of the Thames enclaves, where British-Celtic populations remain ensconced in what were once Roman cities, everything Roman has long since been abandoned. It does not matter whether you go to the shore forts on the eastern coast, once respectable cities like Eboracum [York] and Camulodunum [Colchester], or the villas of the plains. These centres and buildings have been deserted now through the span of living memory. And while the British Celts, whose great-grandparents dwelt within their protected perimeters, retain some respect for their architecture and ambition, the other peoples of the islands despise and fear them as the homes of giants or ghosts. Even a visit to such a site might frighten the locals into lynch mobs or, at least, lead to unwelcome arrest and confinement. Instead, the best place to find the home of the king is to search out the highest and steepest hill in the area, for, since Roman civilisation was expunged from Britain, the British Celts have returned to the hillforts occupied by their ancestors centuries before and their dykes and moats have been settled and laid round with spearmen and sentries. To our eyes, these strongholds – some are also built on coastal islands or cliffs – are hardly impressive: when the Roman armies first came to the island in Claudius's reign a legion usually took the early part of an afternoon to batter one into submission and that was five hundred years ago. But we advise the traveller to always find something to be amazed at, for the locals have a touching attachment to their wattle palaces.

The seat of the king is also very often the site where justice is given and punishments carried out. It is impossible to generalise about the legal customs of the Dark Isles, for each people has its own rules. And, to see the extent of this variety, one has only to think of, say, the status of women in the different kingdoms. So among the Saxons a woman has little greater status than that of an object in the gift of her husband or father; among the Picts, on the other hand, women have a status not on a par with, but closer to, that of a man. British-Celtic and Irish women, meanwhile, stand somewhere between their eastern and northern sisters in terms of their legal rights.

One thing, however, that all four peoples have in common is the *wergild*, to give it its Saxon name. In this barbaric and curious system every individual is given his price, so, for example, a peasant might be worth one gold coin and a king one hundred. Though customs vary, this value is used to determine how much should be paid in the case of insult or injury. It also means that one with a higher *wergild* can outswear one with a lower social status. As the embassy found out twenty years ago, this system has one disastrous and obvious consequence for the outsider: the explorer will have a low or non-existent value. The solution? Always seek out the protection of a powerful man on arrival and so increase both your *wergild* and your likelihood of surviving a trip through the wilds of the country. And should the worst happen and a band of natives turn to violence? If you cannot boast the protection of a local potentate, remember, at least, this: the inhabitants of Britain and Ireland associate foreigners with riches. They are unlikely to eat, sacrifice or otherwise misuse you until they know that a ransom is either not forthcoming, or so small as not to be worth their while.

(IV) PACKING

We are often asked how large a mule train is needed for trips into the British and Irish hinterlands, a question that we invariably respond to with an indulgent smile. The heavier the load that is carried, the more it will be weighed down by the island rains, while the longer the line of trotting beasts the more bandits and local warlords-turned-taxmen will collect in your wake. It is far better to keep luggage at one sack per traveller and to accept that much of the journey will be made without even a lame horse to bear your provisions. We say this, for these beasts are so rare in parts of the islands that, for example, in the Orcades [the Orkneys], some of the population run screaming before them; while in other regions, such as the swamps of the east, the beast itself becomes a burden to the harassed traveller and has to be practically carried. We also advise the serious explorer to gather only a small group of not more than ten including slaves, translators, guides and any dogsbodies or factotums that are picked up along the way. The previous embassy sometimes had as many as twenty in their party and risked being qualified as a hostile warrior band, for large numbers of foreigners are inevitably looked at with suspicion, especially in the areas where war is endemic.

Instead, the ideal group should include five individuals, where at least three have good spoken Latin – a language that is, as we have mentioned, sometimes understood among the British Celts and in the Irish monasteries. Naturally, muscle is also needed and we suggest here that another member of this small party be a mercenary picked from the Emperor's army. And, as there are large numbers of northern barbarians who serve in our forces, we would advise taking one who knows something of the Saxon tongue. As for dress, the party should wear, at the beginning of their trip at least – clothes rarely last long under the conditions encountered there – sailors' trousers and shirts. These prove warm, resistant to water and, in the more civilised parts of the island, they will suggest to the locals that the small group before them are innocuous merchants.

For the contents of the pack we, meanwhile, counsel six items:

(1) A change of clothes, possibly more formal dress for introductions in court, but with material long enough to serve as a blanket during the cold British and Irish nights.

(2) Gifts – teak music boxes, gold rings in the Byzantine style, incense, inscribed spoons – to give to regional chiefs: we have already insisted on the importance of visiting local strongmen.

(3) Some 'exotic' items – Sicilian shells, silk scraps, coral, bronze

coins – that will impress the simpler people and that can be given as presents or used, thrown on the ground, to disperse crowds.

(4) A good all-service knife that is long enough to wield as a weapon, but can, if checked by guards, pass as a kitchen utensil. We suggest purest iron, for this is said to frighten the *sid* or fairy beasts that plague the Dark Isles.

(5) Dried rations for emergencies: meat pellets, hard cheese, protein-rich sheep droppings and stale bread. The most important requirement is that victuals should be able to survive a heavy soaking.

(6) Last, but by no means least, this book, placed in a snug, watertight wooden container.

The reader may be surprised by the absence of fire-making equipment from this list. In fact, we have decided to advise against tinder of any sort on the basis of the embassy's experience twenty years ago. This, it seems, is just the sort of material that is pilfered by border guards. And, if the traveller finds no habitation from which he may borrow fire, then he can be sure that he is in a dangerous neighbourhood and that a blaze would only draw unwelcome attention to himself.

(V) GETTING THERE

There is only one way to get to the Dark Isles and that is by sea. It is for the traveller, however, to decide just how long he will spend on the waves. If he takes the route up the Dalmatian coast, through the Alpine passes and then along the Rhine there will only be the short, but frequently bumpy, North Sea crossing to endure. On the other hand, if he follows the route across Gaul, he will have to add to this time at sea three or four weeks in the Mediterranean on one of the boats that leads to the port of Marseilles. A third possibility is a journey entirely at sea, indeed, some who take this route boast that they do not put their feet on dry land from when they leave Constantinople until they reach Britain. Boats from Byzantine ports typically set out in early spring, calling at Sicily or northern Africa, passing through the Gates of Hercules [Straits of Gibraltar] and then crawling up the Atlantic coast of Spain. Finally, in early summer, they make the crossing of Biscay – the

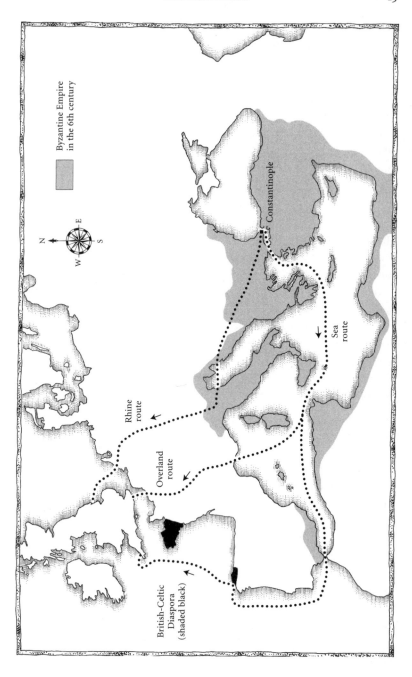

Byzantine Empire
in the 6th century

Constantinople

Sea
route

Rhine
route

Overland
route

British–Celtic
Diaspora
(shaded black)

most dangerous part of the voyage – landing in either southern Ireland or more commonly the region of Britain they call Dumnonia [Cornwall and Devon].

What can be said for and against these different routes? The first, that on the Rhine, has little to recommend it. It is true that some traders still follow these old paths, but only ones with contacts among the Germanic-speaking peoples, who live north of the Alps and who jealously guard the Rhine's long course. Indeed, it has even been suggested that some parts of this waterway are more dangerous than the Dark Isles themselves! We would not go this far, though these are certainly among the more perilous regions of Continental Europe – the ghosts of slaughtered Roman legionaries are said to haunt the forests that line that black river. But, unless the traveller has a precise mission in Britain near the waterway that the Britons call the Humber, which has much contact with the region around the mouth of the Rhine, we find nothing favorable to say about this particular path across Europe. It is certainly the slowest of the three, needing six months to negotiate and bribe the various tribal peoples in ancient Germania.

The second possibility, the trans-Gaul route, can be used the whole year round, for even in the winter months, when the Alpine passes are blocked, a ship captain would probably be found to ferry loyal servants of the Emperor as far as Marseilles. The old Roman roads are still operational and crossing Gaul can take as little as eight weeks out of bandit season and, on fast horses, the journey could be made even more quickly. A lot depends, however, on the situation in the territories north of the Loire, where there are regular conflicts between the various members of the Merovingian dynasty, who lay claim to this region. And so violently and unexpectedly do these bouts of royal bloodletting explode that the traveller preparing to leave Constantinople can have no hope of knowing what he will discover once he actually arrives there. We might also say against this route that the ports of the Franks further to the north bring their ships across to the south-eastern tip of Britain, the most barbarous of all British territories.

Personally, we favour the third option: the long-drawn-out sea journey. Three or four months at sea may not excite the explorer, who wishes to make his name on land. But, as long as a trip in spring fits the timetable of a mission, then it is the quickest way to get to the Dark

Isles. The traveller should search out a berth on one of the Britain-bound traders that two or three times a year set out from Syria, Egypt and even our own city: the merchant captains of these vessels have large overheads and welcome fare-paying passengers. We concede, and we believe no one would deny, that the crossing of Biscay – with winds and snaking monsters – is dangerous, but no less so than the long Rhine valley. And, it is also preceded by a pleasant rest on the temperate coast of Galicia in north-western Spain, while the journey itself is over in three days, when the boat puts in at one of the premier British ports, Tintagel. Do not, however, underestimate the dangers of the crossing even in full summer! Ignatios, the translator of the original Byzantine embassy, was washed overboard in this body of water, becoming in the process the first casualty of that ill-fated party. If rope is available – and if it is not be sure to procure some before leaving Galicia – tie yourself down in any stormy weather!

We have one last, and, we trust, helpful note to the explorer taking either the Marseilles or round-Spain route. As we have already had cause to mention, the British Celts have suffered much in the last decades, and, as we have seen, some of their number, fleeing from their homelands in a many-starred diaspora, came to Gaul and Spain and set up colonies there. And whereas the British-Celtic world in Roman times included almost all of Britain, it has now fragmented into a chain of kingdoms that stretch from the lake they call Lomond in the north all the way down the west of Britain, to the new kingdoms of the diaspora in Armorica [Brittany] and Britonia in Spain [northern Galicia and Asturias]. The cunning traveller can use this chain to his own advantage, for the British Celts are the most friendly of all the world-enders to the Emperor's cause and if they are sufficiently praised as being good Romans they may help voyagers. This is true for the boats about to cross Biscay: indeed, sailors there have long relied on the hospitality and the knowledge of the Spanish Britonians. But the British Celts who live in north-western Gaul [the Bretons] have also been known to ferry Imperial messengers out to Britain. However, be warned: their fear of the Saxons means that they will not even consider putting into port until they are west of Vectis [the Isle of Wight].

The reader, the author and, we hope, the future traveller will now be ready to set out on their own journey to the Dark Isles. And we will delay our departure for only some moments more to remember the ghosts that follow and precede us on our trip: the twelve Greeks who twenty years ago travelled through those north-western regions of Europe. These men, doomed for the most part, were given two instructions on leaving Constantinople: the first, to make contact with the scores of kings that rule in Britain and Ireland, lavishing on them rich gifts; and the second, to record any information that might assist in a later Byzantine invasion. And, as a result, they walked, for more than a year, around the islands searching out wonders, mysteries and the two hundred or so monarchs that rule in those barbaric places. Their failures were legion and often fatal. But they made one undeniably correct decision, a decision with which we will finish our introductory advice: their itinerary once arrived in the islands. With uncharacteristic wisdom, the party had paid for twelve places on a trading ship crossing Biscay and so landed, as do most boats that take that path, on the Dumnonian peninsula. They did this reasoning that a clockwise journey around the Dark Isles, up the west coast of Britain, across to Ireland and then back down the east coast of the larger island, would allow them to adjust gradually to the peculiarities of the world-enders. And they were right, for theirs was effectively a trip of decline from something approaching civilisation in the south-west, to barbarity in Ireland, to sub-barbarity in the far north, to utter bestiality in savage Cant [Kent]. We can recommend their route wholeheartedly and it is, in fact, the one on which we will now ourselves embark.

PART I

CORNWALL AND WALES:
THE BRITISH CELTS

THE SOUTH-WEST OF BRITAIN:
'THE LAND OF THE BRITISH METAL'

(I) SCILLY ISLES

The traveller who has wisely taken the sea paths to the Dark Isles should expect to arrive there in early summer. And, the sea monsters and squalls of Biscay behind him, he will wake one morning, on board the small vessel that for three months has been his home, to find Britain rearing out of the northern seas, its rocky coasts shrouded in that mist that makes navigation so dangerous there. What can the visitor expect here at the ends of the earth? There are, of course, as many opinions as there are adventurers. But one author has painted with words a most pleasing portrait of our destination, one that we think worth quoting as a provocation: 'Like the bride elect', this author writes,

> hung over with blindingly bright jewellery, Britain is made beautiful by long plains and perfectly matched hills well suited to crops; while its mountains contain different pastures and – like a painting – many different coloured flowers are dotted over these same peaks. To water the island there are crystalline streams full of snowy-white pebbles that are pushed slowly seawards and there are, too, wonderful rivers that murmur in the ear of the traveller and whose flow promises golden dreams to those who lie down on their banks and then there are also lakes full of endlessly fresh, cold, deep water.

We confess to admiring greatly the style of this description, but we can hardly agree with its substance. It would be a foolish and soon-to-be-dead traveller that lay down to sleep next to a stream in bandit-infested Britain; and, of its glacial mountains, its leprous heaths and bogs, not to mention its dirty, sulphurous puddles and ponds, there seems no end. The truth is that this island marks not only the edge of the world geographically, but also in spirit. Its people are wild and Britain's harsh landscape conspires against any kind of progress in human affairs, stunting those born there. Indeed, even under the civilising, maturing influence of Roman rule – four hundred years of Roman rule no less – Britain's sum contribution to Europe was a heretic, a bad poet and three mutinous generals.[1]

The traveller, however, may wish to reserve judgement until he arrives in the island and that brings us to the crucial question of a hospitable port. For this we strongly recommend Tintagel in the land of the Dumnonians [Cornwall and Devon], the extreme south-western peninsula of the island. Here we follow the advice of the Mediterranean traders to Britain who, crossing Biscay, always carefully navigate for the Dumnonian coastline. Their choice is a wise one for Dumnonia, as the kingdom is called, is the richest and among the least barbarous corners of dark Britain, much accustomed to visitors from the civilised world.

Dumnonia's wealth and its, at least by British standards, civilisation depend on one fact: tin or, as others call it, white lead, that substance on which so many of our Greek industries are based. Alone in the island and, indeed, alone in Europe the kingdom has sufficient quantities of this precious material to justify mining. It is for this reason that we also name tin 'the British metal' and that many of the traders know Dumnonia as 'the land of the British metal'. Certainly nothing but tin or gold could tempt Greek and Egyptian ships so far north. And so – loaded down with cargoes of olives, honey, walnuts, oil, spices and, of course, Italian wine – Mediterranean adventurers gamble their fortunes and their lives on the crossing of Biscay.

---

1. *Translator's note:* The 'bad poet' referred to here is probably the fourth-century Romano-Briton Silvius Bonus, none of whose work survives, but who was roundly condemned by his contemporaries. The heretic we must suppose was another Briton, Pelagius, whose faith in grace led him into conflict with Augustine and, indirectly, Jerome. The rebellious generals, meanwhile, are probably the three – Marcus, Gratian and Constantine III – who led, one after another, the revolt of 407–9 against the Emperor Honorius. They used Britain as their base.

These ships' captains never land on the southern coast of Dumnonia for the people there have a reputation for wrecking and piracy: these would spill any amount of blood for a carafe of alcoholic beverage. The traveller should follow their counsel and, keeping a sensible distance from the treacherous shores, veer, instead, west along the coast till he comes to Sillina [the Scilly Isles], an island off the extreme tip of Britain; from there it is less than a day's good sailing to the stronghold of Tintagel that stands on the northern flank of the peninsula. The Dumnonians claim that this island of Sillina was once connected to the mainland, but was separated from it by a catastrophic flood that drowned a kingdom – divine punishment for a woman's licentiousness, it seems. This sounds to us like one of their famous Celtic fairy tales, but certainly the waters here are wild and the shores of both mainland and island unstable.[1] In Roman times Sillina was a prison island and even today its population is different from that of the mainland. Many speak Spanish Latin, for Iberian heretics – followers of the despicable Priscillian[2] – were sent there to live out their lives in a place where their words and demons could do no harm. Then later these same Priscillianists, forgetting their precepts against carnal knowledge, bred with the locals, perpetuating themselves. We mention this, not to tempt the reader to Sillina, but rather to satisfy his curiosity so that he might avoid landing on the isle entirely. There is no point whatsoever in a visit for this hump of rock has the economy and lawfulness that one would expect of an ex-penitentiary. The traveller is, instead, again advised to continue his journey along the northern coast of the peninsula to celebrated Tintagel. No matter how brackish his water or low his food supplies, he should not consider docking until he reaches its safety.

1. *Translator's note:* The sea was indeed unstable at this date – and becoming more so. In the sixth century 'Scilly' was a single island; then, soon after, the incursions of the ocean made it into the archipelago that we know today. The chief study of the early medieval Scilly Isles is called, significantly, *Exploration of a Drowned Landscape* (Charles Thomas, 1985).
2. *Translator's note:* Priscillian was a Spaniard who introduced gnostic and apocryphal elements into Iberian Christianity as well as insisting on an exceptional ascetic rigour. He was executed for heresy in 385 and some of his supporters exiled to Sillina.

(II) TINTAGEL

Even in the Mediterranean Tintagel's cliffy bulk has a certain fame and the first sight of it, coming in on a sleek trader, clouds rolling off the heights and shouts from the sentries, is a memory that will likely stay with you through all your days. Indeed, one has the impression that Nature was a warrior, so carefully has she sculpted this rock fortress for a warrior's needs – and through much of the year it swarms with soldiers like an ants' nest. It is, in fact, a demi-island that is attached by an umbilical cord to the shore and that is reached by a simple but easily defended neck of land. All around the coast is rugged and inaccessible and the sailor can only dock on Tintagel at one point: the Iron Gate. No wonder that the Dumnonians hold this their chief settlement and that some ignorant sailors call it the 'capital of Britain'.

If Tintagel is a work of Nature's art, then man has, however, botched its decoration. The British Celts who live there are not great builders. And though they have worked on the natural defences admirably, creating huge artificial platforms, they have also thrown up monstrous habitations instead of the palace that this site cries out for. The king's court is a timber shack, something approximating in size and finish to one of our royal stables. And Tintagel's chapel has gaps in its wall so large that the candles are perpetually blown out by salty sea winds, while at its door there is an incorrectly written Latin inscription, left no doubt with the hope of impressing the Mediterranean visitor.

The traders who arrive in Britain have a boast. They say that they have never stepped on British shores unless on Tintagel. And this we have tested many times talking to such voyagers as we have met – indeed, their ignorance of the land they visit is astounding. On Tintagel, the traders say, all is provided for their delight. The tin is hauled there in ingots so their bartering can be done on the spot.[1] And their ships are protected from the Atlantic breakers by Tintagel Bay. Why, they ask, do they need to cross the neck of land into the interior and so risk their lives? They have a point. For 'the Syrians', as the Dumnonians call all traders from the Mediterranean, Tintagel is a kind of Isle of the

---

1. *Translator's note:* No ingots have yet been found by archaeologists on Tintagel. However, the peninsula is littered with the smashed fragments of Mediterranean carafes from the 'Syrian' ships that traded there.

Blessed. It is a voyage completed, a cargo sold, and a few days of safety before the return to the ocean, where they can enjoy the local speciality, *med* [mead], an alcoholic beverage that is made of honey, but that carries a peculiarly satisfying bitter aftertaste.

The traveller must not be surprised if he does not meet the king of the Dumnonians on Tintagel. We write this for the Dumnonians' kings and, indeed, all the kings of the British Celts, are itinerant, that is to say that they have no fixed residence. They have, instead, a series of courts that they call *lys* and they move from one to another, feasting with their warriors until the local food supplies are all but gone. Tintagel is though the *penlys*, 'the chief court' of the Dumnonians, and it is there that the king spends most of the winter months. Indeed, much trouble is taken to guarantee supply of all the relevant goods through this period, especially drinking water, which is not available in any quantity at the fortress.

The embassy of twenty years ago met the king in his hall on Tintagel in the late spring as he was preparing to leave. There is much that we can say of the strange habits of the monarchs of Dumnonia. But the most noted, and the most important for any newcomer to the kingdom, is the story that all Dumnonian kings are descended from a woman who coupled with a donkey. This may seem an unimportant and rather absurd detail, but it has important consequences. The Dumnonians are convinced that their king has donkey ears and, as tradition dictates that the king must wear a heavy crown that hides his ears, the rumour gains ever more strength. We tell this tale here not for its humour, but because it is easy to offend the king by looking too closely at this crown. Indeed, he believes that any who examine his head are searching out proof of his donkey ancestry and men have been thrown from the highest point of Tintagel for far less. For those who do not believe the king's sensitivity on this point we need only report the gaffe of the embassy. Our Emperor had sent to the Dumnonian king some valuable brooches, one of which had, to the mortification of the court, a horse sculpted on it, the design of which – strange to their barbarian eyes – was taken as an ass! For some days the embassy was in disgrace and the king, unsteady with rage, refused to see them.

The name of the king at the time of the embassy was Constantine, a singularly bad-tempered oaf, who drank far too much *med*. We have since heard, through the traders accustomed to visit these places, that Constantine has died and that another now rules in his place – his name we do not know. However, we recount here too a second incident that took place at the court while the embassy was there and that will be instructive for travellers. A little after the embarrassing donkey episode described above, a holy man pushed his way into the king's hall in a furious tantrum. Rather than come smilingly to the king, on his knees or at least bowing, this lunatic had shouted his way on to the peninsula barging past petrified guards and sentries. We will soon see that the Christianity of the British Celts has strange elements. But it is worth emphasising immediately that one feature of this strangeness is that their holy men are held in such awe that they can get away with almost anything.

This odorous individual – he was a monk from a monastery where evidently there was no running water – caused all the court to flinch with terror and, extraordinary to relate, their king, Constantine, tried to hide from him. An emperor of Byzantium would have had any man who dared to speak out of turn decapitated on the spot, be he bishop or diplomat, commoner or noble. But, though Constantine would have had no fear of another king, he ran like a child from this ecclesiastical thug. Finally cornered, he wept as the holy dervish screamed into his ear all kinds of imprecations. It seems that Constantine had become bored with his wife, putting her away and that he had personally killed some adolescent rivals to the throne on a church altar: the business, in short, of kings in all ages and at all times. But the monk continued with a preacher's voice, saying that Constantine was the 'executioner of his own soul', the carrier 'of the bitter vine of the men of sodom', the eater of 'the filthy food of sin' and much, much more in this vein.

We report this partly so the traveller knows the strange ways of the British Celts – horsewhipping British clerics would be inappropriate, however extreme their actions and however tempting. But we mention it also for a strange sequel that might work to the traveller's advantage, for the embassy here redeemed itself. Our Emperor had sent with his ambassadors the preserved finger of his own personal saint, Ia, as a charm for the journey.[1] But wisely, the leader of the embassy in the

---

1. *Translator's note:* A sixth-century Byzantine emperor, in fact, built a church for St

middle of the hellish sermons described above offered it to the king and the monk as a gift from the holy city. The effect was immediate and significant. Within three days a church had been dedicated in Ia's name and Constantine, the monk and our embassy were all reconciled. The traveller at Tintagel would do well to mention his own special devotion to Ia for we understand that this Byzantine saint is much revered among the British now. A traveller in an awkward corner on Tintagel might even rustle up some other saints' relics as a gift: 'the fingernails of Matrona' or 'a hair from the head of Donatus' perhaps?

(III) BODMIN

From Tintagel the traveller can pass either inland through heavily wooded valleys[1] to the ancient settlement of Botmenei [Bodmin], or he can follow the old Roman road, naturally in a terrible state of repair, along the coast. On both routes and indeed throughout all Dumnonia, the land, he will find, is divided into a series of *cantref*, each with its own royal court and war bands. And each of these *cantref* has its own king, who is subject to the high king of the Dumnonians, the lord of Tintagel. Wherever the visitor travels, he is strongly advised to visit these local rulers and part with some trifling gift to win their favour. The sub-kings are jealous of their territory and would take it as an insult or a provocation if a traveller crossing their land did not at least drop in and exchange some words with them, especially a traveller from the Mediterranean.

How, it might be asked, should one treat these men – with firm words, sycophancy or charming condescension? We favour a frank bonhomie between equals. After all, it must be remembered that the

---

Ia at the Golden Gate in Constantinople. Several churches to Ia are also found in west Cornwall, most notably in St Ives – Ives is Ia – but nowhere else in Britain or Ireland.
1. *Translator's note:* 'Heavily wooded valleys' is worth elaborating on. Specialists in Britain's early medieval landscape suggest that in the south and midlands of the island tree-cover was not very much greater in the sixth century than it is today: extensive clearing had taken place in the Roman and pre-Roman period. However, in the north and the west – for example, in Cornwall, Wales, the north of England and Scotland – tree-cover was much heavier than any that we see in the twenty-first century.

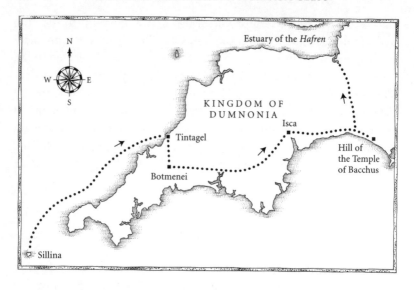

British Celts are convinced that they are Roman, a contention that it is best not to argue with. The inhabitants of Tintagel, for example, often talk of their Roman blood and Constantine even had the impudence to speak of our then Emperor as his 'brother Roman king'. But on Tintagel there is, at least, the refuse of the old Roman civilisation of Britain to excuse such comments, and most of the court and clergy do speak Latin (of a sort). By contrast in the interior the Dumnonians are barbaric in manner and dress so these princes or little kings surprise all when they calmly and sincerely claim: 'we are Romans too'. Luckily, it is not the place of the traveller to argue: he must learn, instead, to tolerate these delusions and talk with them as if they really were fellow-descendants of Romulus and Remus.

Unfortunately, despite their claim to be Roman, none but a very few have any Latin so communication proves difficult. Nor do translators necessarily help, for many Dumnonians claim to speak the language as a matter of pride even when they cannot, in fact, muster more than six or seven words of the Roman tongue. (In these circumstances a series of incomprehensible sounds pour out of the speaker's mouth and, if the listener is fortunate, the first line of the *Aeneid*. The traveller should here be warned: such prestige is attached to being a Latin-speaker that the listener must not be seen to fail to understand. It is best in these circumstances to compliment the speaker on his *bona lingua latina*, nod, smile, bow a little and then walk quickly on.

Each Dumnonian *cantref* is made up of a number of 'rounds', the classic south-western settlement, a circular embankment some forty or so feet in circumference, with a number of oval huts inside. Typically twenty will live in one of these rounds and a *cantref* has up to a hundred spread across its territory. The turf walls of these communities would not stand up to a serious assault. But they do serve for keeping the cattle safe – any animals are herded in before nightfall – and sentries are on watch at all times to guarantee the community's security or at least to give warning of a hostile presence. These precautions are taken partly to protect livestock and round-members from beasts: wolves and bears are an ever-present danger in the peninsula. However, there is also much rustling and one round sometimes finds itself feuding with another, a situation that is then complicated by occasional wars between different Dumnonian *cantref*. In fact, from what we have learnt of this kingdom, it seems that Dumnonia is in an almost constant state of mild civil war.

The traveller working his way across the kingdom is strongly advised to avoid such hostilities by finding a hospitable round where he can at least sleep safely. Most round-holders will be only too happy to offer a room, that is a stall shared with the cows, for the British Celts pride themselves on their hospitality. What, though, should the traveller look for in selecting his round? One with high walls ought usually to be avoided, because any special defences suggest that a feud is afoot. Likewise a quantity of mutilated, war-wounded young men is a bad sign. Running water and a high position are fundamental: the pestiferous, disease-ridden air of the rounds is proverbial; while, finally, the presence of horses can be taken as a sign of wealth and the chances of the traveller eating decent quantities of food increase dramatically.

An evening at a round usually begins badly. On entering his chosen sleeping-place, the traveller will be immediately shown a selection of decapitated heads nailed to the gate, usually unlucky neighbours, Saxon raiders or – be warned – impolite boarders. It is natural that a civilised visitor will feel revulsion at this point. But it is unfortunately customary to show interest in these prizes and the householder will be shocked and perhaps offended if the visitor walks straight past with an ashen expression. Instead, the wise traveller will stand gazing keenly at the boiled, preserved faces, always ready to ask for the vital statistics of this or that head and the circumstances in which a particular guest arrived at the round. The Celts, as headhunters everywhere, take a loving pride in all their trophies and will be overjoyed to go through the personal history of each item in the collection.

There are many ways of expressing gratitude on leaving a hospitable round – though marriage proposals should be refused, no matter how tempting. The preferred method is to leave three or four Imperial bronzes. We say this because the Dumnonians use coins for special purchases, but never mint their own. In fact, take a handful of coins from a Dumnonian and you will find a mongrel selection – an ancient Roman piece of three hundred years before, a few Gaulish barbarian coins and a number of Greek ones. This lack of distinction means that the traveller is quite at liberty to bring with him old and valueless currency and smilingly fob it off on the locals as if he were discarding small fortunes. Some traders have even attempted to purchase tin in bulk, bartering with dozens of Egyptian pennies.

If the traveller is in Dumnonia in the spring, and gains his host's affection, he may, before leaving the round, be invited to see one of the notorious Dumnonian plays. The round-dwellers claim to be Christian, but it is unlikely that anyone has ever explained the full significance of our Lord's nativity and resurrection. And so in their heathen ignorance a round and sometimes two or three in unison meet near one of the region's standing stones, the old pagan temples, to celebrate a despicable drama full of devilish characters and terrible endings. The shame of this in no way strikes them and the embassy witnessed one monk – perhaps the cousin of he that remonstrated with Constantine – chase half a village from just such an evil gathering and then proceed, with his own hands no less, to carve a cross on their stone, hoping, we suppose, to exorcise its demons.

This is but one of their many superstitions. Another, and one that the traveller must be acquainted with, is that concerning Arthur. Arthur, or Artorius as he is called in the Latin language, is the greatest of British-Celtic heroes about whom there are many legends, the most insistent of which claims he will come back to save his people from the Saxons: 'he will come again!' the Dumnonians always say. When the embassy passed through the peninsula, a guide who was with them often pointed out a landmark in connection with Arthur. If he saw a large, circular rock then this guide would say 'Ah! Arthur threw this in anger when "x" did "y": *he will come again!*' If he saw a few trees growing together with a stone at their centre then 'Arthur cooked a meal here: *he will come again!*' or 'this is Arthur's oven: *he will come again!*' Though entertaining at first, if nothing else for proving the extreme credulity of the Dumnonians, it soon becomes tedious to hear every item of the surrounding countryside explained in these terms. The traveller, however, is advised to swallow any annoyance and follow all discourses with care, asking always at least three questions, for, as we will now show, the Dumnonians can become wrathful on account of this Arthur.[1]

There is in the interior a church at the settlement we have previously mentioned named Botmenei [Bodmin], which means in their language 'the house of the monks'. In this settlement the embassy fell into talking with the natives and, as so often happens, these began to speak about their Arthur and to say many blasphemous and wicked things. For example, they said that this Arthur, though slain in battle, was not really dead and would soon come back to life as if he was our Lord himself. They even said, oh infamy, that Arthur was the Virgin's champion!

The embassy soon tired of Arthur and, outraged by such ungodly banter, began to ask awkward questions: where was this Arthur hiding if he was so great a man? The British Celts replied earnestly, in their poor Latin, that Arthur had conquered the antipodes, the islands beyond Arabia and Africa, and was even now preparing his armies to sail north. This statement was the final straw and set all the embassy laughing – a grave mistake, for even though the Dumnonians and the Byzantine party had at this point entered a church, the locals began to push and punch our men. Indeed, if it had not been for the presence

---

1. *Translator's note:* The evidence of the embassy is in conflict with the convictions of many modern Arthur enthusiasts – this is Arthur of Round Table fame – who believe that their once and future king lived in precisely the period covered here, the 500s. However, there are indications elsewhere that the historical individual behind the legend, in fact, belonged to an earlier period of British history and that he was already embedded in British-Celtic myth by the sixth century.

of the local king real blood would have been spilt: as it was, only a nose and several fingers were broken before order was restored.

Let this be a lesson to the traveller, one of the most important that he can learn and one that is fundamental in all the lands of the British Celts: never doubt their fanatical faith in Arthur! For 'he will come again' ... and again ... and again.

The journey across country can finish in only one destination: Isca Dumnoniorum [Exeter], about six days on foot from Tintagel on the southern coast. Indeed, as the Dumnonians say with touching earnestness – it passes for wisdom among them – 'all roads lead to Isca'. When Rome still controlled Britain, the Dumnonians were ruled by the council of this city. And today, the barbarians still have a kind of sentimental regard for the place. In fact, Isca even at its height was little better than a town hall with a wall around it, a kind of administrative village. And now it is almost entirely abandoned with the exception of some industry and occasional visits from the braver Mediterranean traders, who risk the Saxon pirates of Vectis [the Isle of Wight] and come this far east for their tin. No sign, apart from the city walls, remains that this place was once Roman. The proud forum, for example, has been demolished and where once the basilica stood, furnaces and a clay quarry now blight the urban scene. The tedium of the city in this run-down state is almost too much to bear. For the provincial Dumnonians all roads may lead to Isca, but for the traveller these same roads must lead inexorably away.

(IV)   MAIDEN CASTLE

From Isca it is possible either to head east into the richer southern lowlands of Britain or turn back north across the peninsula and pay for passage over the Hafren and its estuary [the Severn and the Bristol Channel]. We strongly advise the latter choice even if it condemns the traveller to many more miles of muddy British roads, for to the east the borders of Dumnonia run with those of the ferocious Saxons. The embassy initially, and against the counsels of the Dumnonians, tried this eastern route, but turned back at the Hill of the Temple of Bacchus

[Maiden Castle]. We quote now directly from their log as a warning to those who are tempted to take a risk:

On the morning of the third day, the coastal plain narrowing, we realised that we were nearing Saxon territory. We moved on nervous but alert, until we came to a large hill that had been described to us as the site of an ancient temple to Bacchus, a few miles from the border. To our delight we found there a religious building, in a beautiful state of preservation, and a frieze of Bacchus with his leopard above its portal (the leopard admittedly seeming a wolf, sculpted as it was in the style of the British Celts). We were also greeted at the hill's top by several men dressed in the green of Bacchus, all lightly armed. At first we thought we had stumbled on one of the plays loved by the Dumnonians. But these people assured us that they were acolytes of Bacchus and this surprised us for many say that the British Celts are, at least formally, all Christian. When we asked them of the faith of Christ, they were dismissive, but pleasantly so in the manner of the philosophers' academy – their Latin was excellent and one even spoke a Greek of sorts. Afterwards, they led us into the building to meet their high priest, a tall man in his late twenties, who also proved affable, though he had that effeminacy so common among the followers of the ecstatic god.

Made comfortable after two days of terrifying journey – food and drink were brought in abundance – our curiosity proved too much for our manners and we began to ask this priest how it was that he and his followers survived so close to the border. He explained that the Saxons, knowing theirs was a holy sanctuary, had feared to venture into its bounds, for they are, it seems, a superstitious people. In fact, the priest and the other Bacchites have had more problems with what they termed 'Christian hoodlums' who have thrice tried to desecrate the temple.

As we were enjoying a light dessert there were yells without and one of the watchmen came in, whispering in the ear of the priest, who then stood and with much authority began to give instructions, sending all the others running. Only afterwards did he turn to us and tell us in Latin that a Saxon raiding party had been sighted and was working its way up from the valley. We could run if we wished, he informed us, but we would be much safer waiting in the bounds of the temple, for the Saxons had turned away on previous occasions faced with what he called 'the majesty of Bacchus'. As he was speaking, he cast a heavy, ermine coat on to his shoulders and moved out to frighten the barbarians away, imploring his god as he did so with charms.

Our first instinct was to abandon the Bacchites to their fate. But, after some frenzied discussion, we decided that we would be better advised to hide in the precincts with our heavy luggage, for escape with the Emperor's gifts on our backs would surely have been futile, and it was unthinkable to leave these to the Saxons. The minutes passed and, peeking through the statues at the entrance, we saw a column of twenty or so tall, armed men walking rapidly up the shoulder of the hill towards the temple, screaming and chanting in their language as they did so. It was our first glimpse of the hated Saxons, and naturally we were appalled.

The scene now unfolded with a terrible inevitability. Between the temple and approaching raiders stood the high priest and a handful of green-dressed men and, as the Saxons neared, the priest began to intone incantations in a loud voice. Perhaps this trick had worked before. But on this occasion it proved useless and the Saxons broke into a run, determined to cut off the spells as quickly as possible. Seeing this, a couple of the priest's disciples immediately fled, the others, meanwhile, unsheathing their weapons. The combat was lost in a rush of limbs and bodies – they were too far down the hill for us to make out any details. But when the fighting was over – a matter of a minute – we saw the Bacchites had all been laid low except the priest, who was gagged and tied in a standing-up position, his furs on the floor. A single Saxon had also been mortally wounded and he lay shouting to his own gods.

The raiding party at this point divided, some running off to find the escaped Bacchites, others to prepare a grave for this dying comrade. We could in no way escape from the hill, and so we tried as best we could to hide ourselves in the bounds of the temple watching all the while the scene below. Working together, the warriors buried the now dead Saxon and then they turned their attention to the Bacchite priest, whom, while still alive, they scalped and cut with their long knives – the *seax* knives[1] –

1. *Translator's note:* The name Saxon actually comes from their short, stabbing *seax* knives, a kind of early medieval machete. The *seax* used in Britain in this period had a flimsier blade than its Continental equivalent, but a longer handle to allow, unusually in Germanic warfare, a two-handed attack.

and then, when he was entirely dismembered, they took his body parts to be buried higher up the slope. Evidently they feared his powers even when dead.

As they came closer we could see for the first time their features. They shave strips of hair back around their forehead and the result is that their faces seem larger and more luminous than those of other races. Their hair is held back with bands but above all with grease – indeed, the northern barbarians use rancid butter for this purpose. By now our terror was palpable and we could barely look at each other. The warriors stood twenty feet from us and it could only be a matter of time before they approached even closer.

In the end their leader, a hulking wedge of a man, walked with two of his deputies to stare at the temple's gate and the statue of Bacchus. At this point we could study their faces and unsheathed weapons, truly the stuff of a child's nightmare. But they reserved a fear for Bacchus's palace that they had not deigned to give that god's servants and refused to enter, peering only through the door into the shadows: it was strange to see our own fear reflected on their barbarian faces. A moment later, they were walking back to their brother warriors and we thanked God for our salvation, left a little time until we were sure that they had retreated and then turned back towards Dumnonia determined to try the northern route where there would be no Saxons to impede us. Cambria [Wales] now awaits.

2

SOUTHERN WALES:
'THE HOLY SOUTH'

(I) ACROSS THE SEVERN

Cambria [Wales], standing across the Hafren [the Severn] from Dumnonia, bravest and most fertile of all the peninsulas of Britain. Or so, at least, claim its British-Celtic inhabitants, who boast that they alone of the Britons bested the Roman legions; and, proud of their martial feats, they swear that they will defend their land too against the Saxons, or the Garmani as they contemptuously call them. We know better though and it is our unfortunate duty to point out that the locals' 'victories' against the Romans were no more than ambushes of cohorts lost on Cambrian moors; and that the British Celts themselves here remain undefeated by the Saxons simply because these newcomers have not yet reached within striking distance. Likewise we must advise the reader against putting too much faith in claims for the peninsula's fertility. As in Dumnonia, the territory is richer in its mines than in its fields: lead, silver, even gold are taken from the earth there, while its soil is mean and over-watered by the western rains. However, one merit we will not pass over: the relative calm of this part of Britain. Out of reach of the Saxons, with well-ordered government and little feuding, there is no other region of the island where a visitor is more likely to die of natural causes.

For the traveller the route to Cambria from Dumnonia is best made across the estuary of the Hafren and, on arriving in the land of Cambria, is best paid for in tin. We have heard rumours of many marvels on this waterway. There is a magical log that, if the sea carries it out into the ocean, will always be carried back at the following tide and left in the same place as it began. There is, too, the ill-temper of the river, for once a year it explodes in anger – the locals call it the *dau ri*, the two kings – when huge waves run along its length drowning villages and inhabitants alike.[1] And others still tell of battles in the mountains of Cambria that are so fierce that the Hafren from source to sea runs red with human blood. But we believe none of these legends, for the British Celts love nothing more than to fill the traveller's ears with their lies and untruths.

However, one fact that we can attest to are the extraordinary hermits of the channel, who live on the Hafren's craggy islands. The holy men among the British and their cousins the Irish love to search out cliff sites or rocky islets for their prayers and visions – indeed, there is no greater praise of a hermit than to say that 'he perches on a cliff like a seabird'. One of these hermit islands is named Silura [Lundy], famous in the times when our Roman eagles flew over Britain for the barbarity of its inhabitants. While, still closer to the coast, on Pyro's Isle [Caldey] another group of monks guard one of the gateways to Cambria with their prayers and fasts. In most of Europe, the traveller sighs with relief to know that there is a monastery nearby, for Christian hospitality means steaming soup, washed feet and a bed for the night.[2] But in Britain this is not necessarily the case, foreign travellers sometimes being treated with a shocking lack of charity. The author can do no better here than quote the passage from the log that describes the embassy's arrival on the second of the isles mentioned above:

> We came within the shelter of the bay after a choppy crossing and found ourselves staring at the famous monastery of which our guides had spoken so enthusiastically, named for its founder, owner, and now abbot, Pyro. This Pyro has, the people say and we were later able to confirm, 'the appearance of an angel sent down from heaven'. And even if greatly advanced in years, he never ceases to worship. All day he works with his hands in small manual tasks to keep his mind straying from God. Then all night he studies the holy scriptures, bringing a burning torch or one of their primitive lamps to his dwelling, in order that he

---

1. *Translator's note:* A confused and legendary description of the Severn Bore. A similar account is found in the ninth-century Welsh text, *Historia Brittonum*.
2. *Translator's note:* At this date visitors to monasteries still had their feet washed by monks intent on imitating Christ.

might either write – three fingers, two eyes, all the body poised over the text – or exercise himself in spiritual contemplation. And, incredible to say, though the man sometimes sleeps, he never uses a bed, but rather leans against walls to close his eyes. We were impressed by these stories and, aware of Pyro's influence, we had already determined to give him one of our precious gifts so he might help the Emperor's cause.

Our task, however, was not to be simple. On arriving at the isle's little harbour we had our first sight of the two thuggish men who were to impede our mission: a couple of monk sentinels standing over the landing place. Their appearance warned us that we were about to enter a brutish and unfamiliar world. They had the normal rags worn by hermits everywhere. But their hair was bizarre. From the front it resembled a circle typical of the western monks.[1] But from behind it was shaved so the rear of the head is entirely free of growth and this, it seems, is the normal tonsure of the Britons and the Gaels.

Nor were their manners any more graceful. Once they learnt that we were 'Syrians' – the word was almost spat – they forbade the boatman to land. We asked the elder of them why we were treated in this uncharitable fashion and reminded him, through our guide, that we were representatives of the Emperor across the sea, his lord. However, the impudent devil was not impressed and replied that he had but one lord, 'He of the Seven Heavens', and that we could not land because we would 'pollute' them. Our guide afterwards explained to us that many British-Celtic holy men believe that any who do not follow their curious customs are not true Christians; so while the holy of Antioch, Alexandria, Rome and Constantinople are all hell-bound, these blisters on the edge of the world somehow guard the one true faith!

We luckily managed to keep our tempers, despite the best efforts of these curs to provoke us. And, eventually, after much negotiation – the mention of gifts was decisive – the younger one was sent tramping off to find his master, Pyro, finally returning to say that we would be allowed to land. However, they insisted that as 'heretics' we could not enter the inner sanctum where the monks pray and that we should on

1. *Translator's note:* In the west at this time the Benedictine or Roman tonsure, the tonsure that we today associate with monks, was the most common. However, Byzantine monks, the monks with which the log-writers would have been most familiar, shaved all their head.

no account speak to the holy fathers. We were then escorted to a small hut on the windy side of the island and our gifts were taken without any thanks – our interpreter explained that they would have to be cleansed of us first, with boiling water.

We expected at least to talk with the abbot over a meal, but that too was denied us for it seems that 'heretics' cannot eat at table with the Lord's elect. Then when a mean spread of cheese on slim bread slices was brought to us we learnt that after the meal the trays we had used were to be scoured with burning sand to purify them, and that any leftovers would be fit only for dogs! Our dirty boatman, however, as 'a true Christian' was welcomed into the monks' hall to feast, and it was not long before a great laughter and cheeriness began to emanate from this place. Then, as the hours of night passed, the din grew for the hermits and monks were celebrating the day of one of their most holy saints.

After several hours of this racket that, at least in terms of volume, resembled an Imperial orgy, a figure stumbled out of the hall and began to stroll drunkenly close to where we were sitting and shivering. We feared a visit from some inebriated monk, but when we saw the age and angelic, alcohol-happy face of the night-walker we recognised, instead, the venerable Pyro. Preparing for a meeting and supposing that the old man had thought better of his treatment of the Emperor's servants, we started to dust ourselves down. However, the poor sot wanted nothing more than to walk zigzaggedly round his domain, hoping no doubt to avoid the temptation of a bed. Sighing, we began to resign ourselves to a night in the cold. But just as we were sitting down once more, we heard a scream and saw to our astonishment that this Pyro had, heavily intoxicated, collided with the stone rim of a well. For a moment he balanced there on its rim and then blindly tipped over, disappearing down into its conical shaft with neck-breaking consequences.

The brothers of the monastery were, as can be imagined, much tormented by their beloved master's death and after matins they held council – to which we were not invited – choosing one of their own as an abbot. The boatman, who was also a little the worse for wear (a result of the superfluity of *med* ingested on the previous night), told us sulkily that this new abbot, a certain Samson, was famous for his abstinence.

(II) DYFED

Whatever the manners of Pyro's monks the island can, at least, be recommended as a useful stepping stone to the most powerful of all the kingdoms of southern Cambria, that of Demetia [Dyfed]. We say this for just across the bay from the monastery is the most famous fort of the Demetians, Tenby of the Fishes, where their king comes to receive tribute from the coastal peoples and gingerly makes contact with the region's holy men including these monks and the ever-cantankerous and soon-to-be-described Watery David. The 'castle' – some baked mud and rough rocks rolled together in the typical British-Celtic style – stands on the heights above the sea and is the subject of a famous song that praises its beauty and its invulnerability. The traveller is well advised to learn and trot off in Latin or better still in the language of the Celts: 'there is a fair fort on the wide water, an impregnable fort surrounded by sea', for a rousing welcome from the locals is bound to follow.

The stronghold itself is guarded by the king's own guards, easily identifiable because, as is typical among the British Celts, the warrior of Demetia shaves his head. Do not, by the way, be misled by the unpromising appearance of their weapons: the preferred Demetian arm is a very puny-looking bow that they cut from a short elm. We say this for what these bows lack in range, they make up for in force and accuracy. In fact, the embassy records seeing one four-inch-thick oaken door that had been penetrated by arrows from such a bow – the arrow tips protruding through the far side! The Emperor's armies would find such allies extremely useful; the careless traveller may find them fatal.

The Demetians live for the most part in simple rectangular shacks, often in groups, and often with no defensive walls around them, for, as we have previously mentioned, this is the safest part of Britain. For the traveller, these buildings can make welcoming though uncomfortable places for a night's sleep. We say 'welcoming' – we will come to 'uncomfortable' in a moment – for the Demetians pride themselves on their hospitality. Any passing visitor will be ushered in on merely asking directions. He will then be seated down in front of the evening fire and the girl of the house will be made to come and play him soothing tunes on her harp, a peculiar type of lyre that is sometimes larger than the player. There are no tables in a Cambrian house. Instead, the traveller will eat with his host family, resting his food on his lap. And, strange to say, there is no pottery or plates either. Water is drunk from a wooden or sometimes – if the traveller is in a household with pretensions – a glass container and food eaten off a thin rolled-out piece of bread: Cambrians love to joke with visitors that they must eat their plates too. Strangely, the natives of this peninsula do not eat hot food despite the cool climate, for they say it injures their teeth. Indeed, they are vain beyond belief about their dentistry, polishing their gums and incisors constantly with green hazel wands.

There are two uncomfortable moments in the evening, of which it is our duty to warn the traveller: the sing-song and bedtime. The Demetians and the Cambrians in general pride themselves on being the only people who sing 'in parts'. Instead of singing in a group with one voice as we do they take turns, different voices reaching different notes. Some visitors to the region say this is half-pleasing, others that it is worse than chickens. But, whatever the guest's feelings, the host should be respected and compliments larded on any family who under-takes to entertain the traveller in this fashion. The Cambrians are so obsessed with the ability to sing that a mother will sometimes present a baby to the foreigner and boast that his or her screams already suit it to one role or another in the communal choir. However, before giving any opinion on this matter the visitor should assure himself that both parents agree, for a baby's singing voice can be the cause of the most terrible arguments.

Even more painful than the sing-song is the Demetian bedtime. The guest is always invited to share the communal bed, for the family rely on each other's body warmth and only cover themselves with one thin sheet, the *brychan*, that is passed over them all, with some, but not many, rushes being laid underneath to give the back comfort. Import-ant note: the traveller need not be worried by any enthusiastic attempt to put him in the middle of the mass of bodies. This is unlikely to be a ruse to rob him in the night, but rather thoughtfulness on the host's part, hoping that the guest will avoid the cold suffered by those on the edges. However, if the traveller is part of a group a sensible compromise would be to seek out the edge near the fire, so combining some warmth with ease of escape.

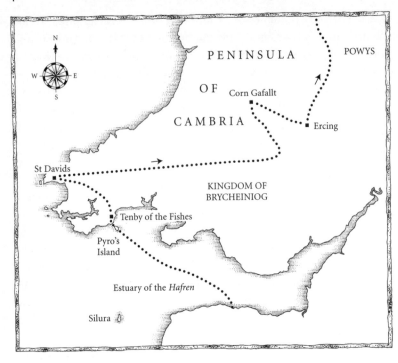

Like Dumnonia, Demetia is split into many sub-kingdoms or *cantref* – seven in fact. But the traveller's work is complicated here for not only are there seven kings, but also seven bishops to placate, one for each of these smaller kingdoms. The high king of all these territories was, at least when the log was written, a certain Vortipor who was already old with grey in his hair when the embassy arrived and bowed their way into his court. He had an unhealthy lifestyle. Not only did he indulge in frequent, violent wars, but he had also tempted the wrath of God by marrying his daughter on his wife's and her mother's death. We do not know whether such obscene marriages are common among the British Celts and we know nothing of Vortipor's successor.

Much as with the Dumnonians, the high king of the Demetians moves constantly with his court from region to region. The locals, for all their hospitality, fear his visits, knowing from bitter experience the burden he and his companions will bring on the local economy: indeed, the joke goes that they would rather be invaded by another king than visited by their own. When their lord arrives they are expected to pay tributes not in silver or coins but in 'feasts'. If the traveller wishes to contribute to this tax – not a bad thank-you present for a night rolling around in the collective bed – he should know that one feast is equal to a horseload of wheaten flour, seven measures of oats, the meat of one ox and a vat of honey.

To the west of Tenby dwells the notorious Watery David or David 'the water-quaffer',[1] so called because the only substance that ever passes his mouth comes from local streams and springs. Pyro's foundation had already a certain rigour in its ecclesiastical customs. But these are as nothing compared to those imposed by David, that stern and superhuman ascetic. His monks work constantly in the fields that surround his monastery dragging their own ploughs, for David has forbidden the use of beasts of burden. And at night the same men are given over to constant prayers or they resort to extraordinary acts to punish the body: some stand neck-deep in cold rivers; others lie in saintly abstinence with lovely virgins, imported specially to tempt their withered members; while others still use nettles to flay themselves into a state of godliness.

The traveller will find David's monastery in the Rosy Valley, though from what we have heard it is rather the 'Rocky Valley', with chunks of marble protruding at every turn. Visitors are frequent for this David believes himself the bishop of all Britain, a claim that must on no account be questioned. The traveller, however, should not rely on a warm welcome. For the closer a British-Celtic priest believes himself to God – and none believes himself closer to the Deity than the watery one – the stronger will be his lack of charity towards 'heretical' strangers. The embassy, bearing this in mind, sent their gift by a British-Celtic envoy and carefully boiled the precious stones beforehand to save this rather frightening monk any trouble. However, a misunderstanding resulted. The embassy later heard that David had been overjoyed to receive certain saintly relics and gems from overseas and that he had built a church to house them. It seems that, due to the imbecility of the messenger, it was understood that our Emperor was

1. *Translator's note:* Today the patron saint of Wales. The city of St Davids is found in the Rosy Valley mentioned below.

a foreign saint and that these 'relics' – the gifts – were memorials of his earthly existence![1] Never give messages verbally in Britain: always write them out in Latin on wax tablets as the western monks do.

If the traveller wishes to risk the wrath of David, we have put together several tips for surviving on the inside of the Rosy Valley. First tip: the interloper should always visit the monastery with crumbs and crusts, for many jackdaws live there and the monks think well of anyone who treats these animals with kindness. Indeed, it is said, we know not on what authority, that the jackdaws never fly from anyone in black, so kind have the monastery's inhabitants proved to these filthy birds over the years. Second tip: on no account be cruel to orphan boys in the bounds of the monastery, nor should the traveller mention illegitimacy there. We say this remembering what we have heard of the circumstances of David's own birth. David was the son of a nun called 'Nun' and a saint called 'Saint'. However, it is told, always in hushed voices, that there was no marriage and that this saint Saint – as we saw with Pyro, the holy of Britain have curious blind spots – raped Nun one day while she was out walking, 'Watery' David being the issue. Tip three: boast about your knowledge of Greek – 'Oh the nectar of the Greeks!' – for though the British Celts believe themselves to be educated, yet they know almost nothing of our language. The school in the Rosy Valley is renowned for its teachers and a Greek tutor would doubtless be welcome there. Unlike other parts of Europe, however, the students do not read the Church Fathers or sharpen their wits on Virgil. Rather they pass over conversational texts, practising to speak Latin in various playful situations, for example, chats at mass or directions on the road to Rome. So if you do choose the master-of-Greek strategy, prepare some likely dialogues for your western students to work their clicking tongues over.

---

1. *Translator's note:* A church to saint Stinian (Justinian – also the name of a sixth-century Byzantine emperor) stands near St Davids. Perhaps this is the misunderstanding to which our writer refers.

(III) CENTRAL WALES

Cambria can be usefully imagined as three horizontal strips. The southern strip, well populated and pocked with valleys, contains Demetia and a number of other smaller states. The northern strip all belongs to the mightiest of the British-Celtic kingdoms, Gwynedd. However, connecting the two is a belt of dangerous, hilly country that runs across the middle of the peninsula, crossed by a number of rivers including the Hafren and the Teifi – one of the homes of the British beaver whose testicles are so valued by the medical profession everywhere. This wide central massif includes a kingdom known as Powys, a name that the traveller will be little consoled to learn means 'the country of the savage people' – another way of saying that the relative safety of southern Cambria ends here.

Given the reputation of this middle region, some understandably choose a boat to visit Gwynedd in the north, though let it be noted that few Mediterranean trading ships head further than the Hafren and Tintagel. In earlier times there was also the eastern route that, leaving the peninsula altogether, took the traveller up through the centre of Britain. (This is now impracticable, for in recent times the raiding Saxons have devastated the area.) The bulk of travellers cross, instead, resignedly over to Gwynedd through the wild and inhospitable central regions, those who can afford to bringing a bodyguard with them.

The most common route overland is to follow the River Teifi up towards its source in the highlands. This takes the traveller into the heart of the small kingdom of Brycheiniog [Brecon], founded many years ago by an Irish adventurer and his pagan band. Brycheiniog is a rare haven of order in the wild, hilly belt that crosses the peninsula and all travellers are advised to seek it out and spend some days there refreshing themselves from the hardships of the road. About its capital we know nothing, though we have heard and repeat with some scepticism that the descendants of these Irish adventurers have a palace built on an artificially constructed island in a lake in the centre of the region.

It was in Brycheiniog that the embassy first saw the bards, or the poets as we would say. Let it be noted that there are many different types of poets in Cambria: seers, satirists, prophet poets, to name but a few. However, there is only one of these that the traveller will find a help or a hindrance on his journeys: namely, the praise poets, versifiers who travel from court to court putting to music the achievements of the great men of the land, be they monarchs, nobles, bishops or even wealthy explorers. These poets have a long training in their art, learning the various metres and games of words over many years. But their bearing is never that of a humble craftsman. Rather they consider themselves kings! They strut arrogantly into a royal court and, almost without asking leave, they begin to compose on the spot, calling the subject of their verse a dragon or a wolf or a dog. And even if the poet is bad or tedious the poem must be finished for the praise poets have the right to give at least one hymn to the king. Some go still further and in their impertinence claim to be the king's spouse, deserving his protection and gratitude![1]

About their poems we know little and have no examples. But those that have heard them say that they are sometimes short and sometimes long, sometimes practised and sometimes extemporaneous, while all are famous for being difficult to understand, the result of the archaic and obscure words used by the bards. Indeed, when one of the poets played for the king of Brycheiniog the interpreter of the embassy blushed, saying that he did not understand enough to translate. And on hearing this the king of that region laughed and admitted that he himself understood only that his name was mentioned from time to time and connected with various ferocious animals. These poets of praise invent many verses for their living, but there is also a national repertoire, examples from which they all know and which are sometimes heard in the Cambrian sing-songs. For example, on the morning before any raid or battle the poet must play for the court a piece known as 'Unbeiniaeth Prydain' or 'The Monarchy of Britain' – a kind of national anthem of the British Celts.

So far the praise poet will have seemed to the reader a preposterous and vaguely amusing character. However, we must warn that he can also be dangerous. The problem is that poets are temperamental. They

---

1. *Translator's note:* There are Irish and Welsh poems from the Middle Ages where a poet claims to be the wife of his patron and demands equivalent privileges. This must be the custom to which our author refers.

will praise one king limitlessly. But if they are treated poorly, mocked or worst of all paid badly, they will search out another patron without any hesitation, writing poems in which a previous master is compared unfavourably with their new lord. This may not seem so terrible in itself, especially to a simple traveller. But the poet's revenge can be carried even further, for if the poet is seriously provoked or not paid his promised sum then he can go so far as to curse a lord. This curse causes blisters to appear on the face and the powerful will go to any ends to avoid this. Indeed, some have even enacted special laws to prevent their praise poets from attacking them in this fashion. Never, never then insult a man with their characteristic lyre on his back – the *cracca* as they call it – for this rash is almost impossible to remove.

The praise poets generally travel a lot for they must constantly search out new patrons. And the poet who performed at Brycheiniog, his name was Taliesin, had already determined to visit the king of Gwynedd for this purpose. As the embassy were also headed in this direction, Taliesin agreed, for a small monetary consideration, to be their guide. He, in fact, proved a boastful, lying kind. But the embassy learnt to respect his knowledge of the country and the many roads and ways. Taliesin also knew, as would be expected of a poet, much of the local lore and he, as all the British Celts, spoke endlessly of the famed Arthur. After the unfortunate incident in Dumnonia the embassy were nervous about asking too many questions. But Taliesin spoke so familiarly of the great man – almost as if he had sung before him – that the poet quite convinced the Greeks, again for a small donation, that he would bring them into what he called 'Arthur Country'.

However, never trust a praise poet asking for money and never trust the British Celts when talking about their Arthur, who, we are convinced, is a phantom of their imagination. Instead of carrying the embassy to the gate of the magical Camelot where this Arthur is said to dwell, Taliesin adopted the maddening habit of the British Celts of Dumnonia and kept pointing to rocks beside the road, claiming that this was the spear, or this the bed, or this the oven of Arthur. Naturally, our embassy soon tired of his games and complained volubly – after all, a considerable sum had already been given – at which Taliesin offered, for a little more gold, to take them to some sites that Arthur would certainly visit while out boar-hunting, a favourite occupation of his. More money was paid. But the results were, as can be imagined, unfavourable. The first 'hunting lodge of the king' was nothing more than a crag named Corn Gafallt [Rhayader in Radnor] where they were shown a cairn that was covered by a large stone with a paw print on it – the mark, it is said, that Arthur's dog made while hunting the world's largest boar.

Seeing the embassy unimpressed by this mark, Taliesin rewarded our people instead with a long and tedious story in Latin about how Arthur had chased 'Old White' (the boar) across the landscape and then into the sea, riding on its back to Ireland. But the head of the embassy was having nothing of it. He pointed out that they had still seen no sign of the great Arthur himself and reminded the praise poet once more of the money that had been paid. Taliesin though, instead of consoling them, brought them a long way across country to a valley that Arthur is supposed to visit, a place named Ercing [Archenfield in Herefordshire]. There they found another wilderness site: a spring next to a strange-shaped rock that the yokels say is the burial place of one of Arthur's sons. It appeared actually to be nothing more than a large piece of sandstone. And once more Taliesin began his legend-spinning, seemingly untroubled by the absence of the British-Celtic hero. The special quality of this stone was, he insisted, that it grew and contracted night by night.

Our embassy stayed there for four days, measuring the stone constantly, and so disproved this stupid heathen superstition: at which point the poet had the cheek to say that Arthur would never appear, nor would the stone change shape for the embassy had revealed themselves unbelievers! As there was no arguing with him and, as no one in the party particularly wanted a permanent rash on their face, they paid up to this master of the tall tale and set their horses north to Gwynedd and the 'highest of the kings of Britain'. However, in the log the embassy record as their unanimous view that Arthur, if he ever lived, is now long since dead and that no matter what the British Celts say about him the traveller should coolly ignore any offers to be taken to see the 'Emperor of Britain' or his remains.

3

NORTHERN WALES:
'THE GREAT PROPHECY'

(I) SNOWDONIA

The capital of the most powerful of all British-Celtic kingdoms, Gwynedd, is to be found on a small offshore isle named Mon [Anglesey] that sits above the kingdom's northern coast. The traveller can be assured of being welcomed once on this isle; the challenge is getting there alive and well. We draw attention to this uncomfortable fact, for the explorer, to arrive, must face the dangers not only of Powys, 'the land of the savages', but also the perilous roads leading through Eryri [Snowdonia], the group of mountains that coruscate Gwynedd's southern border. Eryri has proved fundamental to Gwynedd's success. It can be easily defended in times of invasion – the warriors of Gwynedd flock to it if the foe is too large to be faced in the field. And it is agriculturally rich. Indeed, there is a local British-Celtic saying that all the cattle in Cambria could be fed on the pastures offered by its verdant slopes. However, this agricultural and domesticated description of Eryri should not cause the explorer to forget its many traps, for travel above the meadows is perilous. We have heard, for example, of giant eagles that feast off men and that sharpen their beaks and claws on rock itself. And while we cannot answer for the truth of these bird tales, we do know that in a moment of carelessness the librarian, Stephanos, one of the original twelve, plunged with his packhorse from the high tracks there to death in the blackness of a Cambrian ravine.

Guides normally understand the dangers of this area and the need to hurry through it, but at the southern end of the chain they will insist on taking the traveller off the direct path to see 'famous Dinas Emrys'. We speak here of a mountain-top fort, a forbidding and demon-haunted place with clouds rolling all around it that is only occupied in times of war and desperate straits. The British Celts have a custom that it is best to humour of going to stand respectfully by the lake on the heights of this fort. There they will tell you many hysterical legends about a certain hero Ambrosius, as well as a villain named Vortigern. Again it is best not to question this but to feign interest and when they speak of the 'Great Prophecy' – to which Vortigern and Ambrosius are the keys – to choke back crocodile tears. The poet Taliesin, certainly, did not resist the detour and took the embassy to this peak, raging all the while about 'the Prophecy of Britain' and many other mad notions including a magician called Merlin, his piglets and again this Great Prophecy, at which point he became almost frenzied.

What is the Great Prophecy? The log of the embassy is somewhat incoherent describing events at Dinas Emrys – possibly due to the incoherence of their guide – so we will not quote from it. Instead, we have had to look elsewhere for an answer. Of Vortigern and Ambrosius we have been able to find out little, despite the fact that they were officials in the last age of Roman Britain. Vortigern became the governor of Britain when the Roman legions finally abandoned the island and we have read his missives to the Emperor of the east in the archives of the *curia* – he seems to have been an intemperate man; while Ambrosius, according to these same letters, was sometimes his henchman and sometimes his rival. But none of this helped us to understand any better the Great Prophecy. Indeed, we solved that particular mystery in, of all places, the book market of Constantinople. By good fortune we found there a manuscript written in the demotic Latin of Gaul. This frustratingly short work contained a miscellany of geographical writings relating to various parts of northern and western Europe, and somehow among these had slipped the text below. The story is clearly legendary: Ambrosius and Vortigern have been dragged mercilessly into and through the grinding mill of Cambrian myth. Nevertheless, we translate it in full – only omitting some exceptionally facetious parts – as it explains the Great Prophecy, Dinas's role in it and the nature of British-Celtic delusions generally.

And then Vortigern the king of all the British Celts asked his magicians what he should do. And they told him to go to the farthest borders of his kingdom, and build an invulnerable stronghold, for the Saxons wanted to kill him treacherously and to conquer all of Britain. So the king came with these magicians to Dinas Emrys and they told him to make a stronghold there 'for it is the safest of all the mountains of Britain'. And so Vortigern brought together workmen from all over his kingdom and they found timber and hewn stones but then when the material was brought and piled on the peak of Dinas Emrys it disappeared, all of it, in one night. Three times he ordered the material to be brought and three times it disappeared in the space of a single night. And so frustrated was he at these events that he called again his magicians and asked them again about this magic and how it came to pass. And they consulted for many days and then gave him the answer: 'Unless you can find a child who has no father and unless you sprinkle Dinas with his blood then your stronghold will never be built.'

Vortigern gathered messengers together and sent them to all corners of the island looking for a boy without a father. And these messengers combed the different provinces. Then as they came to a valley in southern Wales they found children playing a game of tig. The children were all laughing at one child whom they mocked for being fatherless. 'You', they said, 'have no father.' When the messengers heard this they interrogated the mother of the boy. She admitted that there had been no father: 'I do not know how this one was born to me for I have never known a man.' And after she had sworn this, they took the child and brought him to the Emperor Vortigern.

The next morning, Vortigern decided to kill the boy and sprinkle his blood over the fort. But the boy spoke to the king earnestly: 'Why do you want me, Emperor?' said he. Vortigern replied: 'So that you can be killed, and your blood spread over this hilltop.' The boy asked then 'Who told you to do such a thing?' 'My wizards', replied Vortigern. 'Bring them all to me', said the child. And so the magicians came all together and the boy addressed them: 'Who told you this about me, these evil lies?' But they did not answer. Then he turned to the Emperor: 'Now I will explain all to you. But to do this fully I must question these magicians.' He turned to them again: 'What is the foundation of this place?' 'We do not know it', said the magicians. 'I know', said the boy. 'There is a lake under us: come and dig and you will see it too.' They dug for many hours until they found it. The boy then said to the wizards:

'Reveal to me that which we will find in the lake.' But again they were silent with ignorance, the Emperor looking on. 'Very well I will show you. You will find that there is a vessel.' They looked in the lake and found, indeed, that it was so. 'What is found in this container?' he asked them. But once more they were silent. 'In it there is a roll of cloth. Open and you will see.' And they opened it and they saw the roll of cloth. Then again to the magicians he said, 'And what is in this roll of cloth learned men?' But they did not know so he told them. 'There are two serpents, one white, the other red. Unroll it.' They unrolled it and there they found two serpents asleep. 'Watch now, O Emperor, what they do.' The two serpents then awoke and began to fight. At first the white serpent beat down the red, but then the red rose up from defeat and drove the white one off the cloth and into the lake. Then the boy turned once more to the wizards and asked them: 'What is the meaning of this?' But they knew not. The boy then explained to them and indeed to all the court of the Emperor of Britain. 'The mystery is simple to me and I will make it simple to you, for this is the Great Prophecy. The cloth is your kingdom and the two serpents are the two peoples of this island that fight over it: the red is the British Celts, the white the Saxons from across the waves. At first the white serpent is victorious but then, when the red is almost defeated, it will surge up and drive the white from out of the kingdom and into the sea.'

This, then, is the Great Prophecy of the British Celts. For they all earnestly believe that one day they will rise again, coming out from the mountains and hills of the west, routing all the invaders and pushing the Saxons into the eastern oceans. The log has many incidental references to this 'rising' and it seems that all among them believe this, speaking of it not as a rumour but as a simple fact, even the most intelligent among them insisting upon it with venom and passion. They grease their psychosis too with other lies, saying, for example, that Arthur will return from the dead, or from fairyland, or from wherever that benighted man sleeps to help them in this task of re-conquering Britain. 'Britain for the British' they brazenly shout.

We are, we must admit, sceptical – especially given that the British Celts are the least impressive in war of the peoples of Britain, having only the Demetian bowmen as a troop of excellence. In the space of a century they have lost half the island to the invaders; in the space of the next century they may well lose the remaining parts. But simple facts such as military defeat hardly seem to worry them, such is their faith in this coming victory; and nowhere is this faith more evident than in the kingdom of Gwynedd, 'the highest of the kingdoms of Britain' as it is called. In Gwynedd it is not enough to nod vigorously when the Great Prophecy is mentioned at tables, one must toast it. We laugh. The reader laughs. And indeed this prophecy is clearly fodder for a gullible people. However, some fact at the bottom of the legend of Dinas Emrys there must be for the embassy reported that ancient wooden foundations protrude from the lake as if Vortigern had truly tried to build his impossible castle there.

(II) THE COAST AND ANGLESEY

There are many pleasing woods on the coast of Gwynedd, woods where the eleven Cambrian trees grow.[1] These lands on the fringes of the northern part of the peninsula are pastoral and have few wild beasts. Certainly, there are no longer bears here; beavers have long since been hunted to death; and the only animal that kills is the occasional wolf that sometimes ventures out of Eryri for easy prey off the farms, coming down the narrow valleys with its whelps. (The traveller who has almost run out of funds by the time he reaches this western extremity of Britain might bear in mind that bounties are paid if any of these strays are killed and that only the tail need be brought to the royal court for collection.) The northern shores of Gwynedd are farmed, and at hand too are the salt treasures of the Irish Sea. Villages as such do not exist, but signs of human habitation are everywhere. In the hills, there are the farmsteads managing the grazing herds. Then towards the coasts there are small rectangular enclosures with wattle huts inside – huts that are built in a simple fashion to last no more than a year or two. In fact, it is uncommon to see permanent buildings in this part of the

---

1. *Translator's note:* According to twelfth-century Welsh law the eleven British trees are the alder, the apple, the ash, the beech, the crab, the elm, the hazel, the oak, the thorn, the yew and the willow.

world and stone structures are almost unheard of. Indeed, even the churches of the British Celts here are wooden and congregations make a point of not attending them while a gale is blowing. A sure sign of poverty – the traveller seeking accommodation would do well to remember this – are houses that have no defensive enclosures. Usually the dwellers here are the despised unfree peasants who are not allowed to become even smiths or poets, so base is their blood. It is better to sleep under the stars listening to lupine howls than creep into their hovels.

The region, however, and this is true even of its better houses or royal courts, is poor. The Mediterranean traders who make a stay in Tintagel bearable rarely reach this far north – there is nothing for them to buy. Coins, as elsewhere among the British Celts, are almost unknown: only a few Roman coppers still circulate. And the population has craftsmen who work for the most part in wood, even a substance as simple and fundamental as pottery being absent from their tables. If the traveller is coming from Dumnonia, tin, the British metal, may prove a useful gift for offsetting the expenses of a bed. But, as we have already noted, the British Celts are famous for their hospitality and are unlikely to begrudge the visitor a night in their home.

A simple way to ingratiate oneself into one of Gwynedd's enclosed communities is to speak about families and pedigree. The British Celts are characterised by their obsession with bloodlines and boast of marrying more for the nobility of a neighbouring household than any vulgar considerations of wealth. Indeed, so obsessed are they with questions of breeding that the people of the region are amazed when a foreign visitor cannot recite, as they can, their grandparents back to the seventh generation. This obsession with the seventh generation means that they define family widely – they call it the *cenedl*, or their clan – referring to even fifth cousins as if they were brothers. And here there is not only a sentimental link, but a living one, for in the law of Gwynedd disputes are often settled with reference to the *cenedl*. So, for example, if there is a murder one clan collectively pays another clan the *galanas* or blood-fee to prevent further violence – psychopathic relations not being encouraged. Family status also decides the honour price of an individual, or the *sarhaed* as they call it. All natives have their *sarhaed*, however small, and this is resorted to in the case of slander. If the traveller insults one of the low peasants we have described, then it is enough to empty a sack of corn over said peasant's head: they are satisfied by little. But if you insult the king of Gwynedd then you will be expected to pay – the traveller has been warned – a *sarhaed* of a hundred cows with one red-eared bull, a rod of gold as tall as the king and as broad as his little finger, and a plate of gold as wide as his face and as thick as the nail of a ploughman who has been a ploughman through seven years.

On the subject of insults and compensation we come now to a delicate subject, one that we find especially painful to write about: relations with the native girls. We acknowledge and have heard and read many times of the pale and striking beauty of British-Celtic maidens. And, what is more, we understand too that some sexual liberty is permitted: young couples can live together before marrying. However, a word of warning to the saucy traveller. A girl's virginity is absolutely sacred. If her maidenhead is taken the consequences are grave, not least because newly-wed husbands have the right to throw their newly-wed brides out of bed and house when they are not 'intact' – so disgracing the girl and her family. As a result the *cenedl* defend their young girls jealously. Nor is marriage to be advised. The traveller must remember that as an *alltud* or foreigner he will have no status except that of his wife and will be treated as a woman in the law courts.

If the traveller is passing through these pages in an emergency – perhaps dazzled by a girl's fey ways and her family's mead, a foolish wedding contract has been made – then we offer the following three tips for escape. Tip one, simulate leprosy: the laws of this people allow divorce for women with leprous husbands. Tip two, simulate impotence: the laws also allow divorce for this, though there is a rather embarrassing series of tests to certify the condition – a large public assembly and a black sheet are involved.[1] Tip three, pretend to be a fairy: the laws do not mention fairies, but the population believe in these strange, malevolent beings as they believe in the sun or the moon. To convince in this new role, the traveller should refuse to speak about

---

1. *Translator's note:* Welsh laws preserved in later centuries also mention that bad breath was a cause for divorce. We do not know whether our author has suppressed this, was ignorant of it or, whether this was a creation of the later Middle Ages.

his true home, but nod longingly at the hills – inside which the fairies are said to live. He must from time to time wave exotic silk around and speak in his sleep about albino cows, or cringe when he comes close to iron, a substance that fairies hate. The British Celts are forever raving about such creatures, who occasionally enter the world to walk off with babies or bed young women. And if a girl can boast of having been seduced by a prince of fairy then she will escape with honour and her husband may escape with his life.

The heart of Gwynedd is not the north coast but the island of Mon that stands just off its shore and where Aberfrau [Aberffraw], the court of the Gwenedotian kings, is to be found. This is the famous Mon that was, we read in the Roman historian Tacitus, the ancient stronghold of the druids. It was here that the druids had their sacred groves and their sacrifices and their schools of knowledge, and it was here that they hissed, danced and cursed the Roman soldiers who stood back in fear before finally mounting the boats to push across and end their evil, pagan rites forever. No druids survive in Britain today – though as the reader will soon see, in Ireland a few linger on – but Mon still has something rather other-worldly about it. Travellers will be shown to the grave of a princess, Branwen, on the River Alau [Alaw], a princess of ancient times whose heart burst from sorrow for bringing about the destruction of the armies of her people. In the Vale of Citheinn there is the stone that walks by night and that should only be observed by day. There is, in the north of the island, though we do not know its name, the hill that turns around three times a year. There are still some wild cats, the spawn of the Cat of Palug that the Emperor Arthur had to destroy with his own hands and the help of some looking-glass armour.[1] Then every day at the fountain of Clarach in the very centre of Mon, two saintly men, 'Cybi the Sun-burnt' and 'Seriol the White', meet, each having walked from their respective homes on the east and the west coast of the island.[2] Finally, we should mention the remarkable

1. *Translator's note:* The Cat of Palug was one of the offspring of a huge boar, Henwen ('Old White'), and is mentioned several times in Welsh legend, always in association with Anglesey.
2. *Translator's note:* The nicknames are easily explained: walking from the west Cybi in the morning takes the sun full on his face, while returning in the afternoon, after his meeting with Seriol, it also burns him; with Seriol, meanwhile, the contrary is true and so he remains white.

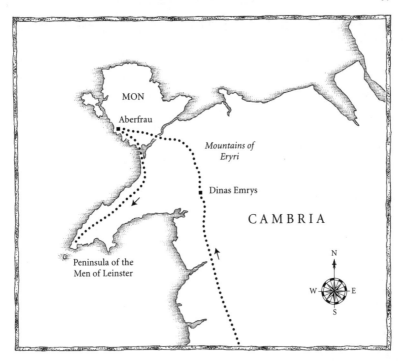

chapel of the Blessed Virgin, where the Emperor Arthur once went when badly injured; there the door is so narrow that you must squeeze through its portal to enter. The traveller needs to work up some guile before arriving at the royal court, for he can lose a week being shown pointless and widely distributed sites such as these: we advise a simulated fever to avoid excursions.

(III) ABERFFRAW

The king of Gwynedd in the time of the embassy was a certain Magloconus, who was known as 'the dragon of Mon'. This 'dragon' had, in his youth, a reputation as a learned and holy adolescent – he had for a time even been a monk. But later he chose to follow the paths of the world, killing many members of his family before finally winning for himself the high kingship of Gwynedd. Nor then did he manage to hold in check his godless lust, but disposed of wife and nephew to marry his nephew's wife.

However, though a wicked man, he was certainly an impressive king. He read Latin and spoke it to the embassy without need of translators. He also had the stature and manners of a monarch even if his was a poor court. So when Magloconus walked into the throne room, before him came his twenty-four royal attendants in ceremonial garb, who were all scrupulously mentioned in the log: the chief of the household, the priest of the household, the steward, the court judge, the falconer, the chief groom, the queen's groom, the chief huntsman, the chamberlain, the queen's assistant, the court bard, the herald, the doorkeeper of the throne room, the doorkeeper of the king's chamber, the chambermaid, the rein-holder, the candle man, the butler, the mead-maker, the royal officer, the shoe-holder and the court physician.

This kind of ceremonial might seem frankly ridiculous for a ruler who, at his strongest, can hope loosely to control a few valleys, mountains and a small island in the Irish Sea. But not the least extraordinary thing about the kings of Gwynedd is that they are under the delusion that they are the lords, not just of this small territory in the corner of a British peninsula, but of the whole of Britain! We say this for they claim that the 'monarch of Britain' held, in ancient times, his court at Aberfrau where the Gwenedotian king holds his chief court today. When this is mixed with the Great Prophecy that we quoted from earlier, a prophecy that also claims that the monarchs of Magloconus's line will one day soon sit once more atop the White Hill on the throne of Londinium [London], the traveller will understand that the kings of Gwynedd have been given ample space to march their delusions of grandeur up and down.

As far as the visitor is concerned it is best to give such delusions room and, if the traveller is an agent of the Byzantine government, to promise our Emperor's full support in so doing. Certainly Magloconus seemed fully aware, perhaps more aware than any other British ruler, of the significance of a meeting with the Greeks. After a long ceremony of introduction where Magloconus asked to be remembered to his 'fellow emperor' in Constantinople – the manners of the barbarians simply defy belief – gifts were exchanged. The embassy gave a fabulous engraved design wrought in the Byzantine style in a surround with precious stones.[1] The Greek Emperor received, meanwhile, a bucking stallion from the hills of central Cambria where the best horses in Britain are to be found. We say his was also a cunning gift for Magloconus already knew that the embassy planned to move on to Ireland and so had to leave the horse behind for 'later collection'. However, a more fitting tribute to our Empire was a stone commemorating the year in the Greek manner that was erected on the mainland nearby.[2] Such stones are regularly put up to remember the dead or mark memorable occasions in administrative centres or cemeteries and are characterised by their large and clumsy scripts.

Magloconus is, as we have noted, a learned man and he played a strange game with the embassy, one that we mention here so that future travellers will not be humiliated in his court. At a time of leisure, between the endless trips to see 'the wonders of Mon' and after the embassy boasted of the excellence of learning in Constantinople, Magloconus gave our people a short sentence written in Greek letters. Smiling and obviously satisfied with himself, he challenged the embassy to unpick the riddle. The 'words' in Greek were in fact all nonsense. It was impossible even to say them. But with much patience the party worked on the code until they found the key, the trick being a simple one. Each letter in the Greek alphabet corresponded to the same numbered letter in Latin. For example, in Greek 'nu' is the thirteenth letter, while the thirteenth letter in Latin is 'm'. When transformed in this way the embassy found that the Greek letters became in Latin: 'Magloconus is a wise king'.

The court was much impressed by such a show of learning – though really the code is elementary, cooked up, we are told, by an Irish monk. Here again we must remind the reader that in Britain none have any real knowledge of Greek, and relatively few read or write Latin intelligibly and so even this modest game with the Greek alphabet can

1. *Translator's note:* A sixth-century intaglio of Byzantine origin portraying a scorpion was found in a grave at Cefn Cwmwd on Anglesey. It is not impossible, given the rarity of this kind of find in western Britain, that this was the central piece of the work referred to by the log.

2. *Translator's note:* A sixth-century stone from Penmachno in Gwynedd mentions, for dating purposes, a Byzantine emperor. Could this be the stone remembered by our author?

seem an accomplishment of wit. It is best not to mock, but rather to congratulate them on their 'Attic learning', shaking the head in wonder many times. They have still more games of which we have heard – the Celts love word puzzles above all other peoples – and we have seen examples of their acrostics, where they make tables of letters with hidden messages. Some even say that they hide wisdom in their lopsided stone inscriptions, including lines from Virgil, rhymes of Plautus and designs of naked men. But this we find more difficult to believe.

(IV) THE LLEYN PENINSULA

We must note here, at the end, the most curious of Magloconus's subjects – the Scotti[1] or Irish who live in a peninsula at the far extremity of his kingdom. The reader might naively be thinking that those who live in Britain are the British and those who live in Ireland are the Irish. But nothing is ever so simple in the Dark Isles. In fact, many Irishmen live in Britain, the descendants of the galloglass that came conquering when the Romans were evacuating their Britannia a hundred years ago or more. Indeed, we have already visited Brycheiniog, where one Irish adventurer carved out a kingdom for himself in the hills of central Cambria. Another Irish group also arrived at that time in Gwynedd and fought for the kingdom, only being defeated by some British-Celtic mercenaries who arrived from the north. The leader of these mercenaries was a certain Cunneda, from whom Magloconus himself claims descent, and who, with elan and passion, fought all the Irish invaders into a humiliating evacuation of this part of Britain. We say 'all' but, in fact, some surrendered to Cunneda and his descendants and to this day live on the neck of land that is named the Peninsula of the Men of Leinster [Lleyn Peninsula], for these Irish serfs, who are

1. *Translator's note: Scottus* was the Latin name for the Irish or Gaels in the early Middle Ages: a word that offered anti-Irish writers much ammunition, for its closeness to the Latin word *sottus* ('idiot'). Indeed, one delicious early medieval anecdote has a Continental king at dinner sarcastically asking his guest, a learned Irish man, the difference between a *sottus* and a *scottus*, to which the scholar cooly replies 'the length of a table'. *Scottus* survives today, of course, in the word Scotland and Scot, the name and the inhabitants of Ireland's most successful colony.

now counted as subjects of Gwynedd, came originally from the part of Ireland named Leinster. On the peninsula, Irish is still spoken and the population follow Gael customs having fear, but no love, for the 'dragon of Mon'. For the traveller, Lleyn remains the perfect gateway to Ireland and he and his party can arrive with the king of Gwynedd's recommendation and from there find their way on to a ship that will cross the Irish Sea and take them to southern Eire and its crowded slave markets. The embassy, who had been ordered by the Emperor to visit all the kings not only of Britain but also of Ireland, certainly departed from there.

On the Peninsula of the Men of Leinster we think we have come to the right and proper place to discuss in more detail the languages of the British Celts and the Irish, for they are best described together, being in many ways similar. Indeed, to speak both it is enough to learn a handful of words in one tongue and then transfer them to the second, changing a little the angle of the mouth and stretching the consonants differently: 'head', for example, is *pen* in British Celtic but *cen* in Irish. However, a bigger difficulty for the foreigner presented by both languages is their habit of changing words in strange ways. Our tongue [i.e. Greek] regularly transforms the last letters, when for example the word is plural. The perversion of these western languages, though, is that one must learn to change not only the end of the words, but also their beginnings and sometimes even the middle!

The British Celts and the Irish barely write in their own languages and so the problem of reading them, other than the odd name of a town or person, hardly arises. However, on the Peninsula the explorer will meet with a strange exception to this rule. The Irish, many years ago, invented a system of writing named *ogam*. To write *ogam* one must take a wand of yew and make horizontal slashes along its length, the number of slashes corresponding to a given letter. So, for example, to write the letter 'e' one makes four slashes across a single vertical line. It is a cumbersome and frankly idiotic way of putting down a sentence. But the Irish have become enamoured of it and include words on silver sticks, swords, bows or even (here the author allows himself to smile) they spend hours grating these lines on to stone. In fact, it is not uncommon in the Peninsula of the Men of Leinster and in other Irish areas to find just such marks, not instead of, but next to Latin inscriptions as if translating them! The traveller must not, as one foolish member of the embassy did, comment that it looks as if a sheep had scratched its back repeatedly against the rock. We say this as the Irish take their *ogam very* seriously.

PART II

IRELAND:
THE GAELS

4

SOUTH-EAST IRELAND:
'A SLAVER'S DREAM'

(I) THE CROSSING AND IRELAND

The island of Ireland lies almost two days' sailing from the Peninsula of the Men of Leinster, across a sea which, although it rarely has the white breakers of the Atlantic, can still prove treacherous to those who have not grown up on its waters. We have heard many things about this sea. We have heard of the villages that were drowned and whose bells still rock under the waves. We have heard of the time when it was possible to wade from Britain to Eire, so shallow was the intervening ocean. And we have heard as well of the many holy men who persist in walking barefoot across the surface of this sea as if it were 'a field of corn and flowers'. They even speak of the Emperor Arthur setting off with several colleagues to raid a fortress made of crystal in the middle of this watery waste, a fortress that inconveniently disappeared on being conquered. But, as we have already stated, the British Celts cannot open their mouths without legends pouring out and they people every landscape, including this forsaken waterway, with their lies. The reader will naturally do as he or she pleases with such stories; but we strongly advise the traveller to ignore these accounts and to concentrate, instead, on finding a capable navigator or better still a passage on one of the trade ships that carry British goods, especially British horses, to Ireland.

Of Ireland itself we have also many things to tell – some so strange that we fear the reader will doubt us or think we have 'picked up' something from the legend-mad British Celts. The most remarkable is the claim that the mild Irish climate proves inimical to all poisons. No reptiles live there, or at least none of those that kill man. And even stinging bees have only recently arrived, coaxed over from Britain by monks who wished to cultivate their honey in monastic gardens. Nor do the wonders cease with this. So poison-proof is Ireland that any tiny scrap from this country works, properly applied, as an antidote. Households in Britain, for example, keep Irish twigs or fragments of Irish manuscripts, and, if one of their own is bitten by an adder, then they are made to drink this Irish object in water as a cure, the swelling coming down almost immediately. We must add some small measure of scepticism, however, to the claim that there is no poison of any type. We do this on the evidence of the log. For the embassy, intrigued by the tales of a poisonless land, took to feeding a slave that they had purchased – we will soon come to the Irish slave markets – all the fungi they could find. And the relatively speedy decease of their 'taster' proved that some venomous substances, at least, do exist there.

Of the Irish themselves we also have much to tell. Like the British Celts they are a proud people, and like the British Celts they are a barbaric people. But there is one difference over their neighbours to which it is worth drawing attention: they do not believe themselves to be Roman, the cause of many embarrassing situations for the embassy in Cambria and Dumnonia. In fact, to be Roman can be somewhat dangerous among the Gaels as there are Irishmen who still guard the memory of their grandparents' wars with legionaries on the shores of Britannia. Some of my more ignorant colleagues and the many troublemakers in our Emperor's court have even expressed surprise that the embassy visited Ireland at all given that our Roman legions never reached these particular shores.

It is true that the legions never came to the island: we admitted as much in our preface. However, it was absolutely right that the embassy was sent, for in ancient times we made alliances with the Irish tribes who sometimes served in our armies. Who could forget the terrible Attacotti, one of whom the blessed Jerome saw eating human flesh? And it is also true to say that today Ireland is almost wholly Christian, thanks to the sponsorship of the Roman Church that sent one of her bravest servants there, a certain Palladius, to convert the Gaels. And as the Emperor has long insisted that he is the rightful protector of all those who embrace the Cross, Ireland too must be seen as one of his rightful domains, a domain that will one day, hopefully one day soon, be taken under the tutelage of his rule.

So much for the theory: what about the practice? Much effort was made by the embassy to convince the Irish clergy of their duties to the Empire and this must have had a good effect, for we have heard only recently that some Irish monks, though certainly still a minority, now refer to themselves as *Roman* Christians. However, their chiefs and warlords were not persuaded and many became positively violent at the thought of bowing their necks to our full-sceptered lord. This is partly a result of their natural stubbornness. But there is also one other surprising obstacle that frequently cropped up: the fact that they believe themselves to belong to another nation, that of the Egyptians. Strange as this may sound, their wise men insist that the Gaels arrived in Ireland, many epochs ago, after a great trek that began in Asia and that passed through the land of the Pyramids. There a certain princess, Scotta, became linked to the Gaelic caravan, and she is today celebrated as the mother of the nation. The reader may sneer at this idea as an absurdity or discard it as an illusion. But there are practical consequences that the traveller can use to his advantage. If, for example, the 'Egyptian' visitor can rustle up a little dry sand in a phial or talk about the Nile in flood and trips to the Mountains of the Moon on the upper reaches of that river, then hospitality is practically guaranteed for a month.

The Gaels have many other strange beliefs. But, before we describe these, we wish first to remark on the reason why so many traders come to southern Ireland. We refer not to Irish dogs – though the island's hounds, we acknowledge, are also celebrated[1] – but rather to slaves. Everywhere the traveller goes there he will have the opportunity to buy these. Indeed so endemic is the trade in humans that the standard Irish currency – they use no coins – is a *cumal*, or female slave, equivalent to three cows. We stress this for many travellers are tempted into a purchase on being told that they will be given ten or twenty female slaves, only to find to their horror that these are simply units of measurement and that they have won instead – and must drag behind them – a mooing herd of cattle.

---

1. *Translator's note:* the Irish laws detail four kind of dogs: the guard dog, the pet dog, the shepherd dog and the hunting dog. No archaeological or textual evidence suggests that any of these correspond to the Irish wolf-hound, a creature that seems to have been bred only in later medieval times. In fact, there is no proof that any Irish dog from this period was bigger than, say, an Alsatian.

One of the most interesting slave markets is to be found where the river they call the Liffey reaches the sea [i.e. Dublin], a useful port, much of the inland horizon being crested by mountains. The log-keeper of the embassy claimed that he had never seen such high-quality slaves so cheaply sold and invested in several to bring back to the Emperor. There he found British Celts, Saxons, Picts, Gaels (of course), and even some Franks, not to mention Spaniards and Africans picked up in raids or sucked along on the waves of war and exchange. There were also many slaves of the third or fourth generation, the children and grandchildren of slaves who had been fathered either by other slaves or more likely by one of their libidinous owners. (Irish masters, it seems, take their slaves to bed as a matter of economics, for one of slave blood is not allowed to become part of the family and so can usefully be sold on.)

We can offer two good rules for buying slaves in Ireland. The first rule is 'buy local' – that is, invest in Irish slaves rather than foreigners. We say this because slaves are priced on the basis of how easily they can escape. A strong young Irishman caught in a raid will cost relatively little money because it is thought probable that he will be able to reach home again if the opportunity arises. A woman from Spain, meanwhile – women rarely attempt escape – is far less likely to disappear in the night and for this reason can prove expensive. Obviously, for the foreign trader, these rules can be used to his advantage. Some of the best slaves for our purposes are strong young Irish warriors who are unlikely to make their way home from the city of the Emperor, but who can be bought cheaply enough on the banks of the Liffey.

A second rule is to avoid the Saxons. We say this not only because they are a barbaric people: as we will later show, they dwarf even the British Celts and the Irish in their incivility and general bad manners; but because they have a strange and secret weapon, the runes. These are small symbols that they scratch on themselves and their possessions and that can magically cause locked objects – such as chains – to open. They also have efficacious prayers and we were told of one Saxon slave whose chains sprung open every time his family – who believed he was dead – prayed for him. Clearly, these types of complications should be avoided if possible. We grant that the young men of their race are of an exceptional beauty; indeed, we ourselves have seen some remarkable specimens in the markets at Rome, for with their long blond hair and a hard cleaning, the type that slavers are accustomed to give before an auction, they shine like-angels. But it is best not to throw away money on goods that cannot be safely moved across country and over the oceans. If the traveller on reading this has already made a purchase, do not fret though. Resale is anyway easy in Ireland as there is no documentation or registration to restrict entrepreneurial flair.

Leaving behind the protection of the Liffey markets, where foreigners, be they Greeks or Gauls, are welcomed and protected, is a decision that no explorer should take lightly. We, at any rate, strongly counsel, before doing so, a meditation on Irish customs and *mores* such as we offer here. The most important point to consider is that their island is split into five different territories. There is, at the very centre, Mide, which in Irish means 'the mid territory'. And around it four larger provinces spin like spokes on a wheel. In the south-east there is Leinster, from where the Gaels on the Peninsula of the Men of Leinster in Gwynedd come and where the slave market we have described above is to be found. In the south-west is Munster, famous for its bishop kings. In the north-west is Connaught, many say the wildest part of Ireland. And in the north-east there is Ulster, where the most warlike warriors are said to live. Each of these fifths, or *coiced* as they are called in Irish, are made up of a number of smaller tribes or *tuath* – we are told that the population of a *tuath* can number several thousand – and each of these *tuath* has its own king. However, the different *tuath* then collectively elect one monarch who becomes the king of the fifth. And from time to time one of these kings is made king of Tara, which means he becomes the king of the whole island. Not the least remarkable point of this most remarkable system is that even higher than the high kings are the Laws of the Irish. For despite the barbarity of this people, they are all fanatical followers of certain injunctions handed down to them from generation to generation, and these even the various tribal leaders dare not flaunt. The different clauses of the Law are remembered – only now are priests starting to write them down for the first time – by a special legal class of professional judges, who travel from place to place peddling their decisions. And though we are loath to speak well of something produced by the world-enders, they make up, in fact, an impressive corpus, the wisdom of which we will see when addressing the territory of Connaught.

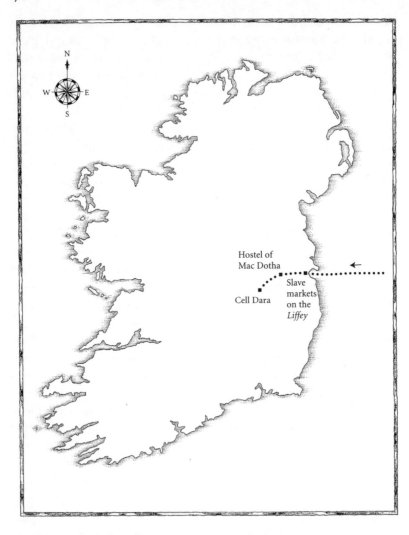

Our knowledge of this system depends not just on the account of the log (which is frequently rather unclear on these points), but also on a visit from a Roman monk who, in his youth, had been sent to the Gaels as a missionary. This man, who served with the most famous of the missionaries to Ireland, the British Celt Patrick, described to us, in compelling detail, the difficulty of passing through the various minor kingdoms. It seems, for example, that when faced with a truculent king or one of the judges who apply the Laws and who have much power, the missionaries had to pay out large sums. At that time – and still in some parts of the island today – the Irish were hostile to the Cross and, on one occasion, our friend and his fellow workers were imprisoned by a local ruler and expected death, only to be ransomed by a Christian king at the last moment. Auxilius,[1] for so this missionary was called, explained to us that the gravest problem for the foreigner is that, according to their Laws, any non-Irish man who lives or travels among them is an *ambue*, or in our language 'a non-person', and the Law offers him no protection. If a 'non-person' is walking down the road an Irishman can spit on him, kick him or jump on him and kill him, and there is no recourse in the Law against such behaviour. Indeed, an *ambue* has no rights to speak of and his only hope is to gain the protection of a powerful man – king, noble or bishop – in the area. How does the traveller arrange such protection? We advise a visit to a local *rath*, that is a stronghold, as soon as he heads inland, followed by prompt payment of a sum of money or – see above – some Nile sand.

Protection is traditionally sealed by the notorious and unappetising act of nipple-sucking. The Irish use many gestures to signal their moods and relationships – for example, pulling harshly at your hand means that you should vanish quickly from the presence of the hand-puller, while hand-clapping is a sign of woe or intense grieving. Nipple-sucking, instead, is a sign of friendship and even alliance. The traveller must never initiate the act, but only move when the shirt is drawn up and the nipple offered. At that point, bowing low, he should bend down and suck for a moment and then slowly return to the upright position. Any prolonged sucking causes social discomfort, quickly rising suggests disgust – both are deemed highly offensive. However unpleasant the sucking proves, the benefits, at least, are enormous. By taking the nipple, the traveller becomes the child of his new 'mother' and 'the mother' will protect him. And any local who then meddles with the traveller will have to face the wrath of this 'mother' in the courts of law.

---

1. *Translator's note:* One of the disciples of St Patrick, who worked in Ireland in the fifth century, was named Auxilius. We may be dealing with the same individual.

(II) LEINSTER

A nipple-sucker or not, the visitor from abroad will meet few other long-distance travellers on the road. Or only very select ones. Men and women from one *tuath* traditionally stay within the bounds of their own kingdom, for only there does the Law offer them full protection. The exception to this rule are the *Aes Dana* or 'the men of craft', which includes poets – Irish poets are, incidentally, even more dangerous than their British-Celtic cousins and can rhyme enemies to death – as well as smiths, doctors, wrights and members of the Church. Such travellers are admired for their various skills and, in a jam, the explorer might even consider imitating one of them. Greek medical knowledge is much respected in all the west and so becoming a doctor is one option; another is to find a sharp knife and perform a rapid tonsure on oneself – remember, however, that the back of the head must be shaved entirely.

Whatever strategy the traveller chooses, he will find one surprising boon on his journey in Leinster and that is the hostel. We do not refer here to the ale halls – may the innocent foreigner be preserved from them! – places of fighting, rape and the drunken forgetfulness of God. We refer rather to the *briugu* as he is known, a man who dedicates himself to freely serving passers-by on the most important roads of the country. Men who become *briugu* are wealthy peasants, for the Law, which decides all things in Ireland, states that those of low blood may not become lords. But if rich enough they can, at least, set up a hostel and so increase their status and privileges in the law courts.

An Irish saying tells us that there are three things that characterise a *briugu*: 'a never-dry cauldron' (the *briugu*'s fire is always lit); 'a dwelling on a public road'; and 'a welcome to every face'. If the *briugu* refuses to take in a traveller, then he loses his status and reverts to being a commoner, so even if you arrive with a band of fifty he will be obliged to keep his smile and provide a free table for all. The Law states that a commoner who wants to become a *briugu* must have one hundred rooms at his disposal – hostels are large – one hundred servants to run errands, one hundred cows, pigs, horses, sheep, goats, dogs, cats, hens, geese and, bizarrely, one hundred bees.

These hostels are found throughout Ireland, though the houses of Leinster are the most famous and the best supplied, and none in

Leinster is better known than that of Mac Dotha's. It is only fitting, then, that we include here the embassy's account of their visit to that famous resting-house, not only for the light it throws on Mac Dotha's home, but also for its insights into the customs of another Irish institution, the war band.

We were greeted with the traditional smile and nod to the unending cauldron by our host Mac Dotha, a friendly, portly individual who was perhaps close to fifty. On establishing that we were foreigners he kindly offered us his nipple, though luckily we were able to refuse being already under the protection of the local king, a fact that, incidentally, impressed him considerably. He then went on to boast that he could offer us entertainment from two specialists that night. The first was a professional farter, famous for his noisy and, as we found, pungent routine: such players are greatly appreciated in the courts of the Irish; while the second was a simple and rather incompetent juggler. Our conversation proceeded kindly enough and then Mac Dotha left, with many bows, to tend to a local war band that had arrived to feast away the night on their way to raiding the *tuaths* of the north.

As we have stated, we were impressed by this Mac Dotha. However, his easy manners and smiles disappeared in a most extraordinary circumstance that we will now recount. Close to midnight, when the feasting was already far advanced and all – including ourselves and the above-mentioned war band – were somewhat drunk, one of his hundred servants came running with some evidently urgent news that sent Mac Dotha stumbling towards the door. Curious and a little tipsy, we followed him to see a mass of men coming down the hostel path. They were, Mac Dotha hurriedly explained, a war band from Ulster, precisely the region that the Leinster war band seated within hoped to raid. Indeed, as we were soon to understand, the men in both bands had fought each other many times before and both sides knew and hated the other intimately.

The leader of the recently arrived band, an Ulster king, strolled arrogantly up to the entrance and Mac Dotha did his best to provide a welcome – though his smile was a shadow of the one he had given us earlier in the day. Formalities over, he then stutteringly explained that some 'friends' of the Ulaid [men of Ulster] were already in residence. At this the Ulster band laughed uproariously and their chief bent bullyingly over little, plump Mac Dotha – hosteliers are well known for never carrying weapons – and hissed: 'Do you refuse us hospitality? Do you deny the Law?' Almost weeping, Mac Dotha stood aside, for, as they explained to us, if a *briugu* ever refuses a guest then he will lose his status. The Ulstermen then filed into the feasting hall smiling and waving provocatively at their enemies, who woke startled from out of their drunkenness.

The two sides settled down surprisingly quickly into burping and bonhomie – we were offered many nipples on this occasion. But, after a few more courses, Mac Dotha entered the hall with a huge swine that had been killed that very evening. In a hostel house, the *briugu* always leaves the carving to a guest and so one of our members kindly stood up to take the knife, only to be dragged down by all three of our terrified guides. These quickly explained that he who carves also takes the first and best piece, known as the hero's portion. We asked how then they would decide who was to carve, for the room had become very silent: 'How else' said a warrior next to us 'if not by sharing according to brave acts? After all, every member of these two armies here has hit the others over their noses before now'. Then, sitting, our mouths wide open, we watched as, one by one, the warriors of the two sides stood up to take the hero's portion, only to be insulted by the other and cowed into sitting down again. Verbal duelling is much admired among the Irish and is well known for its versatility and speed – such that our translator could not always keep pace. However, what we understood was of a rather rough or bloody nature involving genitalia, toilets and the sexual habits of the various warriors' mothers.

After an hour of this sparring the tone changed, though. By a process of elimination in these verbal fights, only two warriors, Conall and Cet, one from each side, were left arguing for the carving of the pig, which was by then getting somewhat cold. However, such was the respect that they had for each other that they did not at first throw insults but sang songs of tribute. (Our translator here admitted again that he did not always understand all the difficult and elusive language.) Then, and only then, did the two hulking warriors return to more vulgar everyday tones – hissing, spitting and shouting.

'Cet, get up from that pig now and don't you dare go back!' yelled

Conall, the taller man, furious at his opponent's presumption in taking the knife in his hands. But Cet's face soured:

'But what, Conall, have you to do with this pig?'

'Oh, if you want to challenge me, Cet, that's just perfect! I accept your challenge to a fight. And I swear what my people swear: since I took a spear in my hand there has not been a night that I have slept without the decapitated head of an Leinsterman under my pillow, and I have wounded a man almost every single day since I became a man.'

We could almost hear the silence as Cet began to consider his position and his response, when it finally came, was muted. 'It is true,' said Cet. 'You are a better man than I am. However, if Anluan, the greatest warrior of the south, were in the house he would offer you a fight. It is a pity for us that he is not here today.' Conall, though, now showed that he was not only the better fighter with arms, but also with words and deeds. 'But Anluan is in the house!,' he said in a stage whisper. And taking a head from off his belt – the head of this Anluan, it transpired – he threw it at Cet's chest with such force that blood splashed through the dead lips. So it was Conall then who carved the hero's portion, his own side cheering, the home side white with anger and humiliation.

(III) KILDARE

The Law splits all Irishmen into two classes: those with cows and those without. This indicates an important truth about Ireland, for although there are many domesticated animals there – sheep, hens, pigs – cows are certainly the most valued; indeed, in wintertime the Irish eat nothing but beef. Nobles do not rent out land to their clients as they do in the rest of Europe. Rather, they rent out cows and the cowless Irish peasant is expected to give back calves with some other goods as rent in the new year. The traveller will find that this system operates wherever he goes in Leinster and, indeed, in the whole island. And in any conversation with the natives, try to establish as quickly as possible whether you are talking to a man with cows or a man without. If the latter, end any communication instantly – for no influence, nipples or help will be forthcoming. If the former, mention the several thousand heads of cattle that the Emperor keeps in Thrace.

Influence and safety in Leinster are best found in the houses or *raths* of the various cow-rich nobles. But they can also be found at a curious site known as Cell Dara [Kildare] towards the centre of the province. Ireland has no cities or villages: a *tuath*'s inhabitants are spread out across the country's bogs and swamps. However, at Cell Dara we find the closest to an urban centre in the island. No enemy is feared there and so secure are its ways that local kings and nobles bring their treasures to the place for safe keeping. There are crowds, some coming for the markets and festivals, others just for the excitement of seeing the rabble of different peoples milling about. And, incredibly, the magnet that brings all these Gaels to one site is a monastery! A monastery should be a place of peace where one goes to escape from the world. But, in Ireland, monasteries with their settled life and defences – holy defences and expertly dug ditches – attract the rabble of people as no other place. And within their limits special laws also apply. So, for example, inside the bounds of the monastery – Irish monasteries are always surrounded by circular ditches – no one should unsheath their sex or bring unclean animals.

Cell Dara was originally the monastery of a certain Brigit who converted to Christ a century or more ago and led her life most admirably, so much so that now her body is responsible for many miracles. We have heard from our friend Auxilius of the tortures that slaves and aristocratic women alike were prepared to go through to become nuns when Christianity first came to the island and we do not doubt that she too – a slave girl with a druid father – suffered the wrath of her masters. She is, we say, a woman who deserves our admiration and we must hope for her celestial prayers. But is it not also true, and have we not seen even in our own time, that when the Gospels are taken outside civilisation to the barbaric races, Christianity quickly grows out of shape and perverts into the savage shoots of heresy? We have heard of this in many of the barbarian countries, not least with the terrible Arian controversy that blunted the message of the Gospel for the best part of three centuries and even now sullies the works of some of our fathers.[1]

So it is among the Gaels and with Brigit, for already the Irish have

---

1. *Translator's note:* Arianism, a heresy that overemphasised the divine aspect of the Trinity. It had great success, especially beyond the lines of the old Roman frontier where Germanic barbarians found it more to their taste than the complicated Trinitarian system of orthodox Christianity.

begun to add their own pagan distortions to the true life of this admirable virgin. We have heard, for example, that in her shrine there is an ever-burning flame kept lit in memory of her, and that, like vestal virgins, some nuns are set to guard it. This might seem a pious gesture. But in Leinster there was in pagan times a mighty goddess named Brig and the custom has been borrowed, shameful to say, from her temples. Indeed, Auxilius informs us that the locals never pray to Christ but always to Brigit and in their confusion they do not know whether they pray to the goddess or the saint. Then, even when the Irish pray through saints – and the saints, for the Irish, like Arthur for the British Celts, fill all their imagination – they cannot avoid blasphemy. For example, the writer of the log recorded, most credulously, a story about the abbot of Drimnagh, a small monastery near the Liffey, who, while out walking one day was changed by fairies into a woman, married the abbot of a neighbouring monastery, had three children and then a decade later magicked back into a man, returning to his old post as abbot again. Incredible to say, the Irish who listened to this story crossed themselves piously at its completion as if they had heard an edifying episode in the life of a holy man!

The first visit at Cell Data should, of course, be to the head of that mighty church. Owing to his situation in the south-east of the island, the abbot there is in more regular contact with the outside world and his hospitality is generous and his manners bearable. He will also remember with gratitude the embassy, for they were responsible for passing on a Greek manuscript of the *Iliad* with a Latin translation glossed above it – a gift that caused him immense joy.[1] Less pleasant but nevertheless unforgettable is the shrine to Brigit, where her body is buried. To enter the church it is best to clap a cloth doused in strong spirits against your mouth and then move into the crawling mass of human refuse that stands there. All those who are distorted by nature – mutes, the blind, the lame and lepers – are gathered in a crowd, some lying, some standing, others squatting before the holy altar muttering prayers in their own language. Fortunately, incense is regularly sprinkled on all, some relief being given to the nose of the traveller.

---

[1]. *Translator's note:* An early Irish adaptation of the *Iliad* – eighth-century? – has long puzzled scholars as it dates to a period many centuries before Homer was read in the medieval west; the twelfth century is normally given for the 'rediscovery' of Homer there. This Byzantine gift may go some way to explaining it.

5

WESTERN AND CENTRAL IRELAND: 'DRUIDS, MONKS AND WOLVES'

(I) MUNSTER

Leinster is hemmed in by hilly and swampy regions in the north and the west; and we advise the traveller strongly against crossing these natural barriers. Living in the south-east near the British seaways and on the merchants' routes, the population in Ireland's most civilised *coiced* [province] have long experience of foreigners and, a useful source of income, these are treated considerately. Beyond Leinster though in the wastelands, where you can sometimes walk a full two or three days without coming to a hostel, and where some of the population have never seen any race other than their own, the dangers mount with the uncertainties.

The embassy was obliged to journey in these perilous parts, for their express order from the Emperor of the day had been to search out all the warlords of the islands, even those who dwell in such marginal places. But we believe that this cannot be held to apply to future travellers. The merchant or spy can have no conceivable reason for going further across the heaths, rivers and lakes of the island – there is nothing to buy, little to sell and absolutely no information worth purloining. And, while we concede that the adventurer or the mapper may be able to make a case for wandering there, the risks hardly justify the rewards: the views from Tara, or the Needle's Eye, or even the chance to see, from afar, one of the last druids, the almost extinct ancient priests of the Celts. Indeed I, who have never been further north than the Alps, shiver just to think of, for example, the Irish werewolves, or some of the customs in the wilder monasteries. If the traveller does insist on risking his life in the province, though – and again we wish to advise against such a foolish and unnecessary course of action – then he could do worse than start off west towards Munster where the bishop kings of the Eoganachta rule. The Eoganachta are the leading tribe of this fifth of Ireland, but they are well known for the carelessness of their government and even a nipple-suck from the king of the Eoganachta himself will not protect the traveller in all corners of the kingdom. 'Yes,' the potential traveller might say, 'but there is always the Law', which is true enough. But as the foreigner is a non-person with no status in Ireland it will hardly prove a trusty shield when bandits descend whooping from the valley sides or out of their hiding places on peaty plains.

One way to facilitate travel in this south-western corner of Ireland – and we grit our teeth saying this – is a marriage. The reader knows that the author has previously spoken against marriage with the natives. This was done not from the point of view of morality; if the traveller wishes to share his bed with a world-ender that is his affair. Furthermore, we have no sympathy for those who argue that the inhabitants of Britain and Ireland are not human; we have ourselves examined corpses that put the question beyond issue. We have advised against this step for the best and most practical reasons: the traveller loses his freedom and often his rights when joined in holy union in the Dark Isles.

However, in Ireland and especially in Munster there is a case to be made for a wedding of convenience. By visiting one of their small, wooden churches with the daughter of minor nobility the traveller is guaranteed half her honour price, which will mean he usefully has a higher price than any peasants he is likely to meet along the way. But even here there are disadvantages. The Irish look down on men who marry outside their *tuath* or tribe, they even call such a one 'a man who has followed a woman's middle parts over the border'; do not expect, then, to be respected for your opportunism. A second problem, and one that has more dangerous consequences, is divorce. We say this for in Ireland women are given an unaccountable amount of choice in this area. And from the log and the brief words of Auxilius the missionary, we have understood that the traveller should, in fact, only marry if he has no land or money of his own to speak of. We grant that we have not heard of any case of a divorced Gael arriving in Greece to claim her sixth of an estate. But we deem it in no way impossible, for the Irish more than any other people love to travel.

The capital of Munster is Cashel – a word taken from the Latin *castrum* [castle] – and a reminder that this part of the island once, when Britain was ours, had occasional contacts with the Empire: trade missions, mercenaries and the like. It is here, anyway, that the kings of the Eoganachta hold their seat and may be visited by the outsider. These kings invite scandal, for uniquely in Europe they combine the office of monarch and bishop or even abbot, while making no bones of marrying and perpetuating their line. However, the most incredible feature of their court is not the royal mitres but the druids; indeed, the embassy was amazed to see these fossils of a bygone age. One can hardly open the pages of the writers of old, Caesar or Lucan, Tacitus or Plutarch, without coming across accounts of the magic powers of this priesthood. What the embassy saw of them, though, proved an anticlimax, for with Christianity growing in strength, they have become less and less powerful and there were mutterings already in the embassy's time that these openly pagan magicians would be soon banned outright from the presence of the king.

But even in their reduced state, these old men – the young with spiritual gifts turn to the Church – have a certain notoriety. Instantly recognisable for their curious cloaks and their shaved heads – each has a short tuft above their forehead – they walk from place to place officiating over oaths and sacrifices (it is better not to ask of which sort). They are also sometimes hired out by kings for help in battle where from the sidelines they cast magic mists, walls of death and the darkness of night on a patron's enemies or fly like birds, so terrifying the opposition. It would be a foolish reader though that travelled to Munster specially to see these druids for the simple fact that the embassy made their trip twenty years ago. And we think it likely that already the last of this kind lies under the turf of Ireland, his soul securely threaded on one of the fiery looms of hell.

One wonder that without question remains in Munster – indeed, our heart races when writing of it – and one that all but sufferers of

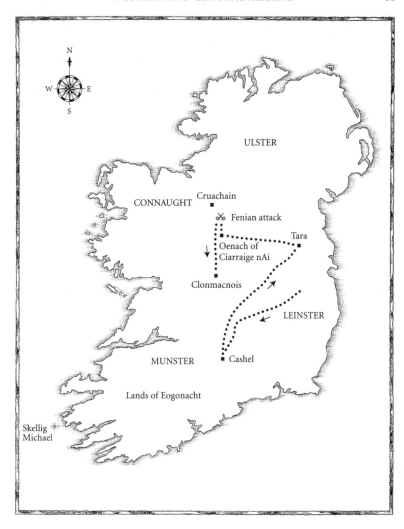

vertigo should visit is the marvellous Rock of Michael [Skellig Michael]. This is a rock six miles off the Munster coast where a group of hermits sit on cliff ledges and pray to the Creator, twelve of them all living in little beehive huts made of smooth sea rocks. The chapel that crests the hulk of this slate leviathan, almost seven hundred feet in height, is dedicated to St Michael, archangel and warrior who fights Satan with lightning. The dedication was well chosen for in stormy weather the place is often struck by bolts while the thunder ricochets around drowning the mumbling prayers of the adepts.

The traveller who arrives there must make his own pilgrimage to the height, and it is a terrifying one, for the penitent is expected to scramble over the jagged path barefoot to a point about two-thirds of the way up named Christ's Saddle. At this outcrop, he will find a number of different crosses made for different classes – we read, for example, of one for smiths – and penitents must pray at this place until they feel ready for the last and most terrifying part of the journey. There is now, before the one to be cleansed, the Stone of Pain, a flat sheer piece of rock that has to be climbed using only the finger and toe holes cut by the hermits. Finally, at the height of this and looking out over the ocean, the penitent sits astride the Needle's Eye, a thin rock finger that extends over the endless oceans of the west. He must then shin along this – we advise calm as a fall would be fatal for body and soul alike – until finally at the end of the rock it is possible to bend and kiss an ornate cross that has been carved there. In this way the penance of St Michael is complete and the sweating pilgrim can return clean to the world.

(II) MIDE

Mide is the central province of the five fifths of Ireland, by far the smallest of the five and yet by far the most important. We say this, for at the very centre of this central province, in the very middle of the island, are the heights of Tara, the traditional place of coronation for the high kings of that country. And from these heights it is possible to make out the other four provinces, spinning around this, the centre of Eire. The hundreds of small tribes that go to make up Ireland mean that it rarely happens that one single ruler is nominated who can command the obedience of the scores of minor kings. A generation ago, though, at the time of the embassy's visit, one of these very rare events took place and, indeed, after a month's stay at Tara, the embassy was able to see, in person, the crowning of one of these high kings. We have heard that this man (his name was Ailill) has since lost power and that no other king has managed to replace him; Ireland is once more in its normal state, that of regular and suicidal, intertribal war. However, as many of the customs are mirrored in the coronations that take place in the *tuaths* or the fifths, we include the relevant passage from the log here for the reader's edification:

We approached Tara over the long plain of which we have spoken and arrived on its gentle slopes already crowded over with people, for the smaller kings had come from all corners of the island to see what they call 'the feast of Tara'. Quite what this feast would involve we did not at that time know. But we soon found ourselves settled on the southern slope near where they say an earlier high king had been buried feet-first, facing his enemies for eternity with sword in hand. The crowds above us milled around a central track on the heights that had been marked off by earlier attendants: the Law has all the particulars of who should prepare the racing way of the feast of Tara. We knew only that as outsiders we were not expected to contribute and so enjoyed ourselves, speculating on which of the many bumps on the hillside was that of the vertically-buried monarch.

Ailill 'the chosen one' finally arrived with a small bodyguard of troops around evening. He was a young man in his late twenties, but a series of scars across his face and on his limbs demonstrated that he had already seen his share of fighting. Our host explained that if, in any of these fights, Ailill had lost so much as a finger or an eye he would not be at Tara on this day. Indeed, it seems that the righteous king is expected to have all his body intact and, if Ailill later had a limb cleaved off or was blinded, famine and disease would fall on the land he ruled until he was replaced by another.

The king-to-be and his bodyguard clustered at one of the far ends of the hill. But already in its centre we could see the paraphernalia for their extraordinary and obscene acts of kingship. A lovely white mare had been brought up from the plain with much care and, frisky and happily unaware of the fate that awaited her, was grazing on the hill. Horses in Ireland fall into two groups. There are the small stunted native variety that can hardly bear a man and then there are the stronger British breeds, the descendants of the horses of the legions in Britain that are regularly traded across the Irish Sea. The mare in question clearly belonged to the second group and was flawless, such that we were told it was probably worth as many as twenty *cumal* or female slaves.

All around the plain of Meath, dusk was rapidly falling and parties and well-wishers were still pouring in through the encroaching dark. Finding it more and more difficult to see, we tried to light a fire, but one of our party was pushed over by a Gael as soon as he took out some tinder. It was then that we first learnt that fire on coronation night is *geis*, or taboo. There are many of these *geis*, which bring about bad luck and in some extreme cases death or blinding. Some are for all – take that of the fire at a king's coronation, as our poor colleague had so painfully learnt – while others are more particular; so, for example, Ailill was forbidden to eat birds, an animal that is holy to him.

The ritual itself lasted most of the night and was thoroughly unpleasant. The king first mounted a stool that had been specially placed and 'mated' with the white horse. We were encouraged to see that not only our party but also many of the visiting kings politely looked in the other direction and talked of the weather during these awkward minutes or played at board games, their beloved *flidchell*, an Irish version of chess.

Seeing our embarrassment our host tried to defend the ceremony, saying that it represented a marriage with the spirit of the land who is said to be incarnate in the animal. We countered that bestiality could hardly be said to represent a marriage and was rather an act of sordid perversion. But he coolly replied that the Irish Church judges bestiality less of a crime than adultery or sodomy, then asked whether we really claimed to know better. Anyway, even if this queenly theme is the explanation for such a terrible deed then the actions that followed the coupling symbolised not so much a marriage as a murder. For, after the mating, the horse was killed and the king undressed. He then, in front of all, climbed into a huge cauldron where pieces of the horse were thrown afterwards, and was cooked along with his bride. Later, before the water boiled he climbed out while the meat was thoroughly stewed and hunks of this horse were handed out to attendants and subject kings, who greedily devoured the flesh.

We ourselves, for piety, were careful not to eat anything, but continued to watch the preparation for the ceremony that now moved on to the chariot. The Law says that he who wishes to be high king of Tara must ride a chariot through two stones placed narrowly together and then along a course that finishes with what they call the stone penis, a small menhir: clearly the theme of marriage continuing. We had heard much of these Irish chariots but had never seen one until now and in truth we were disappointed. They were surprisingly bulky and not as slick or as fast as our own.[1] The guides assure us that no one now uses them in war. But, instead, kings sometimes arrive to battle on them before dismounting and fighting with their swords. Unfortunately on this occasion we were not able to see the chariot managed in normal conditions, for Ailill was expected to ride along a difficult course and through the two narrow stones before grating harshly against the stone penis. Tradition states that he must also do so while using two untamed horses that have never been bridled before. In fact, Ailill took the best part of six hours to persuade these two wretched beasts – which if they were not tame at the beginning of the night were certainly domesticated by its end – to jam their way through the prescribed and narrow way. Onlookers watched in amusement as the king-to-be veered on and off the course, one last humiliation before he grasped the crown of the kingdom of Ireland.

Close to dawn a scraping noise indicated that the deed was done and a weary cry went up from the assembled host, a ceremonial cloak being brought to Ailill and placed around his neck. We were one of the many who now filed past him and gave him rich gifts, ours a fine bird-decked chalice made in the Byzantine style. However, Ailill did not impress us overly, for looking us up and down he merely growled at our translator, apparently asking where we were from. We talked of Greece. But, once he had learnt that Greece was not an island in the Hebrides, he lost all interest and went, yawning, to his next guest. Some in our party were inclined to put this down to ignorance, others to rudeness. But in the preceding night he had copulated with a large white animal, been almost boiled alive and then ridden two raging horses for a number of hours. A failure to give due attention to detail could perhaps be excused in these straitened circumstances.

---

1. *Translator's note:* Referring to 'our own' chariots here the log-writer is presumably thinking of the famous racing chariot of Constantinople. One of the main features of life in that city was the heavy partisan support for the two city racing teams, the greens and the blues, that frequently led to hooliganism and riots.

(III) CONNAUGHT

The reader must excuse our poorly informed account of Connaught. There was only a brief visit from the embassy that was, as we will soon see, cut short by disaster, the log consequently being scrappy and incomplete at this point. Our other sources, meanwhile, Ptolemy the geographer and Auxilius the priest, have almost no information about the north-west of Ireland. Indeed, even pooling all our data we can manage only one reliable sentence: the grandest fortress in the territory is named Cruachain and all the royal blood of Connaught, the issue of which live in the aforementioned stronghold, descend from a mighty warrior named Conn of the hundred battles.

The embassy began their tour of the province by visiting the *tuath* of the Ciarraigie nAi[1], a kingdom that boasts some of the best farming land in the north. By what they believed was great good fortune the Greeks, in fact, came to the Ciarraigie in August at the time of the *oenach* or the annual general meeting of the *tuath*. The place that is picked for this meeting is generally a strategic hill from which the tribe can see the surrounding plains – the risk of neighbours attacking at festival time is heightened – or they sometimes choose the shade of the sacred tree of the kingdom.[2] Those who attend the *oenach* come not in their working clothes, but rather their 'party' outfits – new belts, shining brooches and brightly woven tunics – to enjoy horse racing, wrestling and the general absence of their womenfolk, an absence that they boyishly celebrate from dawn to dusk. There is at these *oenach* an inexpressible jollity and the community is sworn to *blai* or non-violence, weapons being left at home under the bed.

The log has a vivid description of the law court of the *oenach*, where the most controversial cases of the *tuath* are decided. Seats – thrones of a sort – were placed under the holy tree, and there the judge sat with the chief poet, the bishop and the king behind him lending him their authority and occasional advice. Several difficult cases were brought to the judge's attention and resolved and we record them here to show the

---

1. *Translator's note:* Another branch of this tribe gave its name to modern County Kerry.

2. *Translator's note: Tuath* had sacred trees that marked the spiritual centre of the territory and that were often cut down by their enemies or defiled in times of war.

complexity and wisdom of the Law of the Gaels. In one, a dog had worried a sty of pigs into breaking out of their home and these had then savaged a child, biting him no fewer than fifty times – Irish pigs are big, black, furry devils that are much to be feared. The judge demanded that the pig-owner pay sick-maintenance – that is the doctor's bills while the child got better. But the king disagreed, overturned the judgment, as is his right, and then charged instead the dog-owner with paying for the child's care. Another case involved the pet dog of the queen. This dog had been killed by a bunch of boys with catapults who had subsequently been brought to justice by her highness's kin. Here there were clear precedents in the Law and the teenagers' families were sternly ordered to pay for a priest to read continuously from the Bible for three days the next time the queen was to give birth. The ruling went thus for the Irish believe that a woman's pet dog prevents the fairies from taking babies from the cot in the hours immediately after a child is born and the priest was the best substitute for its yapping.

The most curious part of the court proceedings, however, took place 'on the outside' so to say. The king had provoked the anger of a local farmer who had lost some cattle in a raid and this matter was settled in a singularly bizarre way. The farmer was 'worth' far less than the king in legal terms and so had no recourse against him in the court. However, the Law still left open one road to judgment, namely fasting. The farmer sat outside the court and refused to eat, so sullying the king's reputation and making him vulnerable to magical attack. The embassy thought this quite amusing. But the rest, especially the king, looked on in horror and eventually the lord of the Ciarraigie nAi agreed to a discreet payment. This most peculiar custom, we have heard from fellow researchers here in the palace, also takes place in India. Is it not a strange coincidence that two such distant peoples should have adopted the same form of barbarism?[1]

Of the many games played at the *oenach*, the one in which the

---

1. *Translator's note:* The ritual of 'fasting against an enemy' is an extremely ancient one. In origin it seems to be Indo-European – the people who overran Europe and parts of Asia in the early millennia BC and from whom most modern European people are descended in linguistic and cultural terms. It survived only at the two extremes of the Indo-European continuum: India and Ireland. In India it was used as late as the twentieth century against British officials in the Raj.

embassy excelled was the poetry duels. Here groups of young scholars named faminators, that is 'speakers', dressed in purple, meet to spar with each other in lines of Latin poetry that they have to invent spontaneously, so defeating their opponent with their wit and knowledge. The reader will note from this example that the duellists, judged by their peers, choose the most obscure words possible in improvising their verses.

> You skilful, skilled man I invite verbally to duel
> With slicing red rods in the mouth we can passionfully combat
> Before, often, oftenwards I brought to book unlearned warriors
>   and paced them
> Slamming down grand melee-ers, filling mouths with dust
> And erupting word founts with heat, pulsing steamwards
>   my vic-t-ory.

Deciding to take up the challenge, one of the embassy borrowed a purple coat and threw himself into the fray. His Latin may not have been of the best (he often confused the cases). But his constant use of Greek – the British and the Irish know little of this language, though from a distance they adore it – caught the imagination of the scholarly crowd, who applauded enthusiastically. We leave his winning speech for posterity here:

> You opponents of the twisted word prick me not
> With crueller darts and sparkling arrowblades
> Burning the wounded column-limbs of my body
> And the pillars of soul.
> But availing warful I turn on you
> Brandishing my iron daggeret
> Whose deadly tormenteror pulls expert archers
> From marginalised parts and onto evil duel.
> Gymnasticing my heart pulses your destruction
> And then we brick up across the empty foundations
> But you meatily suffer bleeding tongue
> Mellifluous rivers of words will engage and drown you.

Regrettably, a certain carelessness came over the embassy after their victory at the *oenach* poetry contest. Passing through some of the nearby valleys that lead to the highlands further to the west, they had evidently dropped their guard or not scouted ahead sufficiently. For without any warning they heard running and yelps from the under-growth above and below them, their guides clutching at weapons. We will not quote the passage in the log relating to this episode for we consider it hysterical and unhelpful. One of the embassy, Petros, the physician, lost his life there; while another, Sallos, the bodyguard, had to stay permanently in an Irish monastery because of the wounds meted out on this occasion. But let us say only that the blood spilt was the work of the despised Fenians or werewolves: bands of juvenile delinquents who roam the countryside and prey on travellers and locals alike.[1] These kill. These steal. And they also love to boast of their frequent sexual encounters with any woman they come across, by which, of course, they mean rape.

Good Christians hate and fear them, calling them the 'sons of death'. However, curiously they are not made up only of the bad stock of the locality. Sons of good families commonly run away into the countryside before their beard properly sprouts and live the life of the Fenian for a matter of months, 'wolfing' around as they say, sometimes with the approval of indulgent parents. Usually this phase lasts only the time it takes for a terrible oath they all make to be fulfilled and a victim killed; at this point, his year out over, the young sinner returns to his community and is allowed once more to settle down with his family now a man. However, some Fenians remain in a lupine state all their lives and these, the hard core, tattoo themselves, even their faces, in the most fearful way. The appearance of the wolves, incidentally, is uncompromising and you will never mistake them. As well as the tell-tale tattoos they wear their hair long and matted, carry only a spear and, dirty beyond recognition, are mostly nude. They claim, of course – the vanity of criminals everywhere – that they actually work for the good of the people. They steal only portable objects; they give food to the needy; and they help their *tuath* in times of war – little consolation,

---

1. *Translator's note:* the Irish hero Finn was the original wild boy, hunting and tres-passing his way through the Irish countryside. And from him subsequent 'wolves' were known as *fian*, from which comes the adjective Fenian. The word then had an afterlife – perhaps more familiar to the reader – describing a tendency in nineteenth- and twentieth-century Irish republicanism.

though, this to the man who has had his throat slit by one of their bandits.

It does not matter what protection the Law offers the travellers – through marriage, nipple-sucking or some other stratagem – the Fenians will not care, but will kill and steal as it pleases them. What to do then if the traveller should come across these beasts? If the attack takes place outside Leinster then remember first of all that the present author 'told you so': you should never have left the safe trading stations of the south-east for foolish reconnaissances inland. Then you might consider this: despite the noise the Fenian youth make while out wolving, they often hunt in small numbers; some bands are as small as three, others as large as nine. Do not depend on the charity of these thugs, but face them with force and fight! The embassy only escaped further bloodshed because their guides understood this and were determined not to surrender.

(IV) CLONMACNOIS

After disaster, fortitude and rest. It was the embassy's fortune following the attack to be shown by kindly locals to the monastery of Clonmacnois, whose monks are the enemy of Fenians everywhere. Indeed, it strikes the present writer that a foreigner in poor straits of food and comfort might well tear his clothes a little, claiming to have been brutalised by 'the wolves', turning up at a local monastery in tears. Clonmacnois is, by all accounts, a magnificent site on the edges of the wide central plains of Ireland and the Greeks received much hospitality from the monks and the best of Irish company for almost two months while they recovered from the attack. The foundation is famous for collecting wonders and even though the monastery itself was young in the embassy's time it had already gathered together a veritable freak show of inanimate objects that its abbot, a Briton, Finnian, had had brought to him from throughout the world. The embassy were, for example, shown the thigh bone of a giant, who had once stood thirteen feet high; then there was the anchor of a ship that had floated over Clonmacnois in the sky one sunny day; the skeleton of a headless man, who had lived and walked in the region; not to mention a flying, biting mole. Some of these wonders were clearly fallacious – the flying, biting mole was actually a desert locust, the thigh bone of the giant appeared to come from an elephant. However, we mention them here for the traveller should easily be able to ingratiate himself into this community relying on this passion for the strange. Indeed, any small gift from the Mediterranean, especially ones enhanced by a story, will excite interest in these curious monks and their abbot Finnian.

It was at Clonmacnois of the Wonders that the embassy saw, suitably enough, a special marvel in the heavens, a marvel that the monks there described as 'dragons fighting' [aurora borealis]. Having showed an unwise scepticism about the existence of these monsters in the monastic refectory, our embassy were woken at about midnight a week after they had arrived and rushed from the cells and out into the courtyard. There in the sky they saw strange reddish and greenish lights flashing in and through each other that, truly, seemed to be duelling. Afterwards the abbot described many other wonders they had seen watching the astral spaces including eclipses, two moons, the flying ships related above and lunar rainbows. Indeed, the Irish are keen observers of the night, and at Clonmacnois lists of unusual happenings are kept and astronomer monks left on duty without sleep to observe different quarters of the celestial vault from tall stone towers. In fact, by the time the embassy had to leave this haven in November, the monks were already talking excitedly of an autumn full of blazing stars and spectral orbs. But the Greeks had before them a difficult road and the apprehension of travelling into one of the superstates of the Dark Isles: the empire of Dal Riada. With some regrets, but not too many, they bade farewell to their cowled hosts.

6

ULSTER AND THE HEBRIDES:

'THE EMPIRE OF DAL RIADA'

(I) ARMAGH

There is only one territory in the Dark Isles that might be called an empire. We refer here to the lands of the Dal Riadans, who not only dominate the Irish fifth of Ulster, but have also seized and now claim as their own many of the islands in the Irish Sea and even some of Britain itself.[1] Their fourteen-man fighting ships, powered by oar, are known everywhere in the north; while their campaigns to wrest the Isles of the Little Pigs [Orkneys] from the Picts and their successful conquest of British-Celtic Manu [Isle of Man] have become the stuff of legend. It was they, reader, who provided those most feared of all Irish mercenaries, the cannibalistic Attacotti who served in our Roman armies to such devastating effect. And it is they who sit on the sacred throne of Emain Macha [Navan Fort] on the southern borders of the Ulaid some three days' ride from Clonmacnois, their royal heirs, incidentally, claiming descent from a man dog. This dominion of the Dal Riada stretches from the southern tip of Manu to the Hebrides and from the western fringes of Britain to the marches with Mide, from which it is possible to glimpse the Hill of Tara. To them are subject a score of peoples, including the warriors of the Western Isles, the chthonic Cruthini who live in eastern Ulster, and the proud but now submitting Manx lords.

1. *Translator's note:* These nascent Gaelic colonies in the Inner Hebrides and Argyll were to play an important role in later British history. Three centuries after the embassy visited Britain Viking attacks created a power vacuum in the north and the Dal Riadans expanded to the north and east founding Scotland, 'the land of the Gaels'.

Have we here then at last a race worthy of alliance with our crown? Is this a people like the Negus of Ethiopia or the Sassanians of Iran who deserve our recognition as a rival imperial power and whose armies are the equal of our own? Hardly. The embassy reported, during its time in this empire of sea salt, heather and peat, the mustering of the Dal Riadans for war. Expecting to cast their eyes over a full contingent of warriors stretching to the horizons, they trooped dutifully out with the king of the province only to be bitterly deluded. The entire army of British Dal Riada amounted to a bodyguard, little more than one thousand men; the homelands not offering much more. And these warriors, so talked of in the Dark Isles, had as weapons only the most primitive spears. Nor do they fight in the polished and tightly formed shield walls of true armies. But rather they undertake uncoordinated attacks so that each battle is really a series of individual, screaming duels. As to the much praised navy of mighty Dal Riada, there are several score ships, all warriors being expected to row and fight: ships whose crew could easily be decanted into the water by a few rounds of our Greek fire.[1] Indeed, on the basis of the log, it is our considered opinion that a Byzantine legion placed in the hands of even one of our more incompetent generals and accompanied by a few state ships would be enough to tear up this 'empire' in the space of a week. The difficulty, of course, would be in logistics for, as opposed to the mediocre general, the Emperor would need a quartermaster of genius to arrange the transport, feeding and arming of this legion on its long journey to take issue with those Celtic warlords.

While, however, we wait for our Empire's re-conquest of the Dark Isles to take its inevitable and glorious course, we need to reflect on more mundane and practical problems. In short we must address the likely difficulties that the traveller will meet in passing through the lands of the Dal Riadans. Obviously a sycophantic visit to the court of the 'emperor of Ulster and the Isles' would help to smooth the journey. But it is not always so easy to find the leader of this Dal Riada, who hides sometimes in the Hebrides, sometimes in the thatch halls of Emain Macha and sometimes on distant Manu. For the traveller

---

1. *Translator's note:* Byzantine weapon, a primitive version of napalm, sometimes used against ships.

conscious of influence it makes far more sense to search out the church of Ard Macha [Armagh], within easy walking distance of the capital. Certainly it is better than wasting time with a small regional king. Indeed, let the explorer take note, one of the lessons of travel in Ireland and one that was underlined too by the writers of the log is that the various kingdoms are too tiny, too dispersed and too weak to be worth courting for anything but the most immediate aims. Even the high king of Ireland and the emperor of Dal Riada depend on loose coalitions of submitting sub-kings and are regularly challenged or overturned. The churches, on the other hand, are now deeply rooted and it is, above all, the abbots of the larger monasteries – especially Cell Dara, Clonmacnois and Ard Macha, the house we are about to describe – that most deserve the bows and cringes of the traveller.

Finding Ard Macha, the most powerful of all the Irish monasteries, is a simple matter. It takes the traveller an hour to walk from the fortress of Emain Macha; and the activity on Ard Macha's heights – like Cell Dara, it is virtually a city – can be seen from even further afield. However, unlike friendly Clonmacnois, foreign visitors to the monastery find the place prickly and unwelcoming. For this reason, we give three counsels for getting along with the abbot and monks there. First, don't mention Brigit, the saintly queen and founder of Cell Dara – the monks of Ard Macha hate her name and consider her a dangerous rival to their founder Patrick, evangelist extraordinaire of Ireland.[1] Second, don't ask where this Patrick's body is. Though Patrick was bishop of Ard Macha, he died while away from home and his body is buried out in the sticks, a cause of much regret to his household who have failed in several attempts to steal the corpse. Third and most importantly, mention Patrick *a lot*. A 'praise be' to Patrick here, a 'may Patrick help me' there, and even some general talk about his life and works will go down splendidly.

By now the reader will be commendably curious to know who exactly this Patrick was, for there is no place in the Gaels' island that you can go without hearing his name. This most unconventional British Celt was, in fact, born into a wealthy family on the banks of the Hafren [the

---

1. *Translator's note:* This Patrick is, of course, the patron saint of the Irish. He is generally held to have lived in the fifth century, though his precise dates are a matter of controversy.

Severn] more than a century ago. As an adolescent he was, by all accounts, something of a brat, but this period of carelessness ended abruptly when, aged fifteen, out walking near his family's country home, he was set upon by a group of Irish raiders and dragged scream-ing away to their boat. Within a week he was auctioned off in an Irish slave market from where he was sent to the Wood of Foclut [location uncertain] and constrained to look after a flock of sheep. After these extraordinary events the young Patrick was understandably desperate and, searching for consolation, this one-time Romano-British rich kid turned to God with all his heart and adored Him with as many as a hundred prayers a day.

Patrick stayed on the hills of western Ireland, where he learnt the language and ways of that people for six years until, in his early twenties, inspired by a vision – God had begun, by this time, to speak back – he decided to escape. His daring run for freedom meant a fraught journey from the west coast to a boat at harbour in eastern Ulster. Then, paying for passage with prayers, he got to Britain and, once there, fought his way through the barbarian-infested country until he came to his own family. However, after the initial celebration, both sides found a lot had changed. The years had, as we have seen, transformed Patrick and in the times of tension and slavery he had become a mystic. Frequently he was woken in the night by dreams and frequently he saw and spoke with angels; and in one of these encounters a messenger of God ordered him to return to Ireland to convert the pagans there. For the reader and, indeed, for the author there may seem little to choose between the barbarism of the Irish and the barbarism of the British Celts. But the British Celts haughtily despise 'the savage Irish', and his family, who had already once lost their son, vainly begged him not to go back to the country of his enslavement.

We have heard much said for and against Patrick's mission. The disagreement does not involve its success: all are agreed he converted thousand upon thousand of the pagan Irish. But rather his integrity has been called into question, for many accusations were brought against him and, towards the end of his life, scandal's terrible wings flapped down on to his shoulders. The most serious charge was that he accepted bribes from his congregation; but there was also a dreadful early sin that he had committed while still an adolescent. No one seems to know exactly what this was – we have heard, though, dark rumours of murder, of buggery and of many other unspeakable things.

Our friend Auxilius, the Roman monk who worked in the missionary field in Ireland, knew Patrick personally and disputed these accusations. He claimed that the saint had something of a holier-than-thou attitude and that this annoyed a number of his colleagues, who then sought to discredit him by every means at their disposal. Auxilius did, though, express serious doubts about the orthodoxy of the mission and gave us some frightening examples of the saint's megalomania. Patrick, for instance, had a widely reported vision where he saw himself as Christ crucified on the cross – modesty was certainly never a forte. He once fasted against God, making demands of the Deity much as before we described the farmer who fasted against his king in Connaught.[1] And, worst of all, this western apostle believed himself to be the last of God's missionaries and thought that with his death the end of the world would come!

As the inheritor of Patrick's legacy, the abbot of Ard Macha has a similarly high opinion of his monastery, and claims to be the ecclesiastical suzerain of all of Ireland, the Pope of Ireland, much as Watery David, across the Irish Sea, claims to be bishop of all the British Celts. Ard Macha, however, is greedier than David and desires to win not only authority, but also taxes from its subject churches. And to get such taxes the monks of this foundation take extraordinary measures, including fakery and violence.

Typically, the abbot decides that he wants church x in his tithe books and demands that this church pay an annual tax. Church x naturally refuses. One of Ard Macha's legendary forgers is then brought in – forgery is common throughout the monasteries of the Dark Isles, where it is used for justifying the ownership of property – and this skilled artisan of deception writes a 'history' describing how Patrick originally built church x and that it paid, in ancient times, an annual tax to him.

---

1. *Translator's note:* According to later legends St Patrick fasted against God on top of Croagh Patrick (County Mayo) and, challenging 'the Lord of the Seven Heavens', wrung from Him a number of concessions including a guarantee that the English would never invade Ireland. Patrick's hostile fasting is possibly the single most outrageous act ever to have appeared in hagiography, a genre that includes hundreds upon hundreds of works.

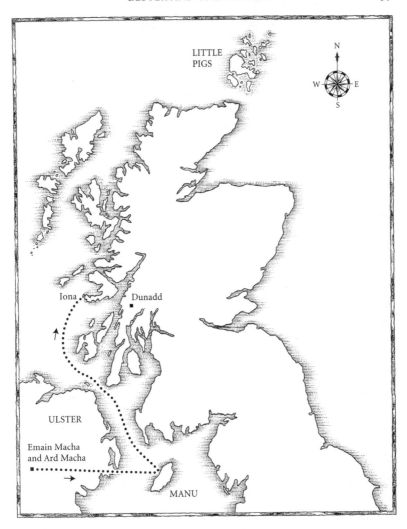

Next this account is placed in a life of St Patrick where the saint performs miracles helping Ard Macha, while cursing several powerful enemies, a copy being kindly forwarded to the about-to-be-conquered foundation. If the church continues to deny its 'true' origins as one of Patrick's churches and still bucks at paying the tax then an 'error' is found in the life and it is rewritten. This time the tax that Patrick claims from the church is raised and any family who attends mass there is said to be damned. And if this too fails then Ard Macha encourages or bribes friendly dynasties to burn the holy trees of the *tuath* where the church is found. And if, even after this, stubborn church x continues to resist then the monks of Ard Macha rally out and fight, hand to hand, the priests and deacons of this other monastery. Lest this sound incredible, the embassy itself reported the abbot meeting them with a stout pole and other monks carrying weapons and preparing for battle, strapping on rudimentary armour and sharpening blades.

It will come as no surprise that, with these efficient methods, Ard Macha now controls the bulk of churches in Ireland. Its power, its influence and its wealth are almost unlimited and friendship with it will guarantee a welcome in many distant parts of the Gaelic world. However, note carefully that the almost industrial level of forgery in the scriptorium of Ard Macha means that other intellectual and holy pursuits are left to one side. The embassy found the monks unlearned, and the abbot hardly seemed to notice the gift of some Egyptian Gnostic texts for the library.[1] Instead, playfully pounding his mace into his open palm, he concentrated on the embassy's greetings, carried hundreds of leagues from the many-pillared palace of Constantinople.

This sadly secular climate does not mean that you will find no saints at Ard Macha, however. The truly wise and holy do live there but only outside the monastery in a modest wilderness area, where they pray most efficaciously to God. These White Martyrs, as they are known – we will shortly explain the term – are the only genuine holy men to be found in the grounds of Ard Macha. They despise as 'sons of death' the monks that live within the monastery itself and refuse to be involved in their unseemly and violent property speculation. Indeed, the White Martyrs believe themselves the true successors of St Patrick and only loftily receive food and other supplies sent from the monastery because it comes, they say, from Patrick. (The monastery, enjoying some reflected prestige, is happy to provide these rations.)

---

1. *Translator's note:* The embassy may have been overly pessimistic. Some later Irish texts show the influence of eastern apocryphal texts and one vision of the afterlife – *The Evernew Tongue* – uses motifs and details that can be most closely paralleled in Egyptian mythology. (John Carey, 'The Sun's Night Journey: A Pharaonic Image in Medieval Ireland,' *Journal of the Warburg and Courtauld Institute*, 57 (1994), pp. 14–34). Could the embassy's gift have brought this particular legend to the far north of Europe?

The name – the White Martyrs – is simple to explain. They are known by this peculiar appellation because in Ireland no one any longer dares to shed the blood of a holy man and so the old-fashioned red martyrdom has passed out of fashion. Instead, by fasting and lack of sleep they personally martyr themselves over the thirty or forty years they manage to survive before being released from their attenuated, famished bodies. The traveller may be thinking that he can spare little time to visit such hermit dens, perhaps even that these are to be despised as fools of God. But the embassy wrote of one special power in their gift, a gift that they referred to cryptically as the 'malefic psalms', a kind of song, we deduce, that can render an enemy helpless and vulnerable to attack. Our patron, the Emperor, would dearly like to know more about these terrible cursing hymns, and we humbly suggest an Imperial commission to discover their true worth.

(II) ISLE OF MAN

The embassy's present to Ard Macha may have gone unnoticed. But it was thanks to this church that they arranged to cross the waters again to Britain. The abbot had a boat heading out to one of their principal churches on Manu to collect a yearly tribute, and from there the Greeks were able to pass over to the larger isle. Manu itself – a useful stepping stone in the Irish Sea – was named in a less happy age for the Celtic god of the waves, Manawadan, and there is hardly a place on its long thin body from which you cannot watch the breakers of its patron crash across its beaches or against its cliffs. Its equidistance between Britain and Eire, meanwhile, has made Manu an important strategic centre and the Dal Riadans had to fight over several years to prise it away from the kings of Gwynedd. Indeed, Magloconus the dragon of Mon still talked, when the embassy met him, of revenging the humiliation to his father's arms and dragging the island once more under his dominion. And he is far from being alone. We have also heard reports that some of the Saxon warriors of the north have designs on Manu; and that the Pictish navy has also considered an expedition there. Nor is the war-making left to warriors. For many years the wise of the various peoples of the Dark Isles have also fought over Manu, debating whether it is a British or an Irish island. There is still much controversy on this point, but one extremely powerful argument in favour of its belonging to Britain is the fact that snakes and other poisonous reptiles dwell there; Irish soil cannot, as we have seen, tolerate such creatures.

The population of the place, as befits a midway land, is neither British-Celtic nor Gaelic but speaks a strange hybrid language of both.[1] And they live not only on a strategically important territory, but also one that grows rich crops and that is verdant and well watered by rain. Strangely, this same population do not fear the Dal Riadans or, indeed, any of the other invaders who every generation overrun them, but only the fairies who plague their cattle and sometimes steal their babies. Indeed, it is often said by the peoples of the Dark Isles that nowhere do the fairy folk have more power than on Manu. Bear this native eccentricity in mind and never climb a hill or cross a bridge there without first asking the fairies' permission.

Several landmarks come to mind if the visitor to Britain intends to sail near the island. There is the Calf of Manu, a small jut of rock off the south-western coast where the traveller can usefully and safely put in for the night. The visitor may even have a pleasant surprise there. We say this for the embassy were flabbergasted to be greeted at its limits by shouts in Greek, for a hermit from our homeland lived out his days on the clifftops of that rock.[2] We can also recommend the north-western coast, where much craftwork is produced in the Irish style. Then again there is Maccuil [Maughold] on the northern side of the island. This is a trading outpost that feeds off the richest of Manu's land immediately to the south, creams off the few, bold merchants from the Mediterranean who make it this far north, and also caters to pilgrim traffic. Pilgrims are mentioned here because several packed boats leave Ireland monthly on their way

---

1. *Translator's note:* The Manx language that died in the 1970s was a hybrid Celtic-Norse language. It was brought to the island in a later period – the ninth and tenth centuries – by Vikings and Gaels from their colonies in the Hebrides and has nothing to do with the tongue described here.

2. *Translator's note:* This isolated Greek hermit may have left a trace in the archaeological record. A golden altarpiece in the Coptic style has been found on the Calf of Man.

to a small chapel named the Luminous House in Britain [the White House, Whithorn, Galloway], which is dedicated to St Martin. On the crossing, these same pilgrims traditionally stay the night at Maccuil and many scratch graffiti on to the rocks there to commemorate their passing.

Of Maccuil itself we know of one story that we relate here and, though the reader may think it a distraction, it proves an introduction to another curious Irish custom – that of casting adrift. Our source is a folio – pressed into the log of the embassy – from the scriptorium of Ard Macha, pilfered by a Greek while being shown around that building. It is naturally as dubious as anything else to come out of that most dubious room, and it is written too in the difficult script of the isles. Yet nevertheless the embassy felt it interesting enough to preserve and so we give a brief summary here.

It seems that when St Patrick was converting the Irish of the eastern coast he was one day set upon by a demonical robber king with a single eye and his thievish band – in short by the thuggish Fenians that we have already encountered. Patrick, however, was made of stern stuff and, raising his arms, he sent out terrifying curses blighting them and making them turn their tails. The one-eyed leader of this mob, a certain Maccuil, was so impressed by what he had seen that, recognising a greater power than his own, he went to the saint and surrendered himself up to that man. Patrick had little time for forgiveness though and, wishing to punish this penitent to the limit of the Law, followed the custom of the country and placed the bandit king in a small rowing boat without sail, tying him to the base of the craft with a chain: for this it seems is the punishment the Irish have for especially deviant criminals. The boat was then dragged out to the ninth wave and there left to drift, as in this way it would be blown wherever God wished through the waves, the currents and the winds. And, after many days of journey, it so happened that Maccuil was washed up on the northern shore of Manu where he founded a settlement that was named Maccuil in his honour and in this way he became bishop of the island. The truth? Or an attempt by Ard Macha to stretch its tentacle-like claims even further? Only God and the monks of the scriptorium of that monastery know.

(III) IONA AND THE HEBRIDES

The rest of the territories of Dal Riada are to be found to the north in the honeycomb of islands and rocks and peninsulas that hang or stand off the north-western coast of Britain. Here the different clans of this people have settled and built their farms, driving the original inhabitants into the mountains to the east where the hated Picts live. These clans – there are three, the Cenel Loairn, the Cenel nOengusa and the Cenel nGabrian – from being the poorer colonial relations of the Dal Riadan empire have now become its richest part. They provide the kings of Dal Riada and, while the Dal Riadans are often defeated on Irish soil, they have rarely lost a battle in Britain. Their capital is at Dunadd: a cold, forbidding fortress at the head of the Great Glen, where a footprint carved into the rock proclaims their sovereignty.[1]

The Irish invaders of Britain have also brought with them their holy men. And indeed, a far better destination for the traveller than chilly Dunadd is Iona, a small, sandy island that sits off a larger neighbour, Mull, one of the main strongholds of the Cenel Loairn. Here a tiny community of Irish Christians built a monastery that has already won fame throughout the whole world, for their abbot Columba. For example, it was his prophecy that foresaw but, alas, could not forewarn of the terrible earthquake that destroyed much of Naples and through which many thousands died.[2]

As the embassy were coming to shore on Iona they found almost the whole monastery out to meet them, a Latin translator on hand and a Greek copy of the Psalter, which the Ionans had somehow got hold of, set on a platter for the visitors' use. Asking how the monks had known to expect them, for the ship had flown rapidly from Manu to the place, they were told offhandedly that it was the abbot Columba who had been shown their coming in a dream. The embassy were so amazed at this that they gave to the abbot a gift that they had once hoped to present to the high king of the Picts, a sword mounted in a fabulous

---

1. *Translator's note:* Several Dark Age sites have footprint shapes carved into their rock. It has been sometimes suggested, and our author seems to share this interpretation, that these were used in rituals of king-making.

2. *Translator's note:* Strangely, this earthquake is only recorded in our *Itinerary* and Irish sources.

ivory sheath. However, knowing that such accounts are easily written but less easily believed, we include one more story from the log that we think demonstrates Columba's powers beyond any reasonable doubt:

We had seen the proof of his prophecy on our arrival, but we confess at first we hardly believed it and speculated that the old man must have seen we were Greek from something on the boat or even the cut of our hair. However, all doubts were swept away on the afternoon of our second day. While we were sitting around him he rang a bell and brought a servant running: 'In a matter of hours', he said, 'a guest will appear on the west coast of the island. Her strength will be almost gone and she will collapse on the shore as soon as she reaches you. You must go and wait there and pick her up and bring her to me. There you will feed her at our expense for three days and nurse her till she is strong enough to move on. Afterwards she will want to return to the part of Ireland from where she came.'

The brother nodded as if this kind of instruction was a normal one and we, with no small curiosity, followed him to the west side of the island. We watched and watched and before long began to think that the old man had finally revealed himself a sham – no boat appearing on the horizon. But after almost exactly three hours had passed a large bird, a crane, evidently tired from a day over the sea, fell from the sky and collapsed on the sand before us.[1] Again, as if nothing could be more normal, the menial in question picked up the fluttering wreck and gently, as if it were a child, took it to the nearby guest house where it was fed and rested.

Cranes are much respected among the Irish. Some refuse to eat the bird, while others keep them as pets in their halls, for they are easily tamed and love human company, proving amusing fellows. Was it for this reason that our host had shown such care in welcoming the bird? He, anyway, continued to show an interest. That evening Columba, not questioning but simply taking it for a proven fact, told the menial: 'God bless you my son! You have taken good care of our visitor. She will stay here for three days only and then pick her way home in the sky.'

For three days we heard nothing more of the 'visitor'. But on the

---

1. *Translator's note:* Cranes, now extinct in Britain and Ireland, did dwell in the islands in the Middle Ages.

morning of the last day we walked with Columba to the monastic hospital and we Greeks watched amazed as the crane cockily walked out of the place and, with barely a thanks to those who had rescued her, took to the air. There she wheeled, looking for her path, and after some minutes making circles, higher and higher took to the west and home. We, of course, could not follow the others in their nonchalance and, curious beyond telling, we asked the holy man how he managed to know these things so clearly. 'You ask me' he told us kindly 'about a very peculiar subject. There are some – very few indeed – to whom God has given a special gift. These few can see with perfect clarity and brightness, with a single thought, the entire world and the sea and the sky around them in one sunbeam.' The monks call this 'the second sight' and we ourselves have now no doubt as to its efficacy.

Many will say that a miracle is wasted on an animal. But the traveller should be careful before sharing such an opinion, for among the Irish Christians the mute creations of our Lord are greatly appreciated and trained by saints to their service. We have heard of tame foxes that guard chickens; of a fly domesticated as a bookmark – it runs from line to line on the manuscript to keep its hermit master at his place; and even of a stag that allows his prickly horns to be used as a bookstand. Treat animals well in the west, then – at least in public. But nor, though, should you write off the western saints as sentimentalists. As has been indicated already, they also have a temper. Even wise Columba sometimes gave indications of a nasty streak and had, in fact, been banished from his homeland for taking part in a battle. When asked by a member of the embassy whether he had prayed in the rear, the saint laughed and pulled up his cowl to show a terrible scar across his side. As we noted while discussing Ard Macha, monks too fight in Ireland.

PART III

SCOTLAND:
THE PICTS AND WORSE

THE NORTHERN SEAS:
'UNKNOWN LANDS'

(I) TOWARDS ICELAND

We must begin this section with an important warning. On no account travel to northern Britain in the boat of one of the monks of Iona. We say this for the embassy made a fatal mistake at this point of their journey, a mistake that miraculously cost the life of only one of the eight remaining Greeks. Their error was to take passage with a party of tonsured 'desert seekers'. 'Desert?' the good reader will ask, remembering the description of green Britain and Ireland, 'are there Saharas in these northern islands?' No. But for many years Irish holy men have enviously read the stories of the fathers of northern Africa, tales of men like Anthony,[1] who travelled into the wastelands there to escape from the world, to do battle with demons and to find God in His purest and most simple form. Naturally, these enthusiastic northerners wished to emulate our saints of the south. But to their considerable frustration there was an almost insurmountable obstacle – the lack of wide, sandy expanses. Some Irish monks found an empty field or, better still, a marsh where no man went and pretended it was a desert – indeed, their country is littered with places called 'Desert of Fintan', 'Desert of Colman' and so on.[2] But others came up with an even more remarkable solution. They turned to the only true wasteland they had – the ocean – and set off to look for God there.

The embassy did not know of the desert seekers when they thanked

1. *Translator's note:* Anthony the Great, died 356, an Egyptian ascetic who spent much of his life praying in the desert.
2. *Translator's note:* The Gaelic word *disert* is frequently found in Irish place names. It denotes a place where there was, in ancient times, a wasteland with hermitage.

a kind Ionan monk named Cormac, who offered to give them a hitch 'up north'. Nor did they know that these monks, instead of depending on the compass and the atlas, rely on God's will, by which they mean the wind, to help them find their way to certain 'desert islands' where they are able to pray. Nor, indeed, were they aware that the boats they use were not made of wood, but were *curraghs*, small wickerwork structures knitted over with branches and then attached to leather skins, such as those that we use to make manuscripts. Nor, finally, did they understand that most of these desert seekers are never heard of again – because, of course, they lose their lives far out in the uncrossable oceans in waves many times the height of their little raft. We include here some of the comments from the log, as the full horror of their situation came home to them.

Day One: We left in the early morning in five of their *curragh*, tied loosely together: four men on each raft. The monks have a most curious method of navigating – they do nothing! They have no sail and the oars that line the boat are left in place. The wind is so reliable, blowing them to the north, that we suppose they very rarely have to use these. We Greeks found it impossible to speak between the boats – the wind drowning our voices – so I chatted instead to Cormac in our *curragh*, the chief of the mission. He is a pleasant enough man, but takes the beatific smiling a bit far, answering all questions with one of two phrases: 'God willing' or 'not difficult'. We asked him, for example, about whether it would be easy to get to the Little Pigs [the Orkneys] and he replied with a 'God Willing' as if even our eventual arrival there depended very much on the grace of the heavens.

Day Two: The wind is picking up even more strongly now and Domitianos, the Greek scholar who shares my boat, is becoming nervous. He is convinced that even when we do get to the Little Pigs, the monks will be unable to steer the craft to land. But have we not heard on many occasions that the monks know the northern waters better than anyone else? Certainly it is the only topic of conversation that Cormac feels at ease with. When we ask him about Ard Macha or even the saints he just gives us a cryptic 'God willing'. But when, instead, we ask him about this or that island there is a stout 'not difficult' and off he goes. We were discussing yesterday the geography of Africa and he began to tell us about certain isles that lie off its western coast, where a small colony of Irish monks or desert seekers has been set up. Can this be true? We also asked him why they call them 'desert seekers', but he retreated coyly back into his holy smile.

Day Three: Domitianos more worried than ever as this strong southerly wind keeps taking us hard and the monks do nothing to direct the craft. Looking at Britain to our right I can't say, though, that I much want to get off – high mountains, snow, while some vegetation there gives them a beautiful purple colour. But the inhabitants will be a problem. This morning we came close enough to the shore to see ten men riding along on horseback – our first Picts. Even from a league we noted that they were blue with tattoos and all rode nude and yelled at us, seemingly keen on committing a martyrdom. The monks just carried on smiling and Cormac opened his arms. 'As God wishes', he said, a new phrase for his repertoire.

Day Four: Left Britain behind today. Waves so rough difficult to write. Wet. Wind continues to blow us, northwards, always northwards.

Day Five: How much longer? They told us a day's journey north of Britain. Food looking mouldy. Mouth full of salt. Must keep codex dry. Write little.

Day Six: The wind died long enough for us Greeks to talk between the boats. We are all worried. Their monks only speak Irish, however, so proper communication impossible. Cormac smiled – for a change – when we asked once more about the Little Pigs and answered in a manner that alarmed me: 'The island of Thule [Iceland] is also interesting.' He seems to have no idea of the incipient mutiny among the fleet; all day he prays and much of the night, while the waves are jolting, he intones a meditation keeping us poor Greeks awake.

Day Seven: Terrifying experience. At midday huge spouts of water began to shoot up around us, coming out of the sea. We had never seen anything like it and the monks prayed so fervently that we confess to having been worried. After ten or so minutes an enormous monster rose out of the depths – a whale of some sort, clearly, but one that was many times bigger than anything that swims in the Aegean. It seemed to have little interest in us and went about sunning itself, but we were terrified that a snap of its tail would overturn the boats. The relief of being spared – it eventually drifted away – brought about a brief return of warmth between us. Cormac told us an absurd story about some monks known to him who once got off one of their *curragh* on to a small ocean island and then, while cooking stew, realised that they had accidentally stepped on to the top of one of these creatures! We can believe it, for covered in barnacles the beast did have a grey, rocky tint to it that might have been mistaken for land. We asked again about the Little Pigs, but Cormac gave us a 'God willing' response and then told us some funny tales about certain monks who go to sea in a boat and let God blow them where He will. We laughed and in the calmer ocean – though those southerlies are still blowing – monks and Greeks alike were rocked gently to sleep.

Day Eight: Realised at dawn! Cormac was not telling a tale about others: he was speaking about himself, that is about us!

Day Nine: Food almost run out. Seems the monks refuse to pack more than enough for a few days as to do otherwise would be 'to show too little trust in God'. We could push the lot of them overboard now. But would it help? The general opinion is that it would do nothing and eventually their expertise might be good for something. If not Domitianos says we'll eat them. When among the barbarians. . .

Day Ten: We have tried to fish using a net that we had in one of the packs. Cormac was not very happy about this. First frown in fact. He said that a net was not giving God space to work his marvels. However, as we were foreign, we had different ways and he would respect these. Though he didn't seem to realise it, never had the damned monk been so close to dying.

Day Eleven: No lands, no birds, some raw fish. Still fresh water but already tastes strange.

Day Twelve: Ditto.

Day Thirteen: Ditto and worse.

Day Fourteen: End of a most amazing three or four hours. Now we have some hope and a tragedy to report. All noticed around midday that the sea was moving in a strange fashion. Suddenly, as if it had been planned, a series of dreadful monsters began to assail the craft. They were like frogs but had long beaks and jumped at us and, as the *curragh* was only lined with leather, we were terrified that they would pierce it and so let the water in; indeed, the panic was tangible.[1] The monks prayed desperately and Cormac – I had never heard him shout before – told us to do likewise. However, it was not, we believe, the prayers that caused the change, but an unwilling sacrifice. Amidst all the confusion one of these terrible animals – an arm's length of it – sprang out of the water and landed on Domitianos whom, writhing, followed it overboard. A moment of horror followed as the water closed around him, and our comrade and the monsters had disappeared. Cormac offered no commiserations for Domitianos, whom his friends knew as 'the wise', but confided in me that he hadn't liked the look of my colleague from the start. It seems that often the desert seekers have problems because, Jonah-like, one of the crew cannot be trusted and must be disposed of. Now, he assured me, all would be well. And strangely enough the wind reversed, blowing us back towards Britain, while a heavy rain allowed us to fill both our parched mouths and the water bottles.

The contrary wind saved them and the malnourished crew of monks and Greeks eventually, thanks to a gale of six days' duration, made land at the Isles of the Little Pigs. There, Columba had sent ahead a messenger to warn the king of the Orcades that soon he would have guests and that these were to be treated with respect and consideration. The relief of the embassy was naturally extraordinary. However, amid the jubilation they also took care to note in the log that further research was needed into the lands to the north of Britain, for in their long hours talking to the monk sailors they had heard many amazing stories, only some of which were quoted above. We were commissioned to write this book by His Majestic Imperial Highness the Emperor and we consider it our duty to relate what information the Greeks heard both from the desert seekers and the inhabitants of the Little Pigs, before we turn to the less important matter of the Orcades themselves. Indeed, it is with some excitement that we come to set down this description of the unknown north, for we believe that there is real potential here for Imperial expansion. And though we refuse to take seriously some of the stories – many of the lands they described were

---

1. *Translator's note:* These animals are also described in a seventh-century Irish text, the *Life of St Columba*. They have been variously identified as flying fish, (most credibly) dolphins or even Greenland mosquitoes!

inspired by the delirium and thirst of ocean travel, brains baked by the sun and addled by the wind – some were talked about so matter-of-factly that we can hardly fail to believe them. In fact, for a fee the Orcadians would have, gladly, taken the embassy to a number of these spits and accidents of islands.

The Pictish sailors whose testimony we trust over the sea-mad desert seekers tell that there are two chains of islands to the north of them, where many sheep and seabirds dwell [Shetlands and Faeroes]. These lands are inhabited by those of the Irish monks who have been lucky enough to come to shore there and they pray on their cliff ledges, ring their small silver bells and read the word of our Lord written out on minute manuscripts. But the islands are also inhabited by an ancient indigenous people. These natives are held up by the men of the Little Pigs as being somewhat behind the times, and given that this comment comes from the almost destitute Picts of the north, it must truly mean something. We suggest that the Imperial army could clear the islands of the aborigines, who would work better in our armies or kitchens, and instead use these archipelagos for large sheep farms, for this animal apparently prospers there.

Beyond these sheep havens the sea loosens, the waves grow and the temperature drops quickly provoked by icy, biting winds. The Orcadians regularly made trips to the Isles of the Sheep. But they only strayed past into this terrible region accidentally and always, in desperation, tried to escape it. The desert seekers, meanwhile, were often blown there, and with joy, for they believe that paradise lies somewhere near! What is true and what is false we do not know. But we place the information before the reader so that he or she can decide for themselves. In this area, they say there are many crystal islands [icebergs] that, not being anchored to the floor of the oceans, drift around. The traveller can even climb on them and stumble over the strange landscapes on which sometimes great white bears are sighted, bears that need five or six men to kill and that have chicken-tasting flesh. They also talk of islands that lead to hell. There is no crystal here, but instead towering portals come out of the sea, through which breaks smoke and sometimes fire, steaming out of Lucifer's pit. The desert seekers claim that the souls of the dead can be heard in the night wind and sometimes the damned come forth into the ocean to escape from their tortures, at least for a while. One of the desert seekers who had travelled with the embassy even said to know one man who had spoken to Judas Iscariot! We confess to not believing a word of these crystal islands and the white bears, they remind us of the British-Celtic legends of islands of glass back in the Irish Sea. But we modestly suggest that the gates of hell are nothing more than volcanoes such as we know from Sicily. The Irish and Picts who have never seen such things cannot, however, believe their own eyes and so ascribe these lava-stained funnels to a murky and fiery underworld.

There is one island in the ocean sitting above the Isles of Sheep, about the size of Ireland, and it is said by those who have strayed into its harbours to be green and full of hot springs. This is the island that the ancients called Thule and that some explorers have visited; we remember especially Pytheas the Carthaginian who trekked the Atlantic a thousand years ago even to the Baltic. The desert seekers know Thule well and if God blows their boats to this place they consider themselves especially fortunate. The men of the Little Pigs, on the other hand, only make very occasional and reluctant voyages to the island and only for large sums – one in two boats do not return – and then only in the height of summer. They do so not just because of the calmed waves – storms can be whipped up at any time on the whale paths of the north – but because of what they call the 'darkness'. We report this again with scepticism, but necessarily, for the islanders talk a great deal of this terrible state of affairs that is said to fall on Thule in the winter months. As we ourselves see in winter, the nights get longer and it is known that this effect lengthens the further to the north one travels. Well, it is claimed by the islanders that on Thule, for several months, not a peep of light breaks through the black. As they never visit the island in these months, we are again disposed to dismiss this as legend. But they do sometimes go there in the summer. And, the embassy met one man who claimed to have seen 'the light', when the sun never stops shining, so that, even at midnight, he could pick lice off his clothes, so bright was the sky. If this is true then the potential for the Imperial economy is obvious. How many textile workers could be packed into this island's small valleys and set to work far into the night?

What lies beyond Thule? Our teachers in school gave us an easy answer. Beyond Thule to the north and the Atlas Mountains to the

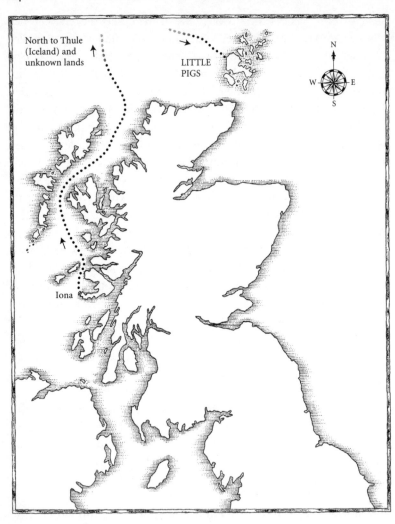

south in Africa there are other lands, and wonderful lands at that. But to reach them is impossible, for they are protected by belts of unbearable cold and heat.[1] For Africa this may, indeed, be the case. But that there is something past Thule, and that it can be reached, seems certain

1. *Translator's note:* Contrary to our modern expectations Dark Age inhabitants of Europe did not universally believe in a flat earth. In fact, many educated individuals

for both the Orcadians and the desert seekers insist upon it. However, quite what these other worlds are we have no way of determining, for the legends and facts come thick, fast and mixed. Is it true, for example, that beyond Thule there is a massive peninsula of ice [Greenland] thousands of leagues long? Or that there are parts of the sea so limpid that you can stare to the sandy bottoms and watch the fishes that flap backwards and forwards [a coral sea]? And what of the dwelling place of the god Chronos, a rock temple that lies beyond the most distant of these seas in a land many times larger than Britain, Ireland and even our Empire? We regretfully must reject these all as mariners' tales. One marvel that we do believe, though, is that of the stunted, ice-eating trolls who dwell in the northern parts [Eskimos]. Many years ago an embalmed example of one of these was brought to the Imperial court. And not long before the embassy reached the Isles of the Little Pigs a troll arrived there in a small narrow raft, clearly blown off-course by the winds and dehydrated from weeks adrift. His boat – who could have believed that trolls took to the sea? – was made of wooden shafts and covered in a bark-like substance. The locals, meanwhile, wondered greatly at his curiously flat face and the strange sounds he uttered; we have no idea of his end, but have no doubt that it was unpleasant.[1]

(II) THE ORKNEYS

From the shadowy rumours of the arctic regions we must now turn to the all-too-real inhabitants of the northern parts of Britain – the Picts. No word that we have yet described in this book, no word at all causes such fear in the Dark Isles as that straight, spat monosyllable. It has a simple, almost pat etymology: it means 'the painted one', a reference to the blue tattoos that those who dwell in the far north of Britain

in this epoch thought of their world as being spherical with distant, unreachable antipodes.

1. *Translator's note:* The 'trolls' described here were northern Amerindian peoples who were probably sighted in Greenland or even, if the 'desert seekers' really did make it that far, on the coast of Canada. These are several instances in European history of North American native peoples inadvertently discovering Europe and arriving in Scotland, Ireland or, in one case, the continent in their small 'bark' boats.

habitually wear. But to those who know it – the Britons, the Gaels and even the Saxons – the word has an effect out of all proportion to its simple form, for like the arrival of winter it causes shudders. Indeed, among the other inhabitants of Britain, these four letters stand as a swear word, such that to call another 'a Pict' is an insult – the kind that in playground or market place signals the onset of punches and kicks.

How the Picts who inhabit the northern islands and the wild highlands of Caledonia earned this status is easily explained. For centuries they tortured the Roman soldiers who patrolled the walls: their strategy was to throw a barbed spear on rope into the back of one of the wall-walkers and then drag him to the heather below, where they committed their horrors. They carried their bestiality southwards too, coming in their slick, small boats dodging around the coastguards and raiding inwards to villages and towns where that very word 'Pict' was enough to empty houses and send fat patricians burying their treasures under elms and oaks. The British Celts, who habitually flinch when they talk of their northern neighbours still remember these terrible times and call the Picts worms, saying that, hidden in the dark places of the north, they only come out in the sun when the spring days begin to lengthen.

But we confess that from our tall, fine tower here in the holy city of Constantinople we have a more charitable view of these northerners. For us, all the peoples of Britain bear the mark of the barbarian, even the 'Roman' British Celts and the Gaels with their Law. And, based on the testimony of our log, we suggest that the Picts are much like any other of the islanders; their barbarity hardly worse than those who mate with horses to crown their kings, or who waste their time on the mad tales of Arthur. The Picts suffer from a worse reputation than they should for two very simple reasons: first, their distance from all other peoples, for they are the last inhabitants of the most northern islands drawn with any confidence on our maps; and, second, their simplicity, for in an age when we use iron, many among them are still carving wood and bone for their tools. The traveller might also work up a sporting respect for a people that for so long and with such dogged persistence defied our legions and that, though many times beaten down – make no mistake, they could not defeat one of our armies in a straight fight – never gave up their patrimony to our emperors. None of this, of course, is to say that we advise our readers to visit their lands – moors, streams and islands bounded by moors, streams and islands – but there is nothing evil about the Picts. Indeed, we would say that, taken into service as bodyguards or bought as slaves, they would make tolerable additions to a household, especially if those inconvenient tattoos could be covered up or displayed in a chic fashion.

The political geography of the Pictish territories is simple and crude. There are seven small kingdoms that are in turn divided into two confederations: the northern and southern Picts. And we begin our description in the north, in the land that in Latin is called the Orcades, this name meaning in Celtic, as we have seen, 'the Little Pigs', the Pictish clan that possess the chain. The reader will, of course, have heard of these islands for was it not the Emperor Claudius when he invaded Britain who claimed to have received tribute from this most northern people? If Claudius did receive gifts from the north – though what could they have given him but pebbles and sand? – then the locals have long since forgotten the fact. Indeed, they were most curious to hear of 'the Romans', a word that even the older among them did not recognise. Their leader, who from time to time visited the court of the high king of the Picts in the south, had heard of it. But he had only an endearingly vague notion of what these Romans – who civilised the world no less! – might be. In these very northern reaches, the legions rarely left their mark in years of wars, let alone those of peace, and the overlong absence of our eagles from these islands has speeded their forgetting.

The embassy were received cordially in the Little Pigs. However, should the traveller wish to arrive at a similar port, be warned. We suspect that without Columba's introduction the friendly welcome the Greeks received may have been rather less so. Whales beached on these shores are regularly dismembered and shared out among the coast dwellers and that will be as likely a fate as any other for a castaway, for the people are still pagan. Indeed, their distance from the rest of the world means that ancient and sacred conventions that we might take for granted even among the Saxons or Gaels – the protection of embassies or of traders – are utterly novel to them. On the islands and in some other northern regions these problems are compounded by language, for the inhabitants speak a tongue unlike any other in Britain.

No one can understand it, and the high king of the Picts – the southern Picts speak a broken-down form of British Celtic – has to take care to send translators with his messages. The embassy, in fact, wrote down some sentences from this northern language to be looked at by the translators of the Emperor. However, only one, a famed scholar who worked with the Imperial army in Spain, claimed to have made any sense of the words. He thought that in some respects it resembled Basque, the language of the mountain people of the Pyrenees.

What struck the embassy most about the Little Pigs was their poverty. There are no trees on these islands – or nothing more than some weathered bushes for firewood – and the soil is so poor that it is only after centuries of smearing it with human and animal excrement that barley, their one crop, grows. Iron and metals of any kind are rare: the embassy was chased and touched by village children for the quantity of beads and buckles on them, a moderate quantity that even their Orcade king in ceremonial garb could not boast. And trade is almost non-existent for the islanders have little to sell; though some amber beads from that legendary northern sea, the Baltic, had found their way to the royal treasury. Even their dead are buried naked and without accoutrements or paraphernalia to take them into the other world; it is almost as if relatives could not afford to lose their few possessions. And it is symptomatic of this general poverty, too, that in return for some trifles, the king gave the embassy charms. These gifts -treasured by the islanders – were rounded sea stones that had been painted with dots and with lines! They were later discreetly thrown in the sea on the voyage to the mainland, so I have not been able to examine them personally; but their crudity was vouched for by all. Another gift was a woollen hood, especially knitted for the Emperor, by the king's wife no less. The embassy got rid of that too – in a bog – but were amazed to see just how long it took to make. With the gathering, spinning and weaving the queen worked for three whole days and far into the night to get it ready in time for the Greeks' departure.[1]

1. *Translator's note:* In 1867 a hood was found in a peat bog at St Andrews, Orkney. We have absolutely no reason for thinking that this item of clothing, today preserved in the National Museum of Edinburgh, and that given to the embassy are the same. But, in relation to the time the queen took over the Emperor's gift, it is interesting to note that when, in 2003, Dr Jacqui Wood attempted to replicate the museum piece using

The islands of the Little Pigs do, however, hold one wonder and that is, surprisingly for such an underdeveloped and primitive race, the dwelling places that are to be found there. We refer not to the round houses or farms that litter the islands. But rather to the brochs, the stone towers in which the richer elements of the population live and that dominate the landscape. The chain of the Orcades is fairly flat and at dusk from a commanding location – we recommend one of the headlands – it is possible to make out a number of these stone, conical constructions like teeth breaking incompletely out of the earth. A tall broch would hardly compare to the artifice of our Imperial buildings. But, by northern standards, they are massive. At ground level they contain many small compartments – we hesitate to say rooms for they have no internal stone walls. Then they reach up to forty or fifty feet, tapering at the end so that their roofs narrow down to almost nothing. Today's population has no idea how they were made for they were a product of their great-great-grandsires, generations and generations ago. But they continue to patch up the collapsing stonework, to thatch the tiny roof when winter approaches and to hide the whole population there in times of war.

While mentioning the dwelling places of the Picts we need to dismiss a myth about another building of this people, rumours of which have even reached Constantinople, namely the underground siesta stations. We have all heard of halls that the Picts have dug underground and that can only be reached by a deep-running stairwell; there, we have been told by the credulous, who had no evidence but hearsay, these northern folk go to sleep, to escape the midday sun. To this we have two responses: first, that the sun in the Little Pigs is so puny – like the moon in winter – that the Picts would hardly need such a retreat. Then, second, there is the evidence of the log. In fact, the embassy were

Dark Age technologies she took thirty-five hours to spin the yarn for the main head part of the hood and thirty hours to weave it, then a further seventy-seven hours to spin the yarn for a lower band that hung down from the hood over the chest and sixty-eight hours to weave the same! Dr Wood's heroic effort might have been slowed by lack of practice in these techniques, but it is suggestive of the care that had to be taken over such trifling objects in pre-industrial times. For her methods see 'The Orkney Hood, an ancient recycled textile, in *Sea Changes: Orkney and Northern Europe in the Later Iron Ages: AD 300–800*, ed. Jane Downes and Anna Ritchie (Pinkfoot Press, 2003), pp. 171–6.

specially asked to investigate this feature of Pictish life. We quote here from their writing: 'As to the underground chambers, they are relatively rare and restricted to richer houses and farms. They are used primarily for grain storage and there is no evidence that any go there to doze.' The final word, we think. But, lest the realities behind these 'mysterious' constructions might, in their very prosaicness, disappoint the seeker of the obscure and arcane, the reader will be reassured to learn that the islanders routinely include human limbs and heads in the foundations of any building they set out to work on.

8

THE HIGHLANDS:
'THE PAINTED PEOPLES'

The Saxons build their sailless boats, the *keels* as they are known, from wooden planks. The Irish use, instead, leather and we have already described their curious *curragh*, where a cow's skin is wrapped around a wickerwork frame. But the most northern of the Picts have an even simpler way of travelling across water – they resort to logs. This is not to say that they do as our Imperial navy that cuts and binds trunks in its shipyards. Rather they scoop out the heart of the tree and sit in it [i.e. the log becomes a canoe] relying on oars for propulsion. It was in these contraptions – several of them – that the embassy were brought south to Britain on a day of dramatic rowing, the sea exploding around them in flights of dolphin and porpoise.

However, when the mainland came within sight, to the embassy's surprise, the rowers refused to land. They did so for the nearest territory to the Little Pigs is that of the Land of the Cats [Caithness], and the king of this tribe is in an almost constant state of unfriendliness with the islanders. But whether or not the two outer Pictish peoples are locked in one of their regular bouts of warfare, navigating, even in these cold and unpredictable waters, remains by far the best way of travelling from one region to another. We say this for the upper-facing edge of Britain is pure rock, with few plants struggling through the cracks of its ambush-ridden paths. And by way of settlements there are only a handful of 'wags' or columned houses built out of local sandstone. The wise traveller is then advised to follow the route the embassy took going south, hugging the coast in one of the native log rafts, watching the seals sun themselves on a dangerous shoreline, until he finally reaches the mouth of Ness, a waterway that infiltrates almost the whole of the northern reaches of Britain.

On the other side of this waterway, which resembles a large river where it reaches the sea, is the territory of the Fidach, a Pictish tribe who generally prove amicable to strangers. But whatever the temptation for the traveller to put his feet back on dry land on the northern side of the Lake of Ness and make the rest of the journey to Fidach on foot and ferry, we urge him to resist. We say this because, as the embassy found to their cost, those who pass across the lake or even walk on its banks are sometimes attacked by a water beast that dwells there.

Our party arrived at the lake edge just after dinner to find a group of Pictish peasants burying one of their number. Enquiries were made, for even with the mean blanket they had laid over him, we could see that the man had marks from a terrible savaging. And they told us that the victim had been out swimming in the lake when one of the kelpy, an animal much talked of in these parts, had risen from the depths and attacked him. A group had left the shore wading bravely to his rescue. But they had arrived too late and by the time they had reached the body the beast had already done its work. Indeed, all that was needed was for them to carry the dead man ashore using iron hooks. Not only would we have to wait for the burial to be completed, but the only boat was to be found across the other side of the lake. And someone needed to swim and lay his hands on it before we had any chance of passing over.

We tried, their funeral finished, to goad the Picts into making the journey. But they, having just seen a friend torn apart, refused even to consider a swim across the lake. Indeed, we were all but resigned to spending the night at this dreadful spot, on the edge of freezing Ness, when we were surprised by the coming of a Gaelic priest, one of Columba's men, on his way to the Pictish high king. He, like us, had no time to waste and after blessing the grave of the dead man rather perfunctorily, ordered one of his own, a certain Lugne, to remove his clothes and paddle over to the other shore. This man, taking his master's word as God's law and shrugging off any fear he may have felt, hurled off all his coverings except one of those typical Irish tunics and plunged into the water, making for the other side. We and the natives watched his slow progress amazed for two or more minutes. But then, just as it seemed he might survive the crossing, the surface began to stir. The beasty, evidently feeling the water above it moved by Lugne's exertions, had started to push up towards the swimmer. Now we Greeks observed fascinated as the creature broke through the water, some little distance from its prey. It was a short, compact animal with horns, a wide gaping mouth and horrible whiskers like those of a cat.[1] As it moved in, those on the bank all cringed, waiting for the inevitable impact – Lugne was too far from the other side for safety and had no weapon to defend himself. But his master next to us rose to a great height and, in the way that a toad when threatened puffs himself up with rage before spitting its poison, the monk seemed to expand before our very eyes, screaming curses in Irish. The monster was clearly perturbed by the noise of the ascetic and, no more than a pole's length from the swimmer, dived, disappearing into the water. We register our opinion that this was nothing more than fear caused by the screaming of the holy man and that no supernatural agency was involved. But the Picts saw things very differently. They began to praise and kneel before the Gael, who promptly baptised them – they were pagan – at the water's edge. We preferred, however, to take our leave from this ceremony and, while the holy man splashed water over the dirty foreheads of these barbarians, we discreetly took the boat from Lugne, whose return with it had been uneventful, and made our crossing to the other bank.

There are said to be many man-eating monsters in Britain and Ireland, though this was the only one seen by the embassy on their journey. For the traveller who wants to avoid such creatures, a useful rule is the following. In the south of the island, fiends are normally cave-dwelling. But in Ireland and northern Britain, water beasts predominate. Stay away then, whenever possible, from lakes, large rivers and sea bays while travelling in these parts.

---

1. *Translator's note:* An almost identical description comes in a seventh-century Irish saint's life, the *Life of St Columba*, that has just such a beast emerge from Loch Ness or Ness river. Cryptozoologists have, however, been rather confused as this 'monster' bears little resemblance to the pseudo-dinosaur of modern lore. It has been suggested that here we are, in fact, dealing with a rogue sea lion!

(II) BURGHEAD

The northerners are known by several different names: Picts in Latin, Pretanni in British Celt and Cruithini in Irish. And these same words may be used with impunity outside Pictland; indeed, when they are said the speaker would do well to screw up his face to show his dislike of 'that demonical people'. However, take care not to use them in Pictish territory. The Picts call themselves, instead, the Albans, Alba being their name for Britain. And these Albani, jammed into their savage peninsula at the end of our world, have taken up some customs that, to say the least, demand patience and understanding on the part of the traveller; for though Christianity has penetrated their southern regions, even there it has not been able to civilise the wilder reaches of the Pictish soul. Take the single fact that is most noticed by outsiders: the place of women in their society. Here, in the far north, it is the female sex that decides descent. So if, for example, a king is to be selected they go to the heirs, not of the monarch's son, but of his daughters. And in some parts this operates too for the simple rules of inheriting a farm or dividing a field – a *pett*, they call it – between children. As a result the marriage of a princess – a simple act of diplomatic chicanery among us – takes on an importance that it would never merit elsewhere.

This custom has meant that the Picts' neighbours fear Pictish women as matriarchs or caricature them as power-hungry witches. Indeed, was it not one of our great Roman writers who described the sexual longing of the orgy-prone Caledonian female, who took as many men as she wished at the time and place of her choosing? The log dispelled these ideas, however. Pictish wives never fight in battle and never speak out of place in court, or at least no more than our own do here in Constantinople. They respect their husbands and the embassy described, for instance, a line of noble daughters demurely riding side-saddle behind their father, rather than taking the more traditional warrior's position on their horses. But even if they are no amazons, it would be foolish to pretend that the bloodline they carry does not give their words some weight in the war council and their bedchambers. In fact, we advise the traveller to remind himself of this every time he sees one of these Pictesses coming down the road towards him, and to take

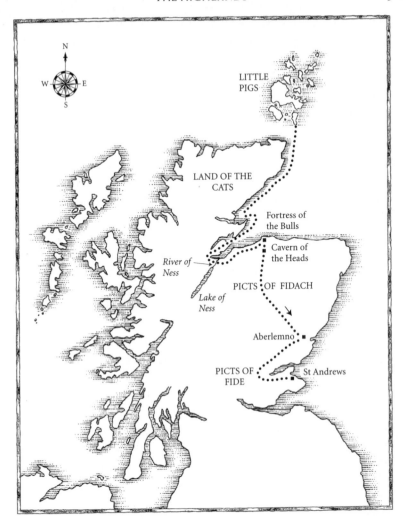

care to bow his head as she passes him by, averting his eyes all the while.

With Lake Ness crossed, the traveller will, anyway, have plenty of practice at dealing with Alban women and men alike. For there, at only a day's ride along the northern coast, is one of the chief fortresses of Britain and the capital of the province of Fidach – the Fortress of the Bulls [Burghead near Inverness]. It was, according to such accounts as we have been able to read, originally an unpromising extension of land with little defensive potential. But, what nature does not provide, humanity corrects and industrious armies of Picts were sent with cartloads of packed soil to subject the place to their king's will. The defences that the embassy saw were certainly impressive. As is typical among the Picts, those who planned the fort hardened the walls by burning wooden ramparts onto slag piles, for these two substances melded together have the consistency of iron. And today the capital of Fidach is reckoned the chief stronghold of the north. Indeed it is the largest of all Pictish defensive works. Its name comes from some of their unfortunate pagan rituals, for at this place they worship a bull deity and all around the traveller will find carvings of the Pictish bull latched on to walls or hanging from wooden catwalks. Their storytellers often make up heathenish tales about these creatures and a favourite sentence among the Picts is to say that someone 'can milk a bull', in other words, that he can do anything.

The fortress itself is the normal British collection of buttresses and ditches, albeit on a larger scale. The sensible visitor will stay put in the quarters assigned to him – it is easy to get lost – restricting himself to a visit to the royal court and its environs. One other site, though, that he will hear of and that he may be tempted to visit is the Drowning Room. We noted at the beginning of our description of the Picts that the evilness of this people is exaggerated by their neighbours. It would, however, be absurd to deny that they have vices – temples to bulls hardly commend them to good Christians – and one of their quirks is the way in which they dispose of their criminal class. In our country decapitation and the garrotte are usual. In other countries stoning or the arrow; in Ireland, for example, they use the noose or pit extensively. Among the Picts, however, they take those convicted of capital crimes and thrust them head first into water until the air is choked out of them. In the Fortress of the Bulls, a subterranean room has been specially put aside for just this purpose, filled from a natural spring. Visitors can, if they want, easily gain access to this chamber which in appearance though not atmosphere resembles an unlit Roman swimming pool. But it is suggested that you avoid those times when justice is being meted out by Pictish executioners – the embassy suffered from nightmares after their visit.

The Picts' barbarian side does then have this habit of sometimes unexpectedly rising to the surface, and, in this light, the log records several uncomfortable but instructive anecdotes. For example, in the wilderness, travelling away from the Fortress of the Bulls and, following the sensible advice I have already given of avoiding caves in the south of Britain and bodies of water in the north, the embassy stumbled on a large cavern and decided to spend the night there. The smell, they reported, was musty. But they put this down to lack of air and were at least happy to be out of the whipping highland rain. After preparing some food and writing up the day's entry in the log Andreas, the youngest member of the party, decided to explore. And he marvelled at the carvings he found on the walls there, for, as we shall soon see, the Picts have curious hieroglyphs that they place everywhere about them. However, on venturing further into its depths he uttered a dreadful scream and the rest of the party, when they eventually found him, understood that he had fainted bloodily against the cavern side, extinguishing his torch. More light was brought and a neat pile of seven decapitated bodies were found in various states of decomposition, stacked against the far wall. Retching and colliding into each other, the embassy ran out into the night and, though driven back by the rain, slept in the entrance, leaving at first light this cult centre that they had so unwittingly come upon.

The reader, shocked by such savagery, may wonder why the Picts have not fallen headlong into foreign dominion. To find out, he need only travel to their Alba, go to the Fortress of the Bulls and then walk due south on the path the embassy eventually took into Cairngorms or, indeed, he could take the alternative route and pass along the coastal roads. There you will find the reason: the best general of the Picts, their merciless, heathered landscapes. Humming in summer – the campaigning season – with bees or smelling of flowers and salt on the spring shore, these territories can be deceptively gentle. Indeed, so beautiful are they that the locals say that many are seduced into lying on the ground there, where the fairies, who live in the earth below, suck away their souls. But appearances deceive. And, though it should fear no fairies, an invading army forced to live off this country would soon begin to scratch hungry bellies; while the Picts love nothing more than to lure invaders deep into their territory, burning all around them, before wedging their opponents into some marshes and then turning, encircling them and finally slaughtering every soul that foolishly took the road to the north and imagined glory. So it was with our legions and both the Gaels and the British Celts have similar stories of warrior bands with brave leaders that rode out, never to be heard of again.[1]

(III) ABERLEMNO

The Picts, as we have already explained, are divided traditionally into seven tribal peoples. And in turn these tribes are split into the northern and southern federations, the boundary between these two groups being the Cairngorm mountains that lie to the south of the Fortress of the Bulls. For he who dares to cross them it will prove a dangerous and challenging route and, during those few hours that the elements do not wrap howling around the explorer with drizzle and wind, there is no guarantee that he will be able to see hidden enemies on the scree-laden mountain sides. Once the peaks and snows fade away, though, an easier landscape opens up, bringing the traveller down to the richer lands of the south. Here, at last, the earth can bear more than just barley, and some deformed fruit and vegetables start to appear.

A key point on this road south is Aberlemno, a landmark high on a ridge between two plains. This place is a traditional camping site for travellers approaching or leaving the northern mountains and is marked by several gravestones of famous Pictish lords and warriors. We talk of 'gravestones'. But the traveller will find no fine-hewn slabs here and certainly no ordered Latin letters. Rather he will discover a collection of what are known in Britain as 'the hieroglyph stones', a form of monument that is characteristically Pictish and resorted to throughout their territory. To produce these stones the Albans take a

---

1. *Translator's note:* The most famous example of a lost army in the Highlands of Scotland, the Ninth Legion, fictionalized by Rosemary Sutcliff, is actually based on nothing but supposition; the legion in question disappeared from administrative records and archaeology rather more quickly than some experts would have expected. Nor do we have any other records that substantiate our anonymous author here. In fact, the best-attested example dates to after the time of the embassy: namely, the disastrous Northumbrian campaign of 685 when the Anglo-Saxon king Ecgfrith led the flower of his kingdom into the territory of the Picts and was subsequently surrounded and massacred with all his men.

flat piece of unprepared rock and then set about etching into it their peculiar symbols. Sometimes they draw a sword handle, sometimes a beast, sometimes a bull, sometimes a rearing sea monster such as that seen on Ness, sometimes combs, sometimes flashes of barred lightning… There are hundreds of these symbols and the Picts use them as a kind of alphabet to represent their different clans and, indeed, their own names. Nor do they limit this writing to tombs or memorials. They also, rather disgracefully, etch these symbols on their raids, as if they were schoolboys out graffitiing. If they defeat a foreign army on its own territory they search out the most visible place and then carve the hieroglyph of the leader of the raid into the hard rock, where it will stand ever after as a proof of our enemy's humiliation.

They too adorn their bodies with these symbols. Indeed, most Pictish tattoos are made up of hieroglyphs that express the lines of descent of the warrior in question. The talented passer-by can learn with some experience to read them, and this has two useful purposes, for it both quickly informs the traveller of the name of the man before him and also mightily impresses the Picts, who consider the hieroglyphs their national secret. For example, a man with a large elephant-like creature on his back – the design is supposed to represent a dolphin – will be called Gartnait. Say 'Gartnait' before the warrior opens his mouth and you will set all a-muttering and a-wondering. Do not, by the way, worry about staring at their bodies. The Picts are, in truth, exhibitionists and love to have visitors passing their eyes over the luminous white skins of the north, puzzling at their excess of tattoos.

The reader may have noted that the present writer has a certain affection for the Picts, a charge we willingly admit to. Our fondness began many years ago in our conversations with the missionary Auxilius, who himself had spent some time among this people trying to retrieve kidnapped Irish converts. Auxilius described with care the different hieroglyphs, and even made sketches of some on hard wax tablets that are now in our possession. Indeed, we sincerely hope, once the present work has been completed, to turn to a study of the Pictish symbols – with a full explanation of their origins in the east and their later use in Etruscia and northern Africa. For this reason, we are desperately searching out exemplars, but unfortunately we have so far managed to bring together only eighty of the hieroglyphs, many of them untranslated. The author would gladly pay for any further examples and is especially interested in tattooed Pict skin that has been removed from its owner – no questions would be asked and the rewards are generous. If the reader sends, instead, a hieroglyph stone it would also be gratefully received; however, we understand that transport might prove prohibitively expensive in this case.[1]

(IV) ST ANDREWS AND FIFE

As the explorer passes deeper and deeper into Pictland down seemingly endless and invariably steep roads, he will find that the need to identify fellow travellers at a distance is especially urgent – not least because, sometimes, he should avoid those who are approaching. The embassy took care in the log, in several scribbled marginalia, to set out all the tell-tale signs. A Pictish male with long hair and tattoos on display will be a warrior. If he is naked (they detest armour that distracts from their body designs) or has one of their axes – the preferred weapon of the Picts – in his hand then he will be going off to battle. In this case we advise the bystander to shout 'Alba! Alba' in a stern voice, bowing at any with ponytails, a characteristic of princes or kings. Another traveller who should be treated respectfully is the royal officer of the high king, who carries with him two signs: a heavy silver necklace that jingles around his neck, and a silver disc that, to prove his identity, he some-times takes off his belt and flashes at those he encounters. As these officers are the servants of the king, they do not always appear dan-gerous; often they travel without weapons or have only small body-guards. But, whatever the provocation, do not offend such men, for the key to the kingdom is theirs!

Most visitors will naturally want to meet and pay their respects to the high king of the Picts. However, this is more easily said than done for the high-kingship rotates among the seven tribes and though the

---

1. *Translator's note:* Our anonymous author seems to have been a good deal closer to cracking the symbol stones – the modern term – than we are. After close to one hundred and fifty articles and books looking at the question, not a single symbol of the many that appear from early medieval times on stone and silver has been satisfactorily deciphered.

south tends to dominate this competition for the crown, even there it swings from one tribe to another with alarming frequency. And, to make life still more difficult, this wrestling match for the throne is so bloody that even when the panting voyager finally arrives at what he believed was the high king's home region, it is more than probable that his intended host has already been drowned by a wilier opponent. Periods of interregnum are frequent and often there is more than one lord of Alba.

The best way to meet the high king is to let him come to you on the coast of the province they call Fide [Fife]. Fide only rarely provides its own candidates to the throne. But it is there, at St Andrews, that the only monastery in all Pictland stands and most high kings visit the place in the circuits they make after coronation. Of the Picts and Christianity we have not yet said enough. A useful rule is that the closer to the old Roman border – the wall of Antonine – the more Christians will be found. So in the Little Pigs there are none. But here in the hinterlands of the monastery of Andrew, where from the sea you can just make out territories once marched over by our legions, there are considerable congregations of the faithful. And now that many missionaries from the Gaels and, above all, from Iona have begun to crawl over the spine of Britain, these numbers are growing every year.

St Andrews is, as we have noted, the only monastery among the Picts and though it is actually nothing more than a chapel with some beds, it has succeeded because of its name. As all good Christians know Andrew was responsible for the conversion of parts of Asia.[1] And, incredible to say, the Picts believe that their distant ancestors, those same that brought their peculiar and unintelligible language to Britain, came too from the Asian steppes. The missionary who settled on the name knew of this delusion. And, after having cleverly chosen Andrew for his foundation, he set about inventing a legend to explain the unlikely arrival of the apostle in cold and distant Britain. Clearly it was impossible to have Andrew come to the island in his lifetime, for his burial place in the east is well known. So, instead, a Greek monk was

1. *Translator's note:* The Church historian Eusebius tells us that Andrew converted the Scythians, the people from whom the Picts claimed descent. (It should also be noted that Scythia was sometimes confused with Scandinavia in the Middle Ages – probably the reason the Picts claimed to be Scythian.)

invented who was said to have brought some of his bones to Andrew's children in distant Alba. The Picts, who, to that time, had treated the founder with indifference, immediately began to visit and see for themselves the miraculous remains – some bones rifled from under a hieroglyph stone – and within a week nosebleeds were healed and hiccuping fits stopped by the saint's intervention. In short, a point of Christian light had entered the dark landscape of the Picts' unbelief. From then on the abbots have been celebrities and the local Picts – pagan and Christian alike – attend ceremonies and pay their respects to the foundation. The embassy followed their example and wisely left a carved ivory casket in the possession of the abbot so that he could let whichever regional warlord next happened to struggle to the high-kingship know of the generosity of the Greeks.[1]

The abbot was most grateful for this small mark of Imperial kindness and spoke at length about his experience among the Picts. His comments were recorded faithfully by the embassy and may be of some interest to the traveller who wishes to civilise this distant and difficult people or, indeed, any other barbarians. According to this warrior of Christ, who had served for many years in the field, there are four cardinal points to remember in converting the pagan.

First, learn the language well before attempting to convert. There were at the beginning of the abbot's mission some embarrassing incidents that led to confusion or laughter: on one occasion, for instance, he accidentally baptised a convert 'in the name of the Daughter, the Fatherland and the Holy Spirit'; while on another he described the miracle of the loaves and fishes as 'the miracle of the loaves and flying ants' to some wide-eyed converts.

Second, pick your clothes carefully. As soon as the abbot had understood the local customs of dress he adopted the native style, growing his hair long to mimic the Pictish male, stopping short only of tattoos and habitual nudity. Here he described, in some detail, the difficult balancing act a missionary must perform, for if the priest is too commonly dressed then he will be ridiculed; one of his monks had been

---

1. *Translator's note:* No such casket survives. However, it is sometimes suggested that the famous early medieval sarcophagus at St Andrews was based on a Byzantine model, perhaps even a small ivory casket such as is described here.

laughed at in the royal court. Then again, if he always goes around in the vestments of mass, these will become dirty and commonplace. He now wears his priestly outfit only when he is expected to go into battle against the pagan priests of the Picts in a magic duel; or when celebrating communion.

Third, talk to kings not peasants. Though some conversions can be achieved by browbeating the populace, the best method is to spend more time on leaders who can order hundreds of their subjects to be baptised at a time. The abbot talked of one six-month period when he had won only a small valley full of souls, and common farmsteaders at that, who were hardly likely to enrich the heavenly kingdom. However, following on from this he had one of his most remarkable successes when he converted a local king and in an afternoon had to baptise several hundred of his subjects. There were so many, in fact, that he huddled up the Picts into groups and poured water on them collectively. The only danger with this method, as he himself noted, is that apostasy is more likely and, at the first sign of an unusually harsh winter, the Albans return to their bestial rites.

Fourth, do not antagonise the old faith unnecessarily. The abbot insisted on making war on the priests of the pagans in his region. But he tried never to go out of his way with, what he termed, 'unimportant details' in day-to-day life. For example, the local populace enjoyed an annual festival where – this being the Picts – bulls were slaughtered. A less experienced missionary, he told the embassy, would have tried to stop this and so be blamed by the population for any subsequent famines or plagues. However, he simply held a Christian mass and sacrificed the bulls himself afterwards in the name of Jesus Christ, the population hardly noticing the difference. Here the leader of the embassy laughed, saying that at least the abbot had prevented the decapitation of human victims such as they had seen in the cave near the Fortress of the Bulls. But this missionary, whose experience stretched over almost two generations, looked sheepish so the point was not pursued.

From St Andrews to the southern borders of the Pictish territories there are three days of hard walking. The embassy, excited by the idea of leaving behind the woaded ones, chilled by the colds of winter and refusing to sleep, made the journey in two.

9

THE LOWLANDS:
'BETWEEN THE WALLS'

(I) THE WALLS

Ask even the beggars in the streets of Constantinople or an illiterate child from the poorer quarters of that same city to tell you one thing about distant Britain and they will begin unhesitatingly to talk of 'the Wall'. And who, indeed, has not heard of that unparalleled act of engineering by which our legions built, from sea to sea, across the north of that island, the defensive line named for the Emperor Hadrian [AD 76–138] in stone? And who has not heard too of the smaller wall, built almost one hundred miles to the north that, in the time of Antonine [AD 86–161], was constructed over the very narrowest neck of the island? For though the second was done in turf rather than rock – even the Imperial treasury of the golden age had a bottom – it too served to protect Britannia from the tattooed Pict and his war cry. Ten thousand Romans manned Hadrian's Wall and five thousand Antonine's. And in between these two territories, client tribes of the wilder British Celts were wedged to provide yet another line of defence.

But 'ah', says the sceptic with a tolerable schooling in the history of the Empire, 'is it not also true that the Picts learnt to row around these land defences in their boats?' So it is. But it was then that the Imperial navy built the *Pictae* ships, camouflaged green to melt into the sea, so they could catch the raiders in the ocean, where they pushed them screaming under the waves. It was also then that the shore forts were built, from out of which rode cavalry to needle at any Pictish warriors who did make it to land and to corral them into a valley or plain where the game could be finished to the Romans' satisfaction. The days of glory, these, when legionaries knelt beside the writhing bodies of dying

Picts and tried in vain to read the strange tattoos they found there.

But then came the disasters on the Continent and, to the woe of this country, the legions had to leave Britain [c. 410]. The walls were abandoned by all but a few auxiliaries and the shore forts and the attendant boats fell away, for, without the guiding hand of Rome, the natives, like children, can do nothing. And so it was that one of the most brilliant defensive structures ever created declined into uselessness, the Picts pouring south as they chose, the results being visible in Britain to this day. Burnt-out settlements still dot the area below the southern wall. Peasants regularly dig up treasures hidden by desperate Roman citizens just before fleeing that were never collected by their owners, death intervening. And though some half-hearted attempts were after-wards made to re-man the wall and hold the border, these failed. Instead, the greatest feat of building north of the Alps slipped into ruins and today remains a curio and a quarry for farmsteaders. Indeed, the only clue that the finest army in history once walked its length and protected the burghers of Britannia comes at its far eastern reaches where a small population of Syrians, originally brought to the north as hydraulic engineers, even today work the land around the River Tyne, though they have long since forgotten the Semitic language of their homeland.

The reader will forgive this historical excursus, especially as most of the details are so well known as hardly to bear repeating. However, these two walls must be fixed in the mind to understand the realities of travelling in the north of Britain, for they still define the region. The land between the walls [essentially the Scottish Lowlands] contrasts with the highland landscapes of the north or the mountains imme-diately to the south – indeed, the place is something of an agricultural oasis of meadows and rich river deltas, caught between moors and snowy peaks.

And the peoples of this inter-mural region, we know of two tribes, are as unique as the landscape that they farm. The Damnonii and the Gododdin, as they are called, control respectively the west and east of this narrow belt, and for the best part of a hundred years now have had to hold their own against the Picts to the north and the Saxons to the south. The westerners, the Damnonii, have their capital on the Rock of the Clyde [Dumbarton], where a mass of stone bulks out of the river, a mass that they guard against all comers. The Gododdin, meanwhile, defended, in the embassy's time, the eastern territories from their fortress at Etin [Edinburgh], a plug of volcanic rock in a range of some of the sweetest hills in the island.

The embassy found that both of these kingdoms were, surprisingly given their far northern position, British-Celtic. Their inhabitants spoke the language of Gwynedd and Dumnonia with only small variations of dialect. They were Christians, all of them. And, incredibly, they believed too in the Great Prophecy and the messiah Arthur, who will return, they say, to drive the Saxons from Britain and so save them. Indeed, the writer of the log reports that, to the Greeks' bewilderment, their guide through the territory had once more that infuriating habit of the British Celts of the south of naming various prominent landmarks on the road as the 'something or other' of Arthur. For example, the exasperated party were taken ten miles off their path to see an 'oven' – actually a barrow with stones covering it – of that most noisome of all British-Celtic heroes, humouring, through gritted teeth, their pathfinder's invocations.[1]

But in one point these northern folks are not normal British Celts and that is in their lack of *Romanitas* or Roman-ness. Though in the distant past they were kept as allies of Rome, they were never given the honour of calling themselves citizens of the Empire – an honour that, even if the other British Celts to the south can rarely speak Latin, they remember with pride. In fact, their only contact with Rome was the flood of gold coin that travelled north to help pay for wars against the Picts, a mutual enemy. And now that the Empire has withdrawn and the gold has ceased to flow to the two kingdoms, the British Celts have forgotten the legions and the old alliances. Indeed, the only clues of earlier contacts are Latin names among the grandparents' generation and the odd architectural flicker of another, happier age; the embassy, for example, stumbled upon a hill in those parts on which a Roman theatre had, bizarrely, been built in wood and on which, more peculiarly still, the local tribal leader was expected to sit and dispense justice.

---

1. *Translator's note:* Probably the ancient tomb 'Arthur's O'en' near Stirling.

(II) DUMBARTON

Other than the walls, the most impressive sight in the lowland region is the previously mentioned Rock of the Clyde, the capital of the Damnonii. This Rock is, in fact, an enormous basalt protrusion that comes out of the River Clyde and that stands like a sentry guarding the northern marches of the kingdom. And even though it is small, it has proved so secure and convenient over the years – the Rock is fed by an internal spring – that the local king frequently holds his court at its peak and, come evening, walks out on artificial platforms that have been grafted onto his palace's stone body, to better survey his kingdom. Lest the reader finds the place difficult to visualise then he or she could do worse than savour the words of the embassy: 'At twilight and from a distance the Rock has the silhouette of a fist coming out of the earth, the wider and higher parts being the timber frame where the guards patrol.' However, the traveller eager to arrive there should also be warned: to climb up to the royal sanctum you must use one of several vertigo-inducing rope ladders.

There is much envy among the neighbouring peoples on account of this superb fortress and the Dal Riadan armies have swarmed many times down the river to try and push the British Celts back from their strongest outpost. But, a testament this to the Rock's defences, the Gaels have never come even close to taking this British-Celtic stronghold. Indeed, so powerful have the defences proved that in Ireland they now tell tales about the sieges of this fortress as if it were a second Troy. Of course, it would be the short work of an afternoon for one of our legions, equipped with the necessary machines of war, to reduce the pile of men and wood that crest this stone to a pulp of bloody splinters. But, for the warriors of the Dark Isles, with their primitive methods of attack, the Rock of the Clyde is justly held to be invulnerable.

Twenty years ago the embassy traipsed across the spine of Britain in early spring and, after traversing many a mountain pass, they arrived at the Rock, just as the snows were melting. Their mission? Once more spies with diplomats' smiles, they had decided to greet the king of the region and give him gifts on behalf of the Emperor of Byzantium, while, at the same time, collecting any useful information for a future invasion. But there was also something else. Ever since they had come

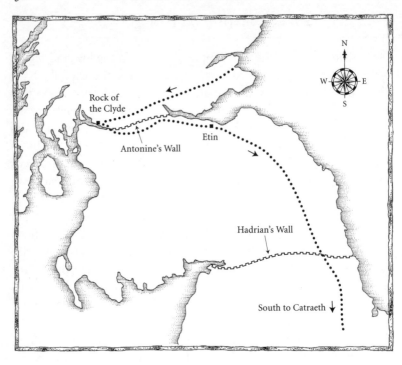

to Britain, they had heard rumours of a hermit who lived close by the royal court, a certain Gildas, who had the reputation of being the 'wisest of the wise of the islands'. And reasoning that the Emperor would never have forgiven them if they had missed this particular individual, they had wearily taken the road to the south-west and the chief court of the Damnonii, the Rock, hoping not only to unload trinkets on the monarch there, but also to fill their log with the wisdom of this guru.

The one they call 'Gildas' was, in fact, born eighty years ago in the kingdom of the Damnonii, the child of one of the leading noble families there. Sent south to civilised lands for his education, he early on showed remarkable talent at the writing of the Latin tongue. However, he at first wasted his gifts and, instead of using his quill to praise the Lord, misspent much ink on the celebration of carnal love and the world, one result being a series of notorious and over-explicit love poems. When finally his conversion came, it was, as is often the case in those who turn late to the Cross, characterised by a malevolent and almost frightening single-mindedness. And in his slovenly hovel – for, after travelling through Britain, Ireland and even the Continent, he returned to his homeland to search for God – he took to writing works of edification including histories, sermons and letters. All the great men of the islands have come to court him and suck at the breasts of his wisdom in that lonely cell.[1] Finnian, abbot of Clonmacnois, for example, arrived begging advice for the foundation of his monastery and was received with affection. King Magloconus of Gwynedd visited to reconcile himself with the Church after his irregular and incestuous marriage, only to be driven from the hut with a storm of shouts. And Gildas has been dragged, too, into high politics: he brokered, for example, an important recent peace on the Isle of Manu.

Though already an old man in the embassy's time, Gildas enjoyed rude health. How could it be otherwise? For the previous forty years he had lived the life and taken the diet of a monk: water, grass and, as a treat, goat's cheese. And we have no doubt that he is still muttering his prayers and that he will be, indeed, for many years to come; the western saints often live to well over a hundred. The future explorer will certainly then be able to approach the hut where he lives. But do not depend on entering it. Gildas, as we have already hinted, is an irascible individual and though he is often petitioned for meetings and interviews, he rarely endures another man's presence for long.

The embassy, in fact, arrived at an uncharacteristically ingenious strategy to gain access to his cell. In the churches of the British Celts and Irish, all good Christians have what they call 'a soul friend' who listens to their sins and ministers to their eternal part. Those who live in a monastery visit this soul friend as often as twice a day, while those at a distance sometimes wait as long as a month before going and admitting their misdemeanours to their surgeon of salvation. And, once arrived, the sinner kneels before 'the soul friend', confesses his sins and then is given a penance that will help him wipe away the blackness that stains him.[2]

1. *Translator's note:* A characteristic early medieval expression.
2. *Translator's note:* Indeed, the Catholic Church's present-day system of private confession with penance may have actually originated in Ireland or Britain in the early Middle Ages.

Well, after first being driven from his door, the Greeks usefully remembered that Gildas was a leading expert on 'soul friendship' and, had written many treatises or 'penitentials', as they are called, discussing which penance (fasts, cold baths, even exile) best matched which sin. And, while Gildas initially said that he would have nothing to do with any 'dirty Syrian heretics', the embassy guessed correctly that he would soften on learning that one of his Greek visitors was weighed down under several horrific sins, for the soul friend cannot refuse to cure. By lots the Greeks chose one of their party – the log does not tell us which – and then sent this pseudo-sinner on his knees into the cooped-up wattle hut where Gildas lived. For some minutes they heard the murmur of confession and then the pained screams as Gildas began to contest and decry the invented crimes. Minutes passed and the yells grew louder until, finally, the pseudo-sinner was dragged out of the house by his hair, stripped to his waist and soundly thrashed with nettles. After this first round of penance, Gildas, now smiling, was more than happy to answer the many questions of the group.

It is our opinion that the log took the 'wisdom' of Gildas rather too seriously. The log-writer enthusiastically wrote, for example, several pages on the correct penance for one who allows ravens to eat Communion bread – six years! – and other similarly scintillating topics. However, let there be no doubt that some of Gildas's recorded words did prove useful both to the embassy and to the present writer in composing this work. Gildas was especially eloquent on the hated Saxons, whom we first met at the Temple of Bacchus and who will loom increasingly large in these pages. So he described, for example, the Saxons' relentless advance across the east and centre of the island, not to mention their almost endless victories over the British Celts. He talked extensively of how the Saxons lack, for the most part, kingdoms and how their war bands simply unite under the most devious and violent warrior they can find. And he warned the embassy too that as they headed south, they would constantly cross what he called 'the line of control' between the British Celts and the Saxons. Finally, and most usefully, he gave the Greeks a series of British-Celtic insults for the Saxons that we include here hoping the traveller will be able to use them profitably. The 'dirty easterners' were, he insisted: *allmyn* ('foreigners'), *granwynyon* ('white cheeks'), *ffoxas* ('foxes'), *lloscit* ('incendiaries'), *du gyweithyd* ('black hosts'), *kechmyn* ('shit men'), *heit* ('a swarm') and many other things that modesty prevents us from writing.

(III) EDINBURGH

The embassy's work among the Damnonii over, they next headed east to the lands of the unfortunate Gododdin. We talk of the 'unfortunate' Gododdin. Perhaps it would be truer to speak – though our notices are still vague and based on hearsay – of the extinct Gododdin. But this we will explain in our own good time. The capital of this people was found, in the embassy's time, at Etin [Edinburgh], on a huge rock platform, and it was here that old king Mynnyddog held his court. Mynnyddog the damned he might be called, for over a generation his lands had been buffeted on the northern side by the Picts – an ancient threat that the Gododdin treated with equanimity; while, in the south, a far more serious opponent, Saxon settlers, penetrated and, acre by acre, the newcomers tore valleys and estates from what had once been the largest of all British-Celtic kingdoms. Some made paltry treaties to legalise their conquests, while others were openly and contemptuously defiant.

Mynnyddog was not the man to resist the invaders: by the time the embassy visited he was over ninety, decrepit and infirm. But nor did his successors rise to the occasion. Indeed, only days ago we heard the news from one of the rare merchant ships that passes Tintagel, and that has since made its way back to the Mediterranean, that resistance has now all but crumbled in the territory. The Saxon colonists and invaders, from their bases in the south, have wrenched even the rock at Etin from British-Celtic hands: the Gododdin, in short, are no more.

Given this state of flux, we can only warn the traveller to stay away from the region altogether. Nor will we pass on any of the copious writings of the embassy on the peculiarities of this northern people, for it is not yet clear whether the natives have been driven out, slaughtered or merely enslaved. Instead, we will limit ourselves to quoting from the log the military habits of the Celts while fighting against the Saxons. After all, if anyone is foolish enough to travel in this area, these are the customs that he is most likely to see.

We were greeted at the court of Mynnyddog on Etin's Rock with only cursory politeness. The time of year being spring and the war with the Saxons mounting, all were involved in preparing a strong counter-attack that would take back a swathe of land that had been lost in the previous three years. In fact, even our gifts failed to distract the monarch; though if truth be told, we were careful to give sparingly, aware that both Mynnyddog and his kingdom might not be around for all that much longer. Indeed, a memorandum should be written to the Emperor suggesting more strenuous efforts to recognise the Saxon conquests further to the south and we will do our best to facilitate contacts in our travels.

The preparations themselves have proved most interesting. Mynnyddog has, despite his age, gone to some trouble to plan the raid, a raid that is widely billed as a last opportunity for the kingdom. He, first, sent messengers abroad many months before warning his neighbours of the coming war with the Saxons and put aside supplies as best he could. And, in answer to his appeals, many of the kingdoms of Britain sent warriors to aid the lord of the Gododdin in his fight: we met men from Gwynedd, Dumnonia and even a Pict among his retinue. It should be stressed, however, that none of these and still less the nobles of the Gododdin consider themselves mercenaries in Mynnyddog's service. Rather they are his household or *teulu*, as they would say, and their loyalty has been sealed in the past year not just by hunting and war play, but through constant feasting on the rock that is Mynnyddog's court. There, as among all the British Celts, *med* is drunk and the warriors have sworn again and again to justify Mynnyddog's faith with acts of courage. And Mynnyddog, a small, wizened old man, gives the assembly gifts in return for their boasts and promises. He hands out rings to the young braves and all carry a golden torque around their neck to show that they have taken his drink and so will defend his land, if need be to the death.

There is an enormous range in age: some are still adolescents, in their mid or late teens; others are old boars with grey bristles. But few have the boisterousness of, for example, the Irish warriors that we met in Mac Dotha's hostel. This is partly because their situation is so much graver: the kingdom is at risk. But it is also the British-Celtic temperament that we have by now seen so much of; for though Mynnyddog's warriors burp, gulp and shout their way through their cups as warriors everywhere are inclined to do, and though they are in some respects ruthless killers, yet they also have a pleasing modesty, the young among them blushing, for example, at the mere sight of a maiden. Yes, there is relish at the soldier's life, but without the sunny bravado of the warriors of Homer. Indeed, it passes as wisdom among them that life is like that drink, *med*, that they all so love: sweet, but with a long, bitter aftertaste that dulls human affairs and that will lead them all, unfailingly, to a soldier's death.

After a week of putting the final touches to the attack the army of the Gododdin marched out to make war on the Saxons and the embassy followed them, reasoning that this would be a great opportunity to observe military practices among the islanders.

For the purposes of the ride south we were given steeds and put together with one Aneirin. When we were presented to the man, we learnt, with some trepidation, that he was in fact a praise poet and that he even knew Taliesin, our guide through the mountains of Gwynedd. But he was, we are pleased to report, a good deal less expansive than Taliesin – possibly the tension of the occasion working on him – and he was not forever speaking of legends and impossibilities, as is typical of this people. In fact, we were soon glad to have been put in his company, for we learnt that all those who go with him are judged non-combatants. Indeed, his sole purpose on the journey was to report on the heroic deeds of his peers through poems that he would afterwards compose and put into the mouths of the Gododdin.

We know that one of our principal missions in Britain was to give an account of the military potential of the various peoples there: it is important that our Imperial Master have a good idea of how easy a Byzantine invasion of the island would be. And with this in mind we should note that the British-Celts that we saw in arms here impressed us. One surprise was, though, as it had been among the Dal Riadans, the size of the army. After hearing of the year-long preparations for the mission we had come to believe that this was a hosting of almost all Mynnyddog's people. But we and Aneirin rode out behind a mere three hundred warriors! Admittedly this was the very cream of the northern cavalry and they were equipped well. However, such a small number would cause few problems to an invading Byzantine army with its higher level of professionalism. And when we confessed our shock to Aneirin, he explained that armies are regularly counted in the low hundreds and that some raids take place with as few as thirty or forty men! At this point we are hardly talking of armies at all, but well trained bandits.

Aneirin spoke no Latin – in this we found him less learned than Taliesin – but, through our guide, we discovered a good deal of their customs in war and of his duties. It seems that, at all costs, he is to hold back from the line of battle and mentally take note of the heroic deeds that are done there, so he can later compose a worthy epitaph to the dead. He admits that, in fact, much of this is formulaic. It is enough to take the name of a man, find a savage animal that chimes with it and then describe how said man died. What annoys Aneirin most about this rather depressing process is not so much the battle as a ceremony that he is expected to go through on his return. Poets are said to compose best in the dark and so he will be taken to some underground place and left there in the pitch black until his poem is complete.[1]

The march southwards to and into Saxon territory took a week. After two days the evidence of Garmani settlement was already all around; though the locals fled from the British Celts and there was no opposition to the Gododdin's passage except for some ineffectual skirmishing. In fact, it was not until the seventh morning that outriders returned to announce that the Saxon army of the north had finally been sighted and that it was fast approaching.

We had broken camp carelessly an hour before, while night was still around us. But immediately the news came, the horsemen rode into some order and began to prepare their weapons. Aneirin hurriedly explained that the army had hoped to drive a wedge through the territory of the Deirans, a major sept of the northern Saxons. But, instead, news had been carried to the enemy of the Gododdin's entrance into his territory and the army would have to fight on the ground of the Saxons' choosing.

1. *Translator's note:* Aneirin and other poets of his era composed orally and may never have written their works down, memorizing them instead.

The two forces met, in fact, on the plain beside the ancient Roman town of Catraeth [Catterick, North Yorkshire] – now a deserted wreck of stones and brambles – and we watched with trepidation the clouds of dust cast up by the approaching Saxon warriors. The Saxons, like many of the Germanic barbarians, prefer to fight on foot. And often battles between them and the British Celts resolve into a cavalry charge against the southerners' shield walls. However, these are not cavalry charges as we understand them, for, as we were to see, the British Celts employ a peculiar tactic. They rush at the enemy hurling, from about fifty feet, short javelins. Then they turn sharply, apparently retreating, and then, once more taking a suitable distance, charge back, plucking a new javelin from the flanks of their horses. Only when their supply is exhausted do they fight at close quarters. Here they either weave artfully with a spear, dodging and thrusting between the ranks of the enemy,[1] or more usually they dismount with their shields raised and fall on the opponents with blood-curdling cries.

The tactic was impressive and even our army could, we humbly suggest, learn from such skilled weapon-workers. However, on this occasion it did not prove enough. The Saxon shield wall had certainly had sections torn out of it. But it was not broken, and by the time that the Celtic warriors dismounted, letting their horses trot off to a distance, there was still much to do. Shouting 'Gododdin! Gododdin', they sank wildly into the fray. But there were too many of the foe and retreat, the British Celts being many miles from home, was out of the question. We began to prick at our horses' sides, looking expectantly at Aneirin, for he had told us many times in the last days that his most important task was to return to the Gododdin to immortalise the deeds of his warriors in verse: he had to get home alive and could not risk capture. But he shook his head at us and continued to look sternly over at the troops meleeing three or four hundred yards away.

Most of the Gododdin collected themselves together into a shield wall, to resist as long as possible the spear jabs of the enemy and their sword-wielding captains. In this position they died fighting, gathering

---

1. *Translator's note:* 'Weave' is interesting here. The absence of the stirrup, which did not reach Europe for another four or five hundred years, meant that warriors could not make frontal attacks with weapons – they would have risked being thrown from their horses – but had to make lateral ones that greatly reduced their force.

around the corpse of one of their senior warriors and shouting useless war cries in the early morning mists that characterise this region – it was an hour after dawn. However, not all the northerners faced death bravely. Two Celts who had become detached from the line of battle ran for their horses, mounted at a leap, and then spurred away from this invitation to eternity. It was a sensible decision: all was clearly lost.

But when we said as much to Aneirin he spat. For the British Celts nothing is worse than abandoning the field on which their leader's dead body lies. These warriors had betrayed their comrades and now Aneirin would betray them. So vile would be their names in his poem, that they would never again be welcome among their tribe or their families. Those who stayed, though, screaming in their death agonies, would receive Aneirin's praise. Praise for what, we ask, for the Gododdin now are doomed? The poem, if it is ever composed in one of the underground chambers of Etin, will last only as long as the kingdom and then disappear into oblivion.[1] With our poet, we watched until the last of the British Celts had fallen, though we had already ridden to the top of a rise near the old Roman walls of Catraeth, and then at something close to a gallop went north with Aneirin to bring news of the disaster to the halls of Mynnyddog.

The embassy followed Aneirin for a day but, deciding that there was no point in making the whole journey, left him at a tidal island that the poet called Metcauld [Lindisfarne]. There they were able to rest and escape some pursuing bands of Garmani warriors, while the Greeks prepared to pass back into the territories of the northern Saxons, the new power of the north.

1. *Translator's note:* The embassy was quite wrong on this count. Aneirin's description of the battle of Catraeth is arguably the most influential of early medieval British-Celtic compositions and it seems to have survived by being brought first from Etin to Strathclyde and from there on to Wales. It is remembered as *Y Gododdin.*

PART IV

ENGLAND:
THE WAR ZONE

NORTHERN ENGLAND:
'THE OCCUPIED LANDS'

(1) LINDISFARNE

We have had already to describe barbarities among the two Celtic peoples, though there Christianity, and, in the case of the British Celts, the memory of Rome, blunts their uncouth ways. The Picts have worse and more unadulterated habits; those who have visited the Drowning Room in the Bull's Fortress or one of their cult caverns will not easily forget the experience. However, it is the Saxons whose territory we now enter for whom we must reserve our most damning indictments. This is a people not only without God. But so horrendously do they live, so horrendously do they kill, that we shy away from thinking that they will ever be brought to the threshold of our Lord. Certainly, British-Celtic priests refuse even to try and convert them; while the Irish, who have made some efforts, confess that they are a difficult and disagreeable rabble. Indeed, we humbly suggest that when the glorious day comes and the legions of our Empire repossess the lost British territories, this entire people be loaded into boats and sent back to the Frisian marshes out of which they crawled a hundred years ago to general dismay. The British Celts can, at least, be trained, as the Roman experience shows, to bear our yoke. One might as well put a plough to a stag, however, as discipline a Saxon.

What then of this people and its origins? We call them 'Saxons', using the name of that northern tribe who have lived in the forests of Germany for as long as man can remember. But though this may pass for a useful shorthand it is, in fact, inaccurate. For, yes, some of the invaders are Saxons. But, in their ranks, the traveller will also find Danes, Angles, Thuringians, Jutes, Swedes and many other nations including even the Alan, those hated, horse-riding nomads from the plains of Asia. The British Celts call them simply the Garmani or Germans, for in origin all lived in or passed through those lands beyond the Rhine about which Tacitus wrote.

This motley collection of vandals began as pirates and raiders when the Romans still controlled Britain, working their way up and down the British and Gaulish coasts, seizing ships or suprising coastal settlements. Already though in those distant times, there were the two elements that characterise them still today: extreme violence and martial excellence. After smashing a patrol or ambushing a cohort, they would return to their boats with slaves, forcing their captives to draw lots from a basket so that one in ten might be crucified on the beach to slake their gods' blood thirst. Then, later, they came to Britain as conquerors, the Roman legions having abandoned the island, but changing little of themselves. Indeed, once they had driven the British Celts out of a territory they refused to settle as normal people, but continued to gather in war bands and under warlords, sniffing out new blood. And still now, almost a century after their invasions, it is only in some very few parts of the country including Cant, East Anglia and the coastal plains of the north that one can speak of stable Saxon dynasties and kingdoms. In the rest of the conquered areas they fight as much among themselves as against their weaker British-Celtic neighbours and their only reason for following one warlord over another is that man's strength in battle. Nobility of blood, in fact, counts for little.

One place that was crucial in their history is the small tidal island to the north of the wall named Metcauld in the British-Celtic language and Lindisfarne in their own. It was here that the embassy left Aneirin, while they recuperated after that hard ride following on so unwelcomingly from the Gododdins' defeat at Catraeth. In fact, the flight – Saxon war bands pursuing all the while – proved a disaster, for the Greeks' mapper, Laurentius, had, with characteristic professionalism, ridden down the wrong valley, falling victim, we surmise, to Saxon thuggery. For the remaining Greeks, the only consolation was that Aneirin, fearing that they would all suffer the same fate, turned off from the main paths and took them to the above-mentioned Lindisfarne to recuperate. The tide wiped away their horses' prints. Saxon war bands raged past oblivious to the poet's deception. And then to entertain them, as the sun set over the mainland, the master bard of the Gododdin told the embassy stories of days long since past. One in particular of these explains the close, tense atmosphere of that island and we think it is worth repeating here.

It seems that many years ago, at the time of the invasions, the first of the Saxons to live in the north held the land about Lindisfarne, after having seized it from the Gododdin. The British Celts of the region, however, rightly feared this inimical presence in the midst of their lands. And so several British-Celtic kingdoms of the region, including the aggrieved Gododdin, Strathclyde, and other realms now long since conquered, agreed to unite and drive the pirates into the sea; while the Saxons, who lived near the island, hearing of this army, and who though strong in war were, at that time, still weak in numbers, fled to Lindisfarne, scenting their extinction. Indeed, even the most optimistic of the Saxon chiefs held out little hope and their final destruction seemed mere hours away.

But, after three days of waiting, something inexplicable happened, something, at least, that in any other people but the quarrelsome British Celts would have been inexplicable. The Gododdin and their allies, finding their victory over the piratical invaders rather too easy, began to fight among themselves. It all started with disagreement, descended into swearing, and degenerated into knife and spear play, until finally on the third night of the siege Morçant, the leader of the alliance, was stabbed as he slept. The Saxons awoke on the fourth morning, preparing themselves for death only to find, to their amazement, that the enemy camp on the mainland before them was dividing before their very eyes, British-Celtic warriors screaming at each other and the wounded being carried away on stretchers. By the evening of that day the Saxon invaders crossed the causeway to find the camp deserted. In fact, all that was left of the occupying force were some decapitated bodies, for the reader must remember that in war the British Celts commonly carry away the heads of the fallen, believing the soul resides there. They leave the corpse or what remains of it to be pecked at by ravens and crows that flock to battlefield carrion as sparrows do to grain.

This was the last opportunity the natives had to halt the Saxon invasions in the north. And when we remember that of the British-Celtic kingdoms that attacked Lindisfarne all but the Damnonii [the British Celts of Strathclyde] were subsequently destroyed by the Saxons, the British Celts must sorely curse their internecine habits. The dictum of 'divide and rule' is never so true as among this people and those who will be responsible for once again bringing our eagles to the north of the island will do well to remember this. The Saxons, meanwhile, who have made the region their own in the last decades, hold Lindisfarne especially dear for the service it did them on those terrible days a generation and more ago. Indeed, the Irish of Dal Riada, who have long had contacts with the Saxons north of the Humber, have even offered to pay and man a monastery there. The Saxons, though, are reluctant to have monks meddling in their territories and have so far refused.[1]

(II) THE PENNINES

The traveller who has, in one manner or another, managed to provide for his freedom of movement through the dangerous territories of the north should remember that the most stable of the northern Saxon lands are on the eastern coasts. In this, the first area that the embassy visited, Saxon settlement is well established and the conquerors are confident and arrogant in their lordships. Indeed, once under the protection of a local warlord the explorer will find that all goes smoothly and the ways are marked out and specially prepared bronze bowls have been set up along the wayside at springs to allow the visitor to refresh himself.

But, after the coastal plains are left behind, then the relative order of those territories gives way to the chaos of a frontier zone. Now, moving inland, the traveller will find an almost endless stretch of mountains and hills with deep wooded valleys and cold streams, the water of which

1. *Translator's note:* They, of course, eventually agreed. The monks of Iona later founded a monastery on 'Holy Island' that became one of the most brilliant and famous in all Britain and that was later immortalized by the Northumbrian historian Bede in his *Ecclesiastical History* and *Life of St Cuthbert*.

needs to be boiled before drinking – beavers and dead cattle having seeped disease into it. This wilder country also belongs to the Saxons, who have chased out the old owners and their clergy with sharp blades. However, these new lords are insecure in their rule, treating the older British-Celtic peasant class that survive through most of the region with open hostility. They call the British Celts the *Wealh* – a word that in the Germanic languages means 'foreigner'.[1] And, at every turn, the invaders show their contempt for the original population. They take their human sacrifices from among the native communities. They grab *Wealh* women for their beds and for breeding, as not enough of their own women crossed the oceans with them. And they treat any display of *Wealh* tradition with disdain. Not surprisingly, the Saxons who rule over these areas, with small armies of twenty or thirty in their train, are regularly ambushed in the wilderness by surly native gangs.

The traveller must try always to remain neutral, sidestepping as best he can the hostility between the two communities. He is advised to wear no jewellery or decorations that betray a visit to the British-Celtic territories and likewise no items that are Saxon in origin. This is, ultimately, a matter of common sense. A more serious difficulty, however, comes in determining just which of the two the traveller is dealing with when he meets, say, a small group on the roadway. The inhabitants of these upland regions, of course, have no such problems. It is enough for them to see a face to recognise the characteristic physiognomy of a native or Saxon – all say that the *Wealh* are darker-skinned, while the newcomers tend to be pale. Language also defines the communities but, since the traveller is unlikely to know either, this is hardly helpful: both are based on similar uncomfortable guttural

---

1. *Translator's note: Wealh* meant, as our author notes, 'foreigner' in Old English, so, for example, the *wal*nut – wal=*wealh* – is 'the foreign nut'. However, by extension, it then took on the meaning of 'British Celt', the 'foreigner' most familiar to the Saxons. In this guise it has passed into modern English, for when we walk of *Wel*sh, *Wale*s or Corn*wall* – the ancestral territories of the British Celts – we are actually reverting to this ancient term. Likewise when we speak of certain modern English place names, including *Wal*ford (the ford of the British Celts), *Wal*den (the valley of the British Celts) and *Wal*cot (the cottages of the British Celts), we also are speaking of the *Wealh*. Finally, it should be noted that *wealh* had a third meaning that our author does not cover. In Saxon it could also signify 'slave'; it is a striking proof of just how little the invaders thought of their British-Celtic neighbours that this ambiguity of meaning sprang up.

sounds. Easier to distinguish are the adornments that the two races wear. Weapons are usually not carried by the British Celts, for only the serfs remain in the conquered territories; while few Saxons go without arms in these lawless valleys, the short stabbing knife, the *seax*, being especially common among them. A cross on an individual marks out a Christian and hence a British Celt. Any strange spangled lines on swords or sewn into clothes, however, are what they call runes and immediately point to the invaders: look out especially for the sign of Tiw, their god of war, it is written thus ↑. These are borne by only the vilest and most uncontrollable of their warriors and could be the first sign the traveller has of trouble and blood and pain.

When a traveller has determined which ethnic group is being addressed life becomes far easier. If there are British Celts before you the traveller should confidentially promise help from the Emperor and talk with winks, making reference to the Great Prophecy and the re-conquest in which all this people passionately believe. If the explorer encounters a Saxon, a more swaggering attitude is advised with lots of eye-rolling when 'the bloody natives' come up in conversation. The Saxons also enjoy military stories, so it is best to exaggerate a recent deed in the Emperor's Mediterranean wars and ascribe it to some heroic northerners – 'they wore swords exactly like that one you are carrying!' The embassy found that this usually did the trick and then it was barley beer all round.

In some of the interior, British Celts continue to control certain valleys or hill ranges. We have heard rumours, for example, of the kingdom of Elmet and its capital at Loidis [Leeds] – though no one seems to know the way to this mythical realm and it may be, for all we know, one of their legends. (The embassy, anyway, sought its remains fruitlessly in a series of valleys of stunning beauty.) Another northern kingdom is Reget [locatation uncertain], the warriors of which fought alongside the Gododdin at the previously mentioned siege of Lin-disfarne a generation ago. The Regetwys [men of Reget] had only recently been overrun in the time of the embassy and some of the survivors were said to have retreated with their gold to Ireland or unknown strongholds in the wilderness. The Greeks, however, saw only the ruined halls of the last kings of this realm, burnt black and covered with nettles and bindweed.

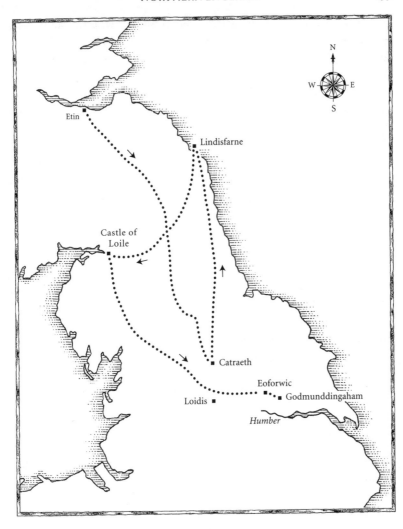

The embassy did, though, find one British-Celtic survivor between the Humber and the wall, that of the Fortress of Loile [Carlisle], which stands not far from where the Irish Sea laps against Britain's western shores. It was a long cross-country journey to reach the stronghold. But, mindful of the Emperor's instruction to visit all the realms of Britain, they persisted through wearying mountain passes and plains, the leaves of overhanging trees whispering 'ambush' and 'bandits' into their fearful ears, until finally they were rewarded with the sight of its walls. At the Fortress of Loile a Roman town has been turned into a defended stronghold. And the embassy were impressed to see that – uniquely, we believe in the north of the island – the inhabitants had kept the city's aqueduct going and were even able to give their Greek visitors a tour of the repaired defences. However, the governors of the city also admitted that they could not resist the Saxons on their own and that their only chance for freedom had been to swear fealty to the kings of the Damnonii across the wall, something that they did with considerable distaste, for they view their British-Celtic cousins to the north as little better than Picts.

Here is an important truth that any future traveller to Britain should try and take with him. Once the peninsulas of the west have been left behind, the explorer will find fragmented British-Celtic communities such as that of the Fortress of Loile. But these differ in two ways from their western cousins. First, they tend to be more Roman: the governors of Loile boasted about their fountains and sewage system in a clipped but not unpleasant Latin. Then, second, to the same extent that they are Roman, they prove weak in war and have to rely on mercenaries and perfidious allies to protect them from the Garmani.

(III) YORK

From the Fortress of Loile it is a four-day ride to the old capital, Eoforwic [York]. In better days, in Roman days, this was the second city of Britannia, Eboracum. Indeed, it was here that Constantine the Great declared himself Caesar on his father's death.[1] But the Saxons, who regularly declare how much they hate everything Roman, cannot be bothered to pronounce the name in the old-fashioned way and so slur it, adding *wic* (another of their words for settlement). The prudent traveller will follow them in this mispronunciation, and try to still his

1. *Translator's note:* The writer alludes here to Constantine I being declared Emperor in York in the year 306, an act that was to start a six-year-long civil war in the Empire and that would after the Battle of the Milvian Bridge (312), pave the way for the official acceptance of Christianity in the Roman world.

rage when he sees how they have reduced the ancient, mortared heart of the north, letting it collapse into ruin.

The most powerful of the northern Saxon warlords (he calls himself a 'king') is based not in, but near the city, to the east of it, beyond a river that is called the Derwent. There at Godmunddingaham [Good-manham] the traveller will discover the torn limbs of men and beasts swinging from the trees of a glade, for an important temple of their gods is also to be found at this place. You will doubtless be thinking that this is the holy enclosure of the Saxon god of which we have already had cause to speak, Tiw, the warrior's inspiration. However, Tiw is only one from a large pantheon of terrors that the Saxons worship. Indeed, he is not even the most fearful. Alongside him is that strumpet of Germany, the evil Frig, goddess of lust and of the fireside.[1] Then there is also Thor, god of thunder and of the smithy, not to mention Eostre, the goddess of earth, 'the Mother' as they call her. But riding astride this cavalcade of demons, and favoured above all at Godmunddingaham, is their king god, one-eyed Woden. He is celebrated in all things and at all times and it is he who requires blood sacrifices and excites the Saxons into their worst savageries. Indeed, before battle has got under way, this people regularly hurl spears over the heads of the enemy, so consecrating them as a worthy tribute to this monarch of hell. These beings and various celestial objects are even celebrated in the names the Saxons give the days of the week: Moon-day; Tiw's day; Woden's day; Thor's day; Frig's day. Our Lord's day is thankfully not polluted by their terrible devils and is simply called the day of the Sun.[2]

Clearly, it does not do to be quite as impolite about their gods when speaking with the Saxons, who, as all barbarians, take such demons very seriously. Indeed, given the British Celts' association with Christianity in the Saxon mind, it is probably best not to carry the cross: a sign that they have learnt to despise. The best approach is, instead, to be and act like one of them. To convince them of your pagan credentials

---

1. *Translator's note:* It is sometimes said that the word 'frig' in modern English (as in 'frig off!') is semantically related to this goddess.

2. *Translator's note:* Most modern European languages use pagan gods' names for the days of the week, e.g. French mardi (the day of Mars), jeudi (the day of Jove) etc. Along with modern Greek one of a few exceptions is Portuguese, which resorts to numbers to avoid invoking pre-Christian deities, so Friday is 'sixth-day' ('sexta-feira').

you should pay on arrival a courtesy gift to the high priest to provide a sacrifice. The gift should not be too large or the high priest will buy a slave – we imagine that no civilised traveller would want to have human blood on his conscience. And the nature of the sacrifice should also be appropriate to the time of year, for the Saxons have a rigorous calendar relating to offerings. In February they have the feast period Solmonath, or the month of the cakes, when they offer dainties baked in the shape of birds to the gods; in that period a sack of flour should satisfy the high priest. March is Rhedmonath, or the month of Rheda, one of their lesser gods, who is normally satisfied with animal blood. In April comes Eosturmonath or the month of Eostre,[1] who also demands blood sacrifices. In September is Halegmonath, or holy month, when the harvest is paid for, naturally, with more blood. Then in November there comes Blotmonath, or blood month, a time when ... well, it may actually be better not to be in these territories at that time of the year. We should also warn the traveller of other cult centres spread through the country. The embassy caught glimpses of a terrible death at a place called Sancton near Eoforwic, where they accidentally walked into a clearing hung with the swastika, the crooked cross symbol of Thor.[2] It was only by walking very quickly the other way that they escaped with their lives and, more importantly still, the Emperor's gifts. Later they were told what an unpleasant fate met anyone who was seen to go unwelcome there, and that the place was dedicated to the terrible lightning-thrower because of the frequency of storms overhead.

What about accommodation in this part of the country? Once the visitor has convinced his host that he is not a Christian, he will be invited to join the family (and hangers-on) for food as a matter of course. In a simple Saxon dwelling dinners are usually Spartan. Indeed, the lowly peasant or farmer is well known for his refusal to adorn his food with any sauce or accoutrement: boiled meat and some vegetables are deemed sufficient. However, in the court there are chefs, there are pretensions to culinary excellence, and the king even boasted to the

1. *Translator's note:* The name of this goddess surfaces in our word 'Easter'.
2. *Translator's note:* The swastika, of course, had a long and illustrious history before it was dishonoured by the Nazis. In other incarnations it appeared as a Hindu fertility charm; the insignia of the Finnish air force in the 1930s; and, as noted here, the mark of Thor.

embassy that he had once drunk 'grape beer', wine, dear reader! What is to be preferred, the simple fare of the peasant's house or the *haute cuisine* of the royal court? Based on the royal menu described in the log – broad bean and spinach broth with saffron bread; smoked fish with buttermilk sauce; honey-glazed chicken with fennel; yellow pea and honey soup; honey crumble and nettle tea – it seems to us that the stomach may be better served in one of the simpler dwellings, above all if the visitor has to cover a lot of ground on the following day.

A still more decisive difference between rich and poor households is the entertainment on offer. At a royal table you will find the *scop* or Saxon poet: *scop* means 'one who shapes' for it is said that they create whole worlds with their tongues. These *scops* sing the deeds of the various Germanic kings with the *hearp* and their boundless memories, since, incredibly, they write none of their thousand-line poems down. As individuals they are prolix, having a certain fame for never using one word when five or six will do. Normal Saxons, for example, call a body a body, the *scop* talks instead of 'the house of bones', while in their contorted mouths a ship becomes 'a steed of the white seas'. At poorer tables, meanwhile, where a *scop* is rare, it is customary instead to pass whatever instrument is available from hand to hand so in this way all take their turn. In addition to the *hearp*, they take out bells, the *shawm* (a kind of oboe), *hwistles* (whistles), *sangpipes* and cymbals that they crash joyfully in raucous passages. The embassy enjoyed themselves enormously in this more relaxed setting and played some Greek tunes, the cause of much hilarity to their hosts.

However, one unfortunate aspect of dining or living with the Saxons does not change in a rich or a poor house, and that is the quality of the conversation. We quote directly from the log:

A characteristic of the Saxons that redeems them from such barbarities as we have seen today is their obsession with wisdom. 'To be wise' is the greatest praise among them and even warriors are expected to enamel their pride and might with that virtue. In itself this is commendable. But in practice it quickly becomes rather tedious for the Saxons have constantly to display this wisdom, throwing strange expressions over you like nets. While we were unloading the horses and preparing them for stables one burly-looking man came along, wagging his finger, to tell us: 'Better often loaded than overloaded.' When we complained to one of the household about the state of our clothes he bolstered our spirits with the reflection that 'The naked traveller fears for nothing' – rather amusing considering the Imperial gold we were carrying in what was left of our packs. Describing later at table our experiences with the werewolves in Ireland, we heard the warlord king mutter, almost under his breath: 'It is better to avenge a friend, than to mourn too much.' When we discussed instead our, for them, strange eating habits the queen politely consoled us with the following words: 'There are as many customs as there are tribes.' Then when we got on to the death of a Greek hero in the Sicilian wars: 'Death is better for any warrior than a life of shame.' When one boy was seen to be bolting his food, 'The one who eats too often is sick' was shouted across the table. When this same boy, a prince or *aethling* as they call them, was seen to hide a table knife in the folds of his tunic his nurse spat at him: 'The person who is ashamed goes about in shadow.' When he denied any wrongdoing his father replied knowingly 'The apple never rolls so far that it does not make known whence it came.' And on and on it went. 'Frost must freeze, fire destroy wood.' 'The ploughman does not plough unless he knows how.' 'The smith follows the exemplar unless he knows better.' 'Fate will spare the brave.'

Just as our endurance was breaking, for it had been a hard day's riding to this mean complex of huts and temples on the edges of Eoforwic, the king stood suddenly and came out with the longest of all: 'Night is the darkest of weather, hardship is the most difficult of fates, sorrow is the heaviest burden, sleep is most like death.' This was a signal for bedtime and sent all scurrying. We, however, not quite knowing the etiquette of the place, were left at table picking at our teeth with Cambrian hazel wood alone with, of all people, the high priest, who had already unnerved us with his hooded eyes and strange smiles. We decided on escape. But we had hardly risen from our seats, when he threw up his arms and too began to expound: 'Life', he soliloquised, looking straight at us, 'is like a little bird that on a winter evening flies through the open doors into a hall where men are feasting. For a moment it is among the warmth, the excitement and the music and then just as quickly it flits out into the night. What comes before and what comes after is a mystery, wrapped as it is in the darkness and the snow. Truly our existence is a sigh between two secrets.'

The hour was late. On the morrow we had to try and cross the distant Humber. And the conversation had progressed from tedious to alarming. As quickly as decorum would allow, we retreated to our quarters.

THE MIDLANDS:
'THE FRONTIER'

(I) THE HUMBER

The Humber is one of the most important British rivers. Powerful in its sedentary crawl to the sea, it divides the upper part of the island, and for the Saxons it is their primary boundary: they call those of their people who live to the south 'South-Humbrians', and those who live to the north 'North-Humbrians'. For the traveller, meanwhile, it is a welcome boon in one of the cruellest parts of Britain. Unguarded and without sentries, it takes ships thirty or forty miles upstream towards the centre of the island and so avoids the uncertainties of the overland route. We have heard of no dangerous animals on its course. And, just as on the Hafren [the Severn] merchants from Syria and Egypt congregate to exchange their wares, so here traders from the Humber's sister rivers in Germany, the Rhine and the even more distant Elbe, bring boatloads of new goods to the northern kingdoms. It is also the point of arrival for Saxon immigrants from across the sea, for many still come tempted by descriptions of a fertile almost uninhabited land and the dream of carving out a farm and some territory for themselves.

Crossing is possible at several points, either by paying ferrymen or, on the higher reaches, scouting out fords. The embassy found an excellent site just south of Eoforwic and, once across the Humber, they made a rare, sensible decision. Exhausted by the road and the still wintry weather, desolate from the recent losses of members – appendicitis carried off Snegdoulos, the geographer, in a hovel on the northern bank of that river – and painfully aware now of the dangers of travelling among the Saxons, they decided to rest for a while in a nearby village until they had fully recuperated. This would allow them not only to put up their blistered feet, but more importantly to examine the customs of this part of Britain and to learn something of the Saxon language.

For this intensive course in Garmani living they chose the first hamlet they came to on the southern banks of the Humber, a typical Saxon settlement that went by the name of Barleytun [Barton-on-Humber], meaning in their language 'village with a lot of barley'. It proved an excellent choice. The population of the place was not at all shocked to meet foreigners. Indeed, because of its proximity to the river traders were frequently seen passing up and down. The natives were impressed with the travellers' stories of the royal court near Eboracum. And, naturally, they were more than willing to make a little extra money in a lean period of the year. ('Spring', as this people say in one of their endless adages, 'is the cruellest season', for their winter supplies are all but finished and yet the new year's crops have not begun to offer fruits.) The entries from the log for the following four weeks proved exceptionally thin, so much so that we are almost tempted to speak of dereliction of duty, what remained of the embassy enjoying themselves rather too much. But the little that was scribbled – usually in incomplete or ragged sentences – showed that the party learnt valuable lessons from their hosts that would serve them well for further travel among the most dangerous people of Britain.

Barleytun was, by the standards of the Saxons, a well-off settlement. The Greeks were struck by the honest, rude health of the population: it seems that, despite appalling hygiene, only a quarter of their children die in infancy. One member of the embassy, who had studied medicine in his youth, confessed himself much impressed by the strength of their teeth – there was none of the decay or wear that is seen among our own people. There were also relatively few terminal illnesses. The plague, for example, much reported among the British Celts to the south, is virtually unknown here. However, consumption was noted; the populace talked of a leper they had had to drive away; and there were, the proximity of the river working against them, several recurring cases of the trembling disease. Nor did the villagers' life expectancy benefit much from the work of the local 'doctor', an aged woman with grimy hands who spat bile. The Greeks were, in fact, introduced to one of her victims, a young man known as Aldhelm the Hole, who was famous for the bore that had, only a few years before, been drilled into his skull to free him of 'demons', by which we presume the savages meant epilepsy. Aldhelm was surprisingly well considering, and charged only a small sum for those who wanted to test with their fingers what repelled their eyes.

The village itself was separated off into wooden communal dwellings, nothing being built in stone. And walking around this settlement, on their first day, the embassy were immediately unnerved by the jealous possessiveness of the men with respect to their womenfolk – never look directly at any Saxon ladies, at least not while their husbands are there! The Greeks stated too that wives and daughters are far less free among the Saxons than among the British Celts or the Irish. They cannot inherit property, nor do they have any autonomous rights in the law. Indeed, if a woman is abused by a man, it is judged to be her husband who has been insulted and it is he who will receive any compensation. However, lest the rich traveller decide to take risks despite these warnings, we remind him that sometimes justice is meted out in an unnecessarily crude fashion, with no recourse to local courts.

This possessiveness that they show for a wife, slave girl or concubine does not, however, extend to the wider family. Indeed, one general impression was that the bonds of family that are, as we have seen, so important among the other nations of the Dark Isles, do not matter much in settlements like this. Yes, certainly, parents and children are strongly dependent on each other. But, beyond that, kinship flags and the fact that a man is a cousin hardly registers in the Saxon mind. The chief of the largest farm at Barleytun said that this had not always been so. In his view it was the fault of the invasions that had mixed many people together and unknotted previous ties on crossing the ocean: he, for example, knew little of relatives in his homeland over the seas and cared even less. He also admitted, whispering, when he was alone with the embassy, that in the past there had been much marrying with the *Wealh* women, and no one wanted to admit to having a *Wealh* cousin, let alone a *Wealh* uncle or aunt.

Instead of family, the strongest bond, at least for the men, is with the local warlord who requires blind loyalty from his henchmen and warriors. The embassy's impression was that this oath was in many ways a more sacred one than the bond between close family members, and described seeing an adolescent kneeling and laying his head on the lap of a battle leader – the sign of total, suicidal obedience. Once an oath is taken and the warrior receives symbolic gifts from this man, it defines him as a vassal for the rest of his life. And, indeed, there is no worse crime among the Saxons than that of abandoning or betraying a master: 'Woe', they say in their wise way, 'to the man who changes lord under heaven.'

One of the early lessons for the embassy was that travelling among the Saxons would mean changing their clothes, for they have outfits that in some respects differ from those seen in the west and north of the Dark Isles. The men of this people are always belted, of course. But their buckles have typically Germanic motifs, above all the boar or wolf. They generally wear tunics with no metal fasteners. And they tote strong helmets when they meet for war, the most aggressive having horns or crests protruding from out of the helm. Our embassy were, at least, able to obtain clothes relatively easily in the village: in fact, some were made to measure there and then for a very reasonable fee. However, they were also embarrassed to find that the locals were fascinated by our own open jackets with the characteristic braids running up past and through the fasteners. With much excitement the inhabitants of Barleytun even tried to copy this fashion and enjoyed aping the embassy in some other minor respects as well.[1]

It is right that we describe here, too, women's clothing among the Saxons. We do not wish to suggest, of course, that a respectable Greek lady would ever travel to Britain. But it is useful to know something of their feminine ways, for the stumped traveller may find a gift of clothes an easy way of impressing a generous or potentially generous host and his wife; though the gift in question must naturally be given, to avoid misunderstandings, with the husband looking on. Most women wear a long tube-like dress that they fasten over their shoulders. They step into this strange item, pull it up to their armpits and then use brooches to attach it, covering their hair modestly with a veil. Some of the more extravagant women – though this is disapproved of by the majority of

---

1. *Translator's note:* The Byzantine fashion for braided coats spread, in the course of the sixth century, to the Germanic world. We may see here one of the rare moments of contact.

the population – use coloured veils that fall to their ankles in what the embassy thought was a most pleasing fashion. Others still have a cloak-like dress, not dissimilar to those worn by our noblewomen. Again brooches are used to fasten the points and, inside, a smaller tunic is worn with a belt fitting tightly around it. As to the fabrics, pretentious types prefer to wear linen, which is reckoned 'superior' to wool, for the vain in all countries care more for fashions than for their body temperature. More curious to our eyes are their accoutrements. Women of all ages and character carry, hanging off their belts, various useful items, sometimes held in small leather bags and sometimes swinging free. These are obvious knick-knacks: keys, tweezers, small knives... But they also carry amulets against the evil eye. Indeed, the Greeks were at first shocked to find that whenever one of the party gazed at a village girl – the husband or father naturally not being around – she would immediately grab at some strange object on her belt for protection. Amulets include many things: boar's tusks, Roman coins and broken combs. And an inventive traveller should easily be able to turn any hand-me-down past use into a much valued gift for a warrior's wife: 'Did this not protect the Empress when...' etc.[1]

The population spent most of the days on agriculture, even the youngest being recruited into the picking, planting and sowing. As a result, they all have permanently bad backs from adolescence on, not least because they spend so much of their time shovelling heavy, estuarial soil. Typically, they put their hands to the tools for an hour, and then rest squatting in a semicircle, talking and laughing. Many of the women instead spend their time at the loom, often indoors. This work was respected and valued by the community. However, as they were unescorted, the embassy wisely decided not to investigate their technique too closely. Occasional hunting was also indulged in. But here the locals excluded the visitors because in an unfortunate incident early on in their stay one of the embassy had accidentally used the taboo word 'bear' while practising the Saxon language. We mention in passing

1. *Translator's note:* One of the most curious finds in the cemetery as Barton-on-Humber was a large ivory horn that archaeologists insist could not have belonged to a native breed. If it, as has been suggested, belonged to a hippopotamus, it is possible that it was originally an amulet gift given by the embassy. We leave the question to researchers.

that the traveller should never refer to this animal. If the word is unavoidable this beast should be called the 'bee-wolf',[1] a euphemism referring to that animal's love for honey.

Anyone who spends even a short period in a Saxon village will have to attend, sooner or later, a funeral. To the reader this may seem excessively morbid for a travel guide. But we insist on including a description, because there are so many opportunities for *faux pas* and gaffes, and the community takes the whole event so very seriously. The Saxons of the north, especially across the Humber, generally (though not universally) bury bodies instead of burning them; their cousins to the south, meanwhile, almost always cremate. North or south, if the traveller is encouraged to assist in preparations he should take care not to remove valuable objects from the body. We, of course, as good Christians, would never include precious items when we bury our dead and keep clothes to a bare and modest minimum. But they put all the dearest possessions of the individual in the grave or, in the case of cremation, on the pyre, not infrequently breaking the object first so that it too will 'die' and follow the corpse to the other world. Indeed, the embassy saw many knives and brooches treated in this reprehensible manner. Afterwards, the fully dressed body is placed in the ground and an animal, in Barleytun a bird, is thrown in to escort it to the other world.

Other objects are brought there too by the elders, picked according to the status of the individual. For example, children are commonly given toys. Adult males always take with them a spear. Teenage girls are given combs. These are then positioned in a special fashion around the corpse, and the traveller should always, always refuse any offers to lay down one of these talismans, for putting an object that should go to the right of the head on the left would cause uproar and bring down perpetual bad luck on all present. Finally, a branch is lain gently over the recumbent body to stop wolves or forest dogs digging it up and feasting on it, while the grave is quickly filled in, food being scattered into the dirt to 'feed' the dead one. A note is needed too on their far-from-typical treatment of babies. The embassy at Barleytun saw one tiny body being buried in the grave of a stranger. Our party did not

---

1. *Translator's note:* The name of the most famous of all Saxon heroes, Beowulf, may derive from this expression.

understand why this was and, because of a number of embarrassing blunders on the same day, feared to ask. However, they guessed it was so that the stranger could keep an eye on the unstable spirit of the child.

The main purpose of the embassy in stopping in Barleytun was to learn the language of the Saxons. And a couple of its members, who already knew Germanic tongues from their days negotiating on behalf of the Emperor, were here surprised. They described the language that the Saxons speak as absolutely bewildering for, in fact, it is almost a pidgin tongue, a, so to say, thoroughbred mongrel. There were five or six words for every fragment of day-to-day life, and verbs and adjectives changed in different ways according to the speaker. In the end, they decided that this was the result of the varied origins of the village's inhabitants for some spoke of their grandparents coming from Scandinavia, some from the marshes of Frisia, some from Frankia and some from plains beyond even the Elbe. In a certain sense this means that the language is uniquely difficult to learn. But it is also simple, for mistakes are more easily accepted by a listener, and there is a generally cavalier attitude to grammar.

It was in the very instability of the language that the embassy made their final and most interesting discovery: traces of British-Celtic. The village universally hated their *Wealh* neighbours to the west and derided scornfully the *Wealh* slaves who lived among them. But the linguists in the embassy noted that a very small quantity of words had been borrowed from the Celtic farmers who had lived in the barley fields on the Humber before the Saxons came. For example, a pig was often called a *hog*, a badger a *broch*, and a container a *bin*, all three words also used among the British Celts.[1] Then, one day, to the utter bewilderment of those Greeks one of the most aggressive and W*ealh*-hating of the natives began to count his sheep in British Celtic![2] On being questioned he

1. *Translator's note:* Three of the handful of words that passed from the language of the British Celts to Saxon and from there to modern English: others include *dun* and *tor*. Philologists often comment on how extraordinarily small this selection is considering that Saxon or Old English replaced British Celtic over a huge territory.

2. *Translator's note:* The use of British-Celtic numbers in mainly northern English areas for the purpose of sheep-counting – 'yam, tain, eddera, peddera, pit' etc. – survived as a lively tradition up until the decades before the Second World War, though there is much debate about just how these numbers arrived or were preserved

admitted that his father had taught him this, though he became furious to the point of seizing up a recently felled trunk when the words' origins were explained to him. Leonidas, the party's cook, who so took to life in the village that he eventually settled there, received heavy bruising across his ribs on this occasion.

The embassy reflected on this rash of British-Celtic words carefully and noticed too that many of the 'Saxon' population actually had, considering their pale Germanic origins, surprisingly dark skin – a product no doubt of British-Celtic blood. And the embassy realised as well that some of the locals had British-Celtic-sounding names: Cerdic or Caedmon, for example. What is incredible is that these quarter- or half-breed British Celts – for most of the population seem to be at least partly of British-Celtic origin – so hate their own people, occasional mentions of a Celtic past being almost immediately hushed up. The embassy wrote, for example, how one old codger, on catching a glimpse of a carelessly hidden cross in the luggage of the embassy, talked of being brought, as a very young child, across the Humber to be baptised by the local bishop. (Of course, by now that bishop, his congregation and his religion have long since been wiped out by the Saxons!) Even the strange habit of burying bodies with birds recalled customs that the embassy had seen previously among the British Celts.

(II) WROXETER

The next destination of the embassy, Viriconium [Wroxeter] was, at least twenty years ago, the citadel of one of the mightiest communities of the British Celts. Unfortunately for inhabitant and visitor alike it was only reachable by passing over stretches of one of the most dangerous territories in the island – Mercia, meaning 'the frontier', where recently established Saxon colonists had carved the land up into dozens of fiefdoms and mini-kingdoms. This Mercia lacks a strong central lordship such as is found among the Saxons of, say, East Anglia or Cant or even Eoforwic and is, in reality, a series of small interlocking peoples,

there. See Michael Barry, 'Traditional Enumeration in the North Country', *Folk Life*, 7 (1969), pp. 75–91.

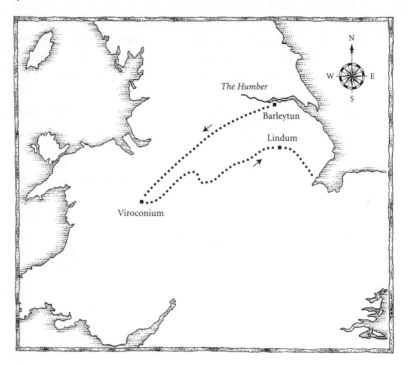

a border territory uniting around the strongest sword. In the embassy's time these various peoples coagulated under a warrior named Icing whose court was near the River Fromed [central Worcestershire] and who claimed, as do many of the Saxon warlords, direct descent from their one-eyed god, Woden. There is little point in explaining the routes to take to reach this place, however, for by now Icing has certainly been replaced by a pretender from a neighbouring kingdom, or the whole confederation will have collapsed into one of its habitual civil wars.

The problem with arriving at the court of Viriconium is not only the insecure state of the intervening part of Britain, but also the constant conflicts that rage between the Saxon Mercians and the British Celts who dwell in this exposed state pushed up against the hills of Cambria. Indeed, Mercians spend months of every year raising bands to march into the territory of Viriconium to drag yet another piece of land under their dominion; and when they are not raiding they are busy defending their own territories from the inevitable British-Celtic counter-attack.

Lines of war are so unstable as to be impossible to chronicle, and they have no doubt changed entirely since the embassy recorded its own impressions. What can usefully be said, though, is that borders, in whichever direction they shift, tend to fix on rivers for these offer lines on which both sides can agree and which are easily defended. And likewise, wars, when they begin, usually start at fords, often with warriors from the opposing sides taking on each other in personal combat before rebuffing or crumbling under a more general attack.

For just this reason, we advise the traveller to take enormous care with rivers and fords in particular, especially if they are guarded. Outsiders who are shot down in sight of the river have no recourse in law – or their family only receive half the compensation that is normally given for a killing. And any foreigner who wishes to cross a river must be greeted by a man from the other side, in sight of the enemy, and then walked across holding his escort's hand. Clearly, contacts need to be made and the whole affair can be rather cumbersome. But do avoid the temptation to do things quickly or to circumvent the law. The first attempt that the embassy made to cross the line of control almost ended in disaster. They found to their horror that they had attached themselves to a band of cattle rustlers of the type that flourish on frontiers everywhere. And as this would have incriminated them in the eyes of both communities they had to slip away at the first opportunity. If the worst does happen and a traveller attempts to cross the border illegally, only to find he has been spotted either by British-Celtic or by Saxon guards, there is but one sensible solution. Fall immediately to the ground throwing your arms before you and crossing your wrists. In the war zone this is a symbol of abject surrender and few will continue to use violence after the victim puts himself in this position. There will then begin the difficult task, however, of providing a ransom, so as to avoid the normal fate of prisoners – an uncomfortable, bundled-up journey to the slave markets of Denmark or Ireland.

When the necessary bribes had been paid and professional escorts were found the embassy crossed the borderline and passed into the British-Celtic statelet centred on the fort at Viriconium, built within the comforting lines of the old Roman walls. And, indeed, they arrived to find a heavily guarded, crumbling city perimeter; not to mention the additional surprise of seeing, on the inside of these, newly rebuilt

Roman-style palaces with all modern features, constructed not in mortar and stone but in wood! As elsewhere on the edges of the Saxon zone of control, the British-Celtic population tended to be more civilised than their cousins in Cambria or Dumnonia, never mind the savage British Celts between the walls. Most spoke Latin, some crisply in rather pretentious tones. But every so often there were reminders of just how barbarous even the best of the British Celts can be. So on their first evening in the stronghold, the embassy were shown into a building that was lit by candles placed in the recesses of partly decayed human heads.

The British Celts in these parts – sandwiched between Cambria and the Mercians – call themselves by a peculiar name. They are the Cumbrogi, a word that means, so the log assures us, 'dwellers of the border',[1] for these are the front line in the war with the Saxon enemy. Certainly, the situation in this, the stronghold of the kingdom, was at crisis point when the Greeks visited. The news came almost as soon as the embassy had arrived that the river crossing that they themselves had used had been broken by the Mercian Saxons. Moreover, the spring had brought with it a plague, much the same as the one that a generation ago emptied our own lands.[2] Dead bodies lay in ditches outside, piled there to try and stop the pestilence's spread, and large numbers had been wiped out in this way for the natives are especially prone to foreign diseases.

On the evening of that first day, indeed in the hall adjacent to that where the human heads gave out a dim light, the embassy were introduced to the chief of the fortress. He had heard of their visit to Brycheiniog and Gwynedd, which lay short miles away over the wastes of central Cambria. But he was flighty and impatient given the difficult situation among his own community and brushed aside their polite-ness: 'Will the Emperor help us? Will he help us against the barbarians?' he asked again and again. The embassy assured him that, of course, the

---

1. *Translator's note:* Cumbrogi became in later British Celtic *Cymry* and it survives today in Welsh as the word for Wales and the Welsh. Hence the Welsh Nationalist Party is *Plaid Cymru*, 'Party of Wales'.

2. *Translator's note:* It is sometimes suggested that the plague that devastated much of Britain and Ireland in the sixth century was brought from the Mediterranean. It is even possible that the embassy were unknowing carriers.

Emperor would. But the city's governor seemed sceptical and only two days later the decision was taken to abandon the fortress definitively – one reason we have limited our descriptions here to the strictly necessary. The plague had killed too many for the walls to be properly manned and reports had come in that Saxon raiding parties had broken the line of yet another river.

The order given, the population that had survived the wretched spring fevers set about the dismantlement of the city with admirable professionalism. Walls were undermined at key points to prevent these defences being used again, and the word went out to take down the palaces and associated buildings by the next evening. The embassy were lodged in a bunkhouse towards the end of the old forum, holding their noses for fear of the pestilence that had left the city deserted, when to their surprise the roof under which they were lying suddenly came away from its bearings and lurched off its walls. It had been dragged by a small crane the British Celts had assembled, the voices of thirty or forty men breaking into what had been the embassy's bedroom. The British Celts of Viriconium afterwards retreated to a nearby hill fort that had been defended in ancient times, for, as is the custom of the British Celts in difficult straits, they had determined to use it to make a stand against the invaders. We have no idea how their campaign fared or whether any of the city's population survive today in the wild lands of Powys. What we have heard, though, from several of our sources is that Mercia and its frontier remains one of the most dangerous and fought-over parts of the island.

(III) LINCOLNSHIRE

For the traveller who wishes to search out the old rulers of Viriconium in the mountains or to break through into British-Celtic Cambria, it may still be worthwhile running the blockades and fords between them and the Saxons. Others, however, are strongly advised to stay away. A far more rewarding destination and a safer one is the kingdom of Lindsey [Lincolnshire] that lay – the embassy once more had to trek long and dangerous miles – five or six days' march to the east, close, in fact, to Barleytun where they had begun. 'Lindsey' comes from the

British-Celtic name Lindum, and this was, too, the name employed by the Romans for the region's main city [Lincoln]. The Saxons call the territory 'Lindsey', that is 'the island of Lindum', because the whole region is surrounded by marshes, bogs, swamps and rivers, as if in reality it were an appendage of Britain rather than Britain proper.

As befits such a territory, its culture is unusual, not least because here the British Celts and the Saxons made common cause in the period following on from the end of Roman rule. So the city at the heart of this diminutive kingdom, Lindum, is occupied both by Saxon pagans and British-Celtic Christians, while the king at the time of the embassy had the Celtic-Saxon name of Caedbald. The embassy even noticed the unusual sight of British Celts and Saxons working together at the pottery furnaces, each producing their own variety of pot. Lest the reader be surprised by this détente, we should explain that the Saxons who settled there negotiated with the locals for land, and this has made the mixing of the two peoples the easier.

The town itself, where they were invited to stay by Caedbald, was also something of a surprise. Three-quarters abandoned, the ruins had been knocked down and overlaid with waste, refuse and sewage in an attempt to make these bare lands useful to what remained of the population. The hope had been to cultivate portions of territory within the city so it could even withhold a siege if one of the Mercian kinglets decided to cross the rivers into Lindsey. In some places the results have been dismal, weeds grow and bricks continue to show through the mess of soil. But in other corners of the metropolis there are orchards and parts of Lindum look curiously like an Olympian garden city.

It was just outside Lindum, on an evening in May, that the embassy were introduced to the most famous sport of the settlers – word-fighting. Frivolous as this game may seem, we have decided to quote directly from the log, for it is a pastime that the Saxons love beyond all others and in which they evidently enjoy embroiling visitors.

The *hearp* had already been passed round three times when the old man challenged us to a word fight. We laughed nervously, not under-standing at first what he wanted to say with this. But their smiles showed that they meant well and he gave an I'll-start sign. Then, clearing his throat, he came out with an extraordinary sentence and demanded an answer of us. In short, it seems that they wanted to play at riddles! Indeed, that night we learnt that the Saxons consider themselves the world's finest riddle-makers.

Thrilled at the prospect of pacifically battling our hosts, we begged them to give us the clue another time and, after listening three times to the passage in question, we managed to translate all the words in it, for our time in Barleytun had advanced our knowledge of their language a good deal. We record it here for the Emperor's edification.

'Hurt always by tips of steel or blades in battle, and tired from the banging and buffeting of war, I dream of sword-play and the foe. But I never heal. Even in peace they batter me with hammers and turn me with knives in the fortresses and villages. No herbs can heal my wounds, no doctor – save a smith – cure me. Instead, the wounds on my body grow bigger and threaten to break my wooden heart. What am I?'

Now we had to solve it. We obviously needed a victim of some sort. Four guesses went by, however, and their contempt had begun to rise before our inspiration came. It was Manuel, the group artist, who found us the way out. He cast his eyes around the barn in which we had been driven by the rain and saw, among other objects of little use, a half-broken buckler: 'Shield!' he yelled to our applause.

The drinking horn returned again and, taking a gulp, the man who had tried previously to confound us consulted in whispers with his colleagues, obviously looking for a more difficult riddle. After a minute's argument they settled on one and another member of the group stood up to give it to us:

'Dropping from the thigh of man a strange shape lurking under the cloak. Chained to the body by a strong bond I am stiff, hard and stand there well. When a man searches for me he lifts his clothes and takes this thing. I am to push my head into a similarly shaped hole of the same breadth which often my hard rod has penetrated before. What am I?'

We blushed and the Saxons roared to see our discomfort. Then, when finally we admitted defeat, for we could not bring ourselves to say *that* word, our kindly hosts screamed for more drinks and told us that they had, in fact, been describing a key! Downcast and sheepish as we felt, they, however, had the good grace to offer us a further riddle, a chance to redeem ourselves:

'I fill women with expectation and though erect and tall is my stem – I stand hard in a bed – and I am whiskered below. A greedy wench will grip me hungrily, putting me in a close place. But soon she will pay for her presumption and this lovely woman who assaults and pulls at me will find that her eyes become wet. What am I?'

This time we were wise to their wicked tricks and discarded the obvious. In fact, after only a minute, it was again Manuel who untied the sentence by thinking intently on the last line: 'her eyes become wet'. They were, of course, talking about an onion! Now it was our turn to laugh and, nettled by our guessing one of their most devious riddles, the Saxons asked us to give them, instead, one of the riddles of the Greeks.

Of course, we are not a riddling people and so had none to hand. But we remembered the famous question of the Sphinx. 'What has four legs in youth, two legs in age and three legs in old age?', while, to add some grandeur to the occasion, one of our number pretended to read it out of the log, for that usually impresses the illiterate. However, it did not work. In fact, all the Saxons made contemptuous sounds, stating the answer, 'man', immediately, indeed, taunting us by asking whether this was really the best the Greeks could do. Now we had to put these swamp dwellers back in their place and so, locking our heads together, we determined to create a new riddle, one in their style that would best them. Our 'masterpiece', for they applauded it enthusiastically when we finally gave the answer, was as follows: 'I grow in a small place, swelling up and rising with the excitement of being covered and hot. I have no bones and so the maiden takes me in her hands and pumps me and then she hides my growing self to perfect.' The answer, of course, is 'dough' and the master of ceremonies assured us it would enter their repertoire as one of the most provoking of all the riddles he had heard.

EAST ANGLIA:
'THE BEASTLY EAST ANGLES'

(I) THE FENS

The territory known as East Anglia, a bulge protruding uncomfortably out of the near side of the island, has one of the bleakest landscapes in Europe. Indeed, the kingdom hardly seems to be British at all, as there are very few woodlands and no mountains. Instead, the traveller will find boggy plains that stretch several hundred miles inland from the North Sea. And so flat is this land that at night, from a rare vantage point, you can see the fires of a thousand Saxon villages. Travelling through such monotonous countryside proves a challenge, and many newcomers end up going around in circles or getting lost. The intelligent traveller will, therefore, before making the journey, commit to memory some basic Saxon for the road so that he can at least pick out landmarks. There is *halh*, a low, damp hollow; *eg*, an island in a marsh; *ford*, a dry-foot crossing of one of the numerous streams in the region; *beorg*, a small rounded rise; *hyll*, a spiky prominence; and *dun*, raised farm land.[1]

As the embassy found, the best gateway to the kingdom is from Lindsey in the north, Caedbald's land, a territory that the Saxons of East Anglia, in fact, regularly invade. However, the journey from Lindsey should be made by boat, not overland – and here the Greeks erred – for between Lindsey and this region is one of the most perilous

---

1. *Translator's note:* Many of these name elements can still be found in East Anglia to this day. *Halh*, Stradishall, Lawshall and Foxhall; *eg*, the parish of Eye; *ford*, Stratford, Bramford, Blyford and Ufford; *beorg*, Chedburgh and Kettleburgh; *hyll*, Haverhill; *dun*, Brandon, Raydon and Thordon. *Hyll* (hill) and *ford*, of course, survive in modern English.

of all British territories, the Fens. These Fens are Europe's largest marsh. They begin at the banks of a river named the Granta, not far from Gronte [Cambridge], and lead from there to the sea. It is a sad and threatening expanse, run through with deep pools covered in fog, full of shallow bogs and occasional sinking mud that have dragged many to their deaths. There are patchily wooded islands, the *egs* and through the whole of these Fens spin twisting, unpleasant streams full of leeches, fish and plagues of mosquitoes. The Fens have grown, they say, in the last years as the sea shrinks back from the shores of Britain. And those who wade in the northern reaches sometimes come across the eaten-out wrecks of ancient farms and settlements that the ocean had once swallowed up, but that now it gives back to the land, at least for a while.

There are five good reasons for not entering the Fens. The first is the smell that is intolerable. The second is the air that rots and pollutes all that it touches; never eat bread made there – the famous hallucinogenic Fen rye – for a terrible mould grows on its surface that induces visions and madness. The third is malaria, which is endemic within the bogs, together with other illnesses that lay down traveller and inhabitant alike in trembles and sweats. The fourth reason is the Celts. We have said that the British Celts are not frequently to be found in the east of Britain, so hated are they by the Saxons who have exterminated or driven out all except a few slaves. But in the Fens, small communities still survive and these, bringing out their weapons, form into war parties and raid the surrounding lands. Then, finally, the fifth reason are the *thyrs*, a race of hominoid beasts that live in the Fens' darkest reaches and sometimes underwater. These creatures can swim in the rivulets and love nothing more than human blood; they attack at night and come with the fogs to the Saxon villages.

The *thyrs* are much talked of in East Anglia. However, we must say that the East Anglians, like the Saxons in general, describe many other similar creatures. They fear, for example, a slighter wood-dwelling humanoid named the elf that can pierce the skin with tiny missiles – the feared elf arrows. Cows and horses are especially vulnerable to these small flint darts that the farmer sometimes finds near his dying cattle. There is the dwarf, another humanoid of spectacular malevolence, that crawls from out of the ground and rides sleeping humans by casting an animal pelt on them as a saddle: 'dwarf riding', it is called, a high fever being the result. Finally, there is the *draca* that lives in barrows and guards treasures; these resemble Nile crocodiles, only they grow up to fifty feet long, have small wings and breathe scorching fire. The embassy were strangely inclined to dismiss such oversized lizards as figments of the locals' imagination. However, we have more faith and suggest an expedition to trap some of them. Certainly, one of these monsters collared and muzzled would be a prize worthy of the sceptred lord of Byzantium. And only the lack of references in the Roman bestiaries prevents us from confidently pronouncing a new British species.

(II) HELMINGHAM

The best way to come to East Anglia is, as we have seen, not overland by the Fens, but by the bay that boards the Fens to the north. Boats are available and the crossing so quick that the wary traveller will be able to avoid the mists and storms of the ocean. An experienced navigator is, however, necessary, for unescorted travellers have sometimes found themselves caught on the edge of the Fens in the sinking pools there. Guides are also needed within East Anglian territory – the route they most commonly take is the River Usa [Ouse], which is in part navigable – for guards will immediately hail those on this waterway and any that have no knowledge of the Saxon tongue will be escorted or harassed.

Do not argue or attempt to bluff guards. The East Anglian temperament, like that of many of the northern barbarian peoples, is unstable and driven by the secret hope of violence; indeed, a favourite local phrase is 'shoot the arrow first, ask the question later'. Be firm but polite, and look carefully into the space beyond an East Angle's head, speaking constantly of business with the king, for the king is feared throughout his lands. If this does not work, speak instead of needing to see the local *eorl* [earl], the lord. Only if this produces no result should stronger tactics be considered. In this part of Britain, bodies are, anyway, easily disposed of.

On the Usa there is the village named Helmsingas [Helmingham] which in the rainy season can be reached by boat. East Anglian villages, even large ones, have rarely more than two hundred inhabitants. And

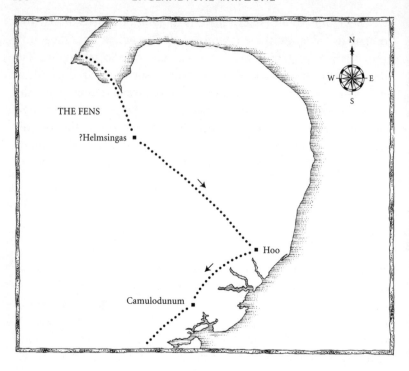

so rare are outside travellers in the region, especially travellers with the olive skin of the south and without beards – East Anglians have faces that are grown over with hair – that they will be followed through the village by screaming hoards of children and curious women. At moments like these, some cheap Greek bronzes to scatter in the mud facilitate easy passage – few of the inhabitants will have seen coins before, still fewer know what they are for, and none be able to read the words on them.

Helmsingas is an important centre for the East Angles, for they say that among the first Saxon invaders there was a queen from Scythia [Scandinavia], a certain Wealhtheow who came to live here with her warrior husband, Beowulf, and so conquered the region. Indeed, the locals can speak of nothing but Wealhtheow, Beowulf and Scythia, 'the homeland' that lies across the sea; and some in their excitement will even begin to point to the north. However, we doubt that this Scythia is any better than East Anglia and may, in fact, be worse. We say this, for so many of the Garmani made the journey to Britain that now the villages of their original territories have been left deserted and the fields fall fallow.

The story of Wealhtheow and Beowulf is one of their sordid pagan fictions. But it is a fiction that the traveller should know for the local kings, the Wuffas as the dynasty is called, claim descent from Wealhtheow and her spouse. Indeed, there is an over-long epic in alliterating verses that the visitor will be made to suffer if he is greeted with favour by the local people. On no account speak or laugh during the *scop* or shaper's rendition, which lasts three hours on a good night, six hours on a bad one. Indeed, any kind of interruption is treated as rank bad manners, and it is best to think of this poem as an extraordinary national anthem. Any prior knowledge of Beowulf and his wife is greeted with much satisfaction, especially if the visitor claims that 'even the distant east knows of his fame' and nods knowingly or openly salivates as the singer raises his voice in dramatic passages. To enable the impression of knowledge to be given, I include here the most important points about this Beowulf and his dam: one, that he killed a *thyrs* in the Fens named Grendel; two, that he swam the ocean in a day and a night; three, that he killed a second *thyrs* that was the mother of the first; and four, that he died fighting an enormous *draca*.

The architecture of the Saxons in East Anglia is almost as curious as their legends. The houses of a typical family in a village like Helmsingas sink in the manner of a badger's sett. If one enters one of these buildings, the burrow is not at once evident. But planks on the floor lift away and there below is a pit between three and six feet deep where they keep animals, naughty children and their carefully wrapped weapons. On no account point to these holes or evince curiosity: the East Anglians have a strong sense of property and treasure their makeshift cellars. To be shown them is an honour and, if they go unshown, casual visitors must learn not to express surprise at the mewing of animals or children beneath their feet.

As well as a collection of such habitations every settlement also has what the Saxons call the hall. This large, free-standing building is reinforced with staves to resist the harsh winds that come across the flatlands and is half palace, half beer cellar. It is here that the village meets and it was in the hall at Helmsingas that the embassy had to suffer the long poem about the hoodlum Beowulf. Other than poetry recitals, the two other primary roles of the place are drinking and duelling, two pursuits that naturally go together. There are also endless, tireless stories about how village 'A' gathered its men in one of the halls to feast, only to have the men of village 'B' come and burn the hall down or fill it with arrows and other unpleasantries – civil war and feuding are widespread among the Saxons. The traveller must *not* enjoy hall-burning stories. The tellers often become tearful, and it is felt to be the height of bravery to have died in a hall fight.

One important point about East Anglian and, indeed, Saxon warriors, that we must note here, is their peculiar relations with horses. This people, who are in so many things violent and uncouth, profess the greatest love for these animals. And it might be this profound sympathy that decided the Saxons never to fight on horseback. True, the most important travel to battle riding, but when they arrive, all, even the king, dismount. Indeed, a question that is often asked the traveller, with no small disbelief, is whether we southerners fight on horses. It is best in these circumstances always to insist that we 'of course' do not, for they have little tolerance or understanding of different ways.

A typical village will put forward a militia of between thirty and seventy men. Of these only the leader, the *eorl*, will be armed with a sword, a primitive stabbing weapon without a proper handle. *Eorls* are also the best-armoured men: as well as chain mail they have helmets, obviously modelled and, in some (rusty) cases, stolen from Roman legionaries. Most of the rest of the army will be spearmen. These fight in close formation with shields as well as javelins that they hurl at their enemies. And these javelins are extraordinary in that they are weighted down, not to hurt the opponents, but to stick into their shields and make them intolerably heavy: battles between equal forces are won or lost depending on how effective the shield wall proves. Finally, for every fifty men there are five or so archers who follow behind the other warriors and who are laughed at and despised.

In battle, the East Angles are said to be splendidly brave. But so much is courage with them that they exaggerate its importance. Even against impossible odds they refuse to retreat, thinking sensible withdrawal a horror. Then if the *eorl* their leader is killed, they stand around his body and fight to the last man. Indeed, one of their battle-cries is 'strength the greater even as our numbers lessen'; and, yelled out over the battlefield, we are assured that this has horrific majesty. Those that flee from a dead lord are forever bound with ignominy, much as we saw among the Gododdin. They are remembered in poems for their tails [i.e. their cowardice] and they are cursed by warrior and woman alike, and must wander from settlement to settlement, stopping there only until the scandal that is their past follows and undoes them.

If the East Anglians miraculously survive a battle – and remember, their wars are as much between villages and clans as against other kingdoms – they return home with their victims' weapons. These weapons are subsequently 'killed' – broken or desecrated – and then thrown into the marshy lands that fill the region. This strange act is not only a shocking waste of good steel, but also of time and sweat as enormous efforts are made and carts full of heavy metal pieces often dragged over tens of miles. (They say it is a sacrifice for their gods: why it should please these bog demons, though, is unknown.)

There is little that one of our soldiers would recognise here in the Saxons' wars and still less that he would admire. With the East Anglians' primitive weapons, their romantic embrace of death, and their pitiful formations, one of our small Thracian legions would reduce them to servitude or extinction in the space of a week.

(III) SUTTON HOO

We do not know where the king of the East Angles lives, nor whether he resides in only one palace, or, like the British-Celtic kings, who travel from estate to estate, has many halls. But he sometimes visits Hoo [Sutton Hoo, Suffolk] on the south-eastern coast and it was there that the embassy met him. He was certainly one of the most powerful kings of Britain, and many of his people called him 'Bretwalda', that is 'the Britain ruler', though this is a title that, as we will soon see, is more often reserved for the even more powerful king of Cant.

The legates of our Greek Emperor recognised this king's might when they gave the Wuffa lord rich gifts: a silver bowl made by Mediterranean smiths, silver spoons with the apostles' names written on them in

Greek and, of course, the obligatory golden coins that so fascinate the barbarians; and these gifts proved a success, some of their ugly twisting Scythian knives being given in return with much incomprehensible breast-beating. The visitor should not, however, depend on being able to point out these gifts when visiting the court, for the East Anglian has the sordid custom of burying his most valuable possessions in the ground on the death of a great man. Indeed, the houses of the East Angles are bereft of precious objects of any kind for just this reason. Our embassy were witness to an orgy of such burying at the death of the old East Anglian king; and as their description gives some excellent insights into the East Anglians and their evil ways, I will quote here directly from the log:

We heard on arriving that the old king had been killed in an ambush, the work of a rebellious *eorl*, and that the whole settlement was working through the night to prepare his funeral. When a king dies they take his wealth and divide it into three separate parts: one third goes to his heir; another third goes for making the clothes for his journey to the next world; and another third for the beer that they will drink on the day of his burial. When a great man is killed, his family say to the slave girls 'which of you will die with him?' When one has said that she will, she is forced to do it, and cannot back out. Two other slave girls are then given the job of looking after the victim whenever and wherever she is, even washing her feet. Then all prepare the king's things, cutting out his new clothes and getting ready everything that should be buried with him, while the sacrificial girl sings all the time and savours the happiness that they say awaits her.

When, finally, all is ready and the funeral comes, the king's body must be burnt. On this day, we went down to the royal cemetery at Hoo with curiosity and not a little foreboding. A boat had been dragged inland seven miles, and next to it had been laid a large pile of wood. All the nobles of the Angles walked around, talking in their language and drinking, and then they burnt the king, whose pyre blazed for many hours. Afterwards, when his body was reduced to its base elements, they took his ashes and put them in the ship with honour, leaving him with many valuable things – though not the silver we had brought, for that belonged to the new king. There was a *hearp*, fruit, furs, his weapons, shields and one of the Saxon helmets. They also took a horse and ran it around until it had sweated and then killed it too, throwing its body near the king's remains.

Then came an old and evil hag who they call the 'death angel', spreading out rugs and preparing the ship. While she was doing these last jobs, the slave girl walked around from tent to tent, and was joined in intercourse with members of the royal household, who asked her to tell the king in the next world that 'I do this for love of him'. Afterwards, they took the girl to a square frame of wood that they had set up. She was sat on several hands and was lifted to look over the highest beam. In all this time, she spoke without fear. She said: 'I see my father and mother', 'I see all my people' and then the last time – she was lifted thrice – 'I see our dead king. He calls me. Let me go to him now!'

The death angel next took off the girl's jewellery. Then she took the girl on board and prepared her knife. The royal household banged sticks on shields and gave the girl a cup, which the angel hurried her to drink. It perhaps made her drowsy, for she stumbled across the ship hitting her head on one of the oar staves. The men beat their sticks more rapidly, for they did not want other slave girls to hear the shrieking, then six men went and copulated with her on the ship. After this, they laid her down beside the casket of ashes with two holding her arms and two her legs. The death angel wound a tight cord around the girl's neck, making the remaining two men pull, and then she took her dagger and began to push it into the slave's ribs in a strange manner, while she was being throttled. And so she died. Finally with speed, the people buried the ship and the girl and their dead king. All, even the young and the servants, had to bring clods of earth to help finish it, the warriors drinking all the while.

That evening one of the drunk East Anglians came to us and told us through our interpreter that we were stupid. We asked, nervously, the reason and he said because we did not burn our own lords. Only by burning, they believe, will their god Woden come down to pluck the soul of the dead man from the earth and a strong wind had in truth blown all day confirming their delusions. Two days later they placed a wooden marker on the mound. The wood had writing in the strange crooked characters that they call 'runes', which spelt out the name of the dead king and his father.

We need have no doubt that the precious gifts of the Emperor, with who knows how many victims, have since been buried below another ship at this haven of demons on the plains of the East Anglians.[1] However, we must also tell of the customs of the common people in their burials which, though less terrible, are just as bizarre and are more likely to be seen by the traveller. The normal East Anglians burn the bodies of their loved ones locally, and then the family walk long distances to deposit the ash-carrying urns in the great communal graveyards. (If the traveller meets one of these families with an urn obviously displayed, it is best to stop out of respect and let them pass.) One of the mass graveyards is found near Gronte, another at the Hill of the Dead [Spong Hill] and other smaller ones are spread out around the countryside. Each urn is specially made, and has strange but suitable designs scratched on to it; for example, women have a spiral like a seashell on theirs. We must also report that some of these barbarians mix the bones of their own dead with the bones of animals: pigs, sheep, even deer, though no one can explain why this should be.

(IV) COLCHESTER

On the road from Hoo to Londinium [London], the traveller will come to the abandoned wreck of one of the proudest of all western Roman cities, Camulodunum [Colchester], originally built by the Emperor Claudius to celebrate his conquest of Britain. It was Camulodunum that resisted furiously the attack of the dirty lioness [Boudicca] in the year of the great rebellion.[2] And it was afterwards here that the mission to make Britain truly Roman was planned by Agricola and other great names from Imperial history. Today, however, the tourist will find Camulodunum a sad sight. There are still traces of the last combat, when the British-Celtic inhabitants were dragged from its walls and killed by the Saxons. Especially unnerving is the breach at the southern gates, the city's mortal wound, where the besiegers used fire to bring

1. *Translator's note:* Our anonymous author was correct. Byzantine silver plate and spoons with Paul's name in Greek were found in a boat burial at Sutton Hoo in 1939.
2. *Translator's note:* The reference is to Boudicca's revolt in AD 61, when British Celts almost drove the Romans from the island.

down a portion of the defences; its ashes still stain the ground seventy years on, and unburied and disintegrating skeletons lie in the vicinity and under the debris. Meanwhile, in the countryside thereabouts are the smaller, decaying British-Celtic settlements and farms that proved impossible to hold and that are now deserted, as well as the puny dykes that the last British Celts built to try and contain the East Anglians pushing south. The locals shun these dykes, which they say are the work of devils, the last grudging memories perhaps of great-grandparents who died fighting across them.

When asked about the British Celts, the East Anglians laugh. They have fled, they say, across the seas or run inside Londinium's walls; there are also some slaves that the Saxons enjoy maltreating. Asked, however, about the remains of once mighty Camulodunum, they become more serious, frightened even. They say that the empty city brings bad luck – they, like all barbarians, fear cities – and stay away from it with the exception of some brave stonemasons who only quarry off the outer walls. The Saxons, indeed, call the place the 'city of the giants' and sing wailing poems about it; strangely, they have already forgotten that it was the British Celts who lived there and ascribe its building, instead, to monstrous superhumans. Guides refuse to take parties any further than the gates, and one party ran away yelling when the embassy decided to investigate further. Meanwhile, the king of the Saxons, when asked why he did not use Camulodunum as his court, became angry: 'cities' he said 'are traps'.

Abandoned and unloved, Camulodunum does prove dangerous to any who walk through it, but not because of demons or giants. The danger comes rather from falling roof tiles and tottering colonnades; and in the streets of what was once the showpiece of Roman Britain, the Roman Britain of only a hundred years ago, run fawns and foxes, and grass grows in the old forum. The British Celts who had lived here at the end were hardly Romans, though. The traveller can still see their shoddy and makeshift repairs. Stone was replaced by wood and skilled calculations by artisans' guesses. When Britain is finally re-conquered for the Empire, it will take many generations to reverse this kind of damage and decline.

From here, the road to the Celtic enclave of Londinium stretches on with its sentries, custom points and potholes. But before we leave behind the territory of the East Angles we will note one more peculiarity of this people. As we have already seen in other chapters, the Saxons despise the Romans, and the traveller is well advised to keep his Imperial allegiances to himself. However, it is typical of the contradictions that characterise the barbarian mind that the Roman-hating East Anglian Saxons claim descent not only from their god, Woden, but also from Julius Caesar! The East Angles have heard that some have the temerity to call Caesar a Roman, but it is, of course, a possibility they themselves will not contemplate, and that they find grossly insulting. The traveller is advised, then, not to argue the point, but to talk in vague and admiring terms about the great man's campaigns and not to show any mirth when a rabidly anti-Roman local calls his son, Julius, to him.

13

THE THAMES VALLEY:
'THE ENCLAVES'

(I) LONDON

AD 410 is a date that, even now, marks Britain and causes the few British
Celts who survive in the enclaves to tremble with rage and fear. 'But
stop', says the traveller 'What have I to do with history? Why baste me
with dates and facts that cannot possibly serve? I want practicalities
and I want to survive. I am in the middle of a dark wood in the middle
of the Dark Isles and I want merely to get from the Humber to the
southern coast, not to learn a schoolboy's crib of historical nothings!'
And normally we would grant him his point. Too many travel guides,
itineraries and verbal atlases graze on the past, hoping in this way to
show erudition and learning, while they abandon the reader to his
difficulties with a shrug of the scholarly pen, the traveller's life dripping
like ink off the quill. We, however, have always eschewed such pre-
tentiousness and the careful reader will bear witness that in this work
learned pieties have come second to difficulties in the field: 'I've accidentally got married to a Cambrian girl, what next?'; 'I'm in an Irish
valley and werewolves are all around. Is there a way out?' etc. However,
in this case we cannot sidestep the details of time, for that one year
explains much of the world that the traveller is about to pass through.

Imagine yourself a century ago in the most distant of the western
provinces of the Empire. A barbaric island, certainly, where many locals
cannot even stutter Latin. But one that is made bearable by imports
from the south and the steady, guiding hand of Roman officials.
Imagine occasional rumours of barbarian activity far away, not so
much clouds but wisping smoke on the horizon blown away every
night as the conceited British citizen lies down to sleep. Imagine now

a crisis in Gaul and rebellions, a crisis worse than any the Empire has ever faced. Imagine an order arriving in the celestial script of the old Roman court. Imagine an overfed, unconcerned British-Celtic official snapping the seal with his thumbnail and his face turning ice-white as he reads the words. Imagine the rumour spreading: the Empire has decided to abandon Britain, the least important of all its provinces – legions and ships were to be removed forthwith. Imagine the archives being burnt; the riots; the legionaries marching to Cant [Kent], trying desperately to get passage for bastard children and mistresses; and a people who had not lifted arms for centuries, indeed, who had no arms, suddenly being left on their own, defenceless. Imagine scuffles as the first Saxon pirates understand that Britain is naked, and the hell as piracy turns to prods, then raids, incursions and then, finally, invasion. A British-Celtic historian describes best the terrible finale of this tragedy:

> 'The arson fed by the hands of the dreadful Saxon grew and ran across the island until the blaze reached from sea to sea. This fire spared nothing, neither town nor farm, and once burning would not die until its orange tongue licked with fiery spittle the western oceans. All the ancient cities were undone and entered by smashing rams, the inhabitants then cut down by blades – burghers, councillors and priests alike – while by the light of the fires weapons glinted. In the old, venerable squares towers and walls gave up their stones, while the corpses that lay there were covered with dried and purpling blood as if crushed in an enormous winepress of destruction. None were buried except in the mouths and bellies of beasts and birds. And only a number of the survivors escaped to the high places – the mountains and hills – where many were also put to the Saxon sword. Those who surrendered were killed immediately – the best they could hope for – or, far worse, became slaves to the enemy.'

This was the result of the invasion of a hundred years ago. The buds and fruit of civilisation that the Romans had cultivated on this strand in the west were scorched away, and even today the evidence of terror is everywhere. Most of lowland Britain was depopulated, the newcomers displacing or enslaving the natives, emptying cities and churches. And in much of the island the inhabitants were not capable of serious resistance, for they – lowly civilians without the necessary training in arms – found themselves helpless when faced with some of the most practised and ruthless warriors in Europe. Shamefully, they made partitions or gave themselves up into serfdom.

However, in a few of the ancient British-Celtic *civitates* [counties], another spirit reigned as the Saxon war bands rode around them – one of defiance. Making alliances among themselves, rapidly erecting defences to supplement those built before by Roman engineers, and raising militias in every corner of their territory, they began the long battle to construct havens that the enemy would not be able to penetrate. Even a hundred years after the time of crises, some of these enclaves still survive in the southern regions of the island. We need only mention Londinium, Calleva Atrebatum [Silchester], holy Verulamium [St Albans], and the Fortress of War [South Cadbury] near the head of the Dumnonian peninsula. It is a strange trick of the geography of the Dark Isles that here, in these British-Celtic enclaves, the visitor will find the most civilised life in the island, while surrounding them in the tracts of conquered British countryside he will find the most barbaric of its inhabitants, the southern Saxons. The tension can hardly hold, can only snap. And by the time the reader decides to pull on his boots and visit these last hubs of Romano-Celtic civilisation, they may already have been overrun.

The most important of the enclaves is, of course, Londinium, the ancient capital of Britannia, where, at one time, the imperial edicts arrived and with them the coin to pay the legions on the Walls. The city is naturally far reduced from its former might. The southern bank, where the wilder nightlife was found in Imperial times – who can forget Bonus's description of the orgies in the tavern next to the temple of Isis – has been all but abandoned.[1] And London Bridge is rickety and near collapse. Most of the great buildings of the past have been pulled down and piled onto the defences so the city walls now have memorial arches and paving from the forum incorporated into their brickwork: the marble that was once, long ago, in a golden age, brought from Syrian and Egyptian quarries and from the islands of the Cyclades, no longer adorns temples, but is jammed into gatehouses and buttresses

1. *Translator's note:* Silvius Bonus, the only named Romano-British poet, who lived in the fourth century. Unfortunately none of his poems survive.

gates. In fact, modern Londinium is like a sandcastle barracked by the sea, where a child has begun to dig out its finely sculpted innards to add a few more desperate inches to its walls.

The city itself resembles a wasteland. Its few remaining inhabitants have had to rope off huge areas of the centre, where the houses are unstable and falling masonry or tiles can easily brain a passer-by. There are other areas where, as at Lindum, they have torn down walls and created vegetable plots among the wreckage to feed the population. Some food, too, gets through from the sea, despite the river having silted up near the old docks. For the sightseer though there are only a few recent constructions worth seeing, most notably the cathedral, a slavish but unusual imitation of the holy church of St Tecla of Milan, while close by is an inscription in Latin hexameter – a reminder of the city's perilous state. It reads: 'the barbarians push us to the sea, the sea to the barbarians. Between these two foes we are either drowned or hacked to pieces.'

There are hundreds who live within Londinium's walls, even if not nearly as many as formerly. And, like the populations of all the enclaves, they are not ruled by kings, but by the council of the *civitas*, much as the city was governed two hundred or four hundred years before. It is true that occasionally tyrants rise, but the council, like the senate of Rome, remains the legislating body of the city and the inspiration and aspiration of the public. The embassy were received with courtesy before it. However, it is fair to say that while these old patricians treated our men well enough, they were sceptical of the Emperor's offer of help in their wars, having had their share of unfulfilled promises before. They were, nevertheless, grateful for a golden gift from the Emperor's treasury. And they gave the high lord of Byzantium two remarkable presents in return. The first was a book from the council's library – a beautifully made manuscript of Virgil with an especially striking illustration of Aeneas and Dido inked on to the parchment in a strange Romano-Celtic style; the script, so the log assures us, was nevertheless one of the worst-copied versions of the *Aeneid* that they had ever seen.[1]

---

1. *Translator's note:* This description closely resembles a manuscript found today in the library of the monastery of St Denis (France), a manuscript that is sometimes said to be British-Celtic in origin.

The second – a real antique, this – was the original copy of the decree ordering the Roman army to abandon Britain: no words were said, but the recrimination was painfully obvious. Then, all bitterness put aside, the embassy were invited to sit on an ornamental balcony over the river. And so it was that, in early summer, the Greeks gazed across the Thames, feasting on Spanish olives and Syrian wine brought up the river by Frankish ships, while the council spoke in their mannered, careful Latin about Petronius and Dio Cassius.

The danger here, for the explorer, is not the Roman citizens of the town. Rather it is to be found in the defensive lines that they have constructed around the city. There are the walls, of course, guarded by men from the militias. There are occasional treaties with neighbouring Saxon warlords that buy peace sometimes for a year, sometimes for a month. But the only defence that really guarantees Londinium's safety are the mercenaries. Long ago the council, in its desperate attempts to protect its boundaries, hired several score Saxon warriors, brought them into the city, trained them, dressed them in a uniform with a characteristic mercenary belt, and then placed them in strong points near the city's perimeter to secure the roads leading to or close to the walls. There are six or seven of these allied camps and till now they have given Londinium breathing space, fighting off attacks from the kings of East Anglia and the Saxons of Cant and the southern coasts.[1] The embassy warned the council of the danger of employing such thugs, for treachery was always possible. But the leader of the council replied dryly that, until the Emperor could provide his own men to guard the town, they would have to rely on what force there was at hand.

(II) THAMES VALLEY

To the north-west of Londinium is another of these enclaves, the ancient city of Verulamium. This centre is sometimes described as the Rome of Britain, for the greatest of all the British martyrs is buried

---

1. *Translator's note:* Several Anglo-Saxon cemeteries have been found on the roads leading to Roman London, at strategic points that seem to confirm the embassy's statement. These include: Orpington, West Tilbury, Prittelwell and Croydon.

here: Alban, who took his place in the legions of Christ and was put to the sword two hundred years ago in the theatre of the city, while arrogant judges and howling crowds salivated and bit at themselves in their bloodlust. And so it happened that even among the barbaric British Celts the Lord our God lit the candles of holy martyrdom to lift the heads of this people to His high throne. The city council – all Christian now – has put Alban's grave in easy reach of visitors to the town and it is possible to pass close to the walls where he was killed, kneel before his covered grave and insert the hand deep into that very box where his mortal remains are kept through a convenient hole. Numberless cures are said to be worked in this way. And even more incredible is the fact that the soil where he is buried and where his blood was spilt is stained red.[1] The shrine has had many celebrated visitors over the years including Germanus of Auxerre, the light of Gaul, famous bishop and fighter of heretics, who a generation ago came to Britain and inspired miracles here. And Gildas the Wise of Strathclyde, whom we met at Dumbarton, also made the journey after his conversion from carnal love and the world. But the Saxons have now taken so much of the surrounding land that Alban's town is almost unreachable without an escort.

The traveller will find in journeying to this city the risks of the road without any rewards. And while not wishing to speak ill of Alban, his grave is such that can be found in any Gaulish town, towns that incidentally boast a far better miracle-to-prayer rate. The city itself lacks the peculiar flair of despoiled Londinium with its marble battlements. The embassy found that all the prefects there could talk about – tediously – was a new water system which they had built and which was for them a matter of enormous pride. Nor are the amenities up to Londinium's standards, for there are none of the luxuries that the Thames brings. Indeed, the embassy described St Albans as, in many ways, a failed city for it is utterly and fatally locked into its Roman past. The locals – though this is also true of the old capital – mint no coins but use old Roman issues from centuries ago; the coins are worn almost

---

1. *Translator's note:* The ground near the shrine is a reddish colour, though this can be more easily explained with reference to the type of clay in the area than the permanence of the martyr's blood. However, the early medieval *Life of St Alban* confirms that the locals preferred the miraculous explanation.

to the point of being illegible. They have also lost the talent of making pottery. At best they spin out some dishes on crude home-made wheels or, more commonly, they use and reuse the pottery that the Roman factories produced over a hundred years ago – for Britain made at this time thousands of plates and bowls a day in its midland furnaces. The result is that the traveller will find himself invited to tea with a local dignitary who is still using the pottery that his great-grandfather gave to his great-grandmother on her wedding day. All of these pieces have, naturally, been broken many times and are bolted together with glue and clips. In fact, an excellent present for a visit to the enclaves would be a new set of crockery.

It was with regret that the embassy advised in their log against any Imperial military aid to this particular British-Celtic stronghold, but it was felt that the population could not hope to resist the Saxon onslaught for long. The Greeks did, however, counsel help for another British-Celtic city in the regions, Calleva Atrebatum [Silchester], the third corner of a triangle of enclaves consisting of Londinium and Veru-lamium. We have very limited records about this particular city, for so carefully guarded is it that, even with recommendations from the council at Londinium, the embassy were not allowed to enter. Instead, they were greeted by burly Irish mercenaries who manned various ditches and mud ramparts in the area, snarling menacingly at all new-comers. The walls of the city looked in good shape, and the embassy suggested that this enclave would be one of the longest-lasting in the south of Britain.

A generation and more ago, after a stunning British-Celtic victory at the siege of Mons Badonicus,[1] it was to the west of Calleva that the treaty line between the Saxons and the militarily more able western British-Celts was drawn. For a whole generation the Saxons, who had taken hundreds of square miles of territory, were happy to remain on their side of the border. However, in the time of the embassy, the treaty

---

1. *Translator's note:* The Battle of Mons Badonicus was a British-Celtic victory described as 'the last victory of the fatherland', dated commonly, but very insecurely, to 516. Later legend attaches the battle to Arthur of Round Table fame. However, the description here seconds that found in our earliest record which connects the victory, instead, to Ambrosius, whom we previously met – such is the sausage machine of Celtic myth! – as a boy prophet in the mountains of Snowdonia.

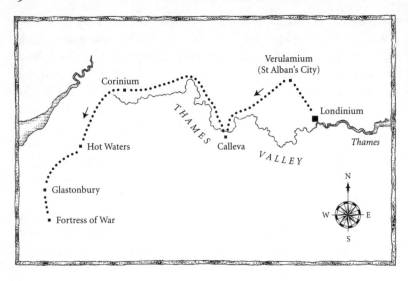

had already broken down. At first, local warriors had ignored it, then individual warlords commanding small armies had ventured across it, then the whole line became a bleeding weal that opened into permanent war between the two peoples. The enclave nearest the old truce line is at Corinium [Circencester], where a British-Celtic tyrant, loath to leave the town of his birth, barricaded the coliseum and made it into his personal stronghold. And today the whole city, incredible to say, lives within its bounds. Plague had recently rolled through Corinium when the embassy arrived, and took the lives of one of the embassy, Andreas, the log-carrier. This Greek was left with the other unclaimed bodies in piles that lined the wall outside the city, some of these unfortunates still vaguely moaning as they were put into the ditches and buried by helmeted men.

If there is no plague and if the road is free of the Saxons, a more interesting site to visit is that natural wonder, Hot Waters [Bath]. There the visitor will find, and the embassy enjoyed, the finest natural baths not only in Britain, but in northern Europe; a small fee being asked for a soak. The locals also follow another worthwhile custom that they taught our embassy with enthusiasm: the curse stones. The visitor who, after his long journey, wishes to revenge himself on those who refused him shelter or those who gave him shelter and then robbed him, should purchase a small flat tablet there. They should then write – better in Latin – the curse they want to come out and then hurl this tablet into the wells or springs with a small gold consideration. For example, if someone has stolen your ring in Verulamium it is enough to write 'may he or she who has stolen my ring lose all sense of movement in their left hand'. The efficacy of these curses has not yet been tested: another Imperial commission is needed. But until we have found out what exactly the malefic psalms are, they represent one of the most potent weapons available to the Empire in Britain. The embassy certainly spent a long day hurling stones into the pools there to avenge their nine lost comrades and to unburden themselves of the many unpleasant memories of their year in the Dark Isles.

Close by Hot Waters – a day's easy ride out of the raiding season – is one of the premier British-Celtic monasteries, that of Glastonbury. The monks here are far more tolerant than those we have previously described – the reader will doubtless remember Watery David and Pyro the Drunken in southern Cambria. In fact, they are in many ways a little lax: the embassy on several occasions saw them eating meat, for example, straying from their normal vegetarian diet. And they also looked rather too avariciously on a copper censer that was presented to them as a gift of friendship from His Highness the Emperor.[1] Yet they were welcoming, not least because as a pilgrimage centre, they are used to foreign guests.

Those who make the journey to Glastonbury are expected to climb the Tor there in dizzying, ever-decreasing circles. And when the traveller has finally reached the top, he is afterwards allowed to light a torch before taking the straight path to the bottom. Many strange stories are told about this Tor, some of which are frankly blasphemous and which we will not trouble to repeat.[2] However, the reader should know that it was here that one British-Celtic troublemaker, Mordred, was said to have escaped with the wife of the legendary Arthur, a certain Guinevere;

---

1. *Translator's note:* Interestingly, a rare Byzantine incense dispenser was found in digs at Glastonbury. However, some experts would date this to the early seventh century, long after the journey of the embassy.
2. *Translator's note:* the legend of Christ coming to Britain might certainly be interpreted as 'blasphemous'; could it be to this that the author refers? It, in fact, seems unlikely, as this legend is first recorded only some eight hundred years later.

and it is told that they lived for a year and a day under the splendid apple trees that grow nearby. We have heard rumours too of serpents in the surrounding countryside, serpents that, though not *draca*, stretch to many feet in length. The embassy saw none of these beasts, so we will neither confirm nor deny their existence. But one rumour we can quash out of hand. Glastonbury is *not* the centre of Britain as some gullible Britain experts have been told and then gullibly repeat. That title is given, instead, to a small settlement to the north-east named the Ford of the Oxen [Oxford], where in ancient times, before even the Romans came to Britain, the holy and royal of the island used to gather together for their councils.

(III) SOUTH CADBURY

Hot Waters, Corinium, Glastonbury... All may have their charms, but by far the most important visit any traveller can make in this part of Britain is to the Fortress of War in the west, a stronghold not overly distant from the borders of Dumnonia where the embassy began their trek. This is the largest of all British fortresses and no other people – Pict, Irish or Saxon, nor the inhabitants of the enclaves – can boast of having such a powerful base. The embassy were enormously impressed by its scale and we quote here directly from the log entries relating to their arrival:

> The mounted escort came out to greet us as we were leaving the bounds of Glastonbury, typical British-Celtic warriors with their shaven heads and beardless faces. Fine horsemen all. We described the slaughter we had seen only four days ago now.[1] And they, after some polite questions

1. *Translator's note:* Our author unfortunately makes no further reference to this 'slaughter'. But modern archaeological digs in the south of Britain have produced evidence, suggesting that such unpleasantries did sometimes happen. For example, in Meaney, *A Gazetteer of Early Anglo-Saxon Burial Sites* (George Allen and Unwin, 1969), pp. 35–6, a 1920s dig at Dunstable found, '*c.* 100 inhumations of young men and women in 10 groups disposed about the barrow and its surround. About 1/3 of the people buried had had their hands tied behind their backs. In some groups, several burials appeared to have taken place at the same time as each other, but since they either overlay or had been disturbed by others, it is clear that the burials took place over a period of time.'

about the shrine, talked of the growing menace of Saxons in their own land, for, with the spring, Saxon war parties had pushed through to them for the first time. Much anxiety and, wherever we rode, they were always looking about them carefully, fearing that the enemy might be on even as well-armed a party as theirs at any moment.

There was a day-long ride to reach their Fortress of War, with frequent diversions for safety and hurried snatches of rest on high, safe places. While riding, they pointed out the lines of ditches that had been built to the west and that had initially held the Saxons. But it seems that these lines of defence have now crumbled, the enemy marching around. Instead, the British Celts of the region have fallen back on the Fortress of War, and rely on beacons and sentinels to warn of approaching robber bands or even invasions. In smaller cases they hope to exterminate. In the case of larger groups they harry the Saxons out of their territory.

The fort was superb. We confess that we had had few expectations, so all were taken aback by its scale and the extent of its defences. There is a massive hill crested with a flat plateau where the British Celts of the region have built a city. And from these heights they can see an area of fifty miles around. In fact, they have taken over a series of large ditches that were dug during the wars of an earlier age; it is even said that in the first century of our era, the Emperor Vespasian personally led an attack on the British-Celtic warriors who held it against him.[1] And over these ditches they have built new walls and fighting platforms, so the new defenders can meet intruders in their accustomed fashion, defending high ramparts and throwing boasts and rocks on the heads of the enemy below.

When we first saw it, night, an early spring night, had come upon us and the top of the hill glimmered with torches, and voices reached us when the wind blew in the right direction. Even in the dark, it was mesmerising. Our escorts, who on seeing their home had become more

---

1. *Translator's note:* Vespasian was Roman Emperor from AD 70–79. His campaigning in Britain – though our author suggests otherwise – relates to an earlier period of his career, before he had taken the Imperial purple. At the time of the conquest in Britain, he was legate to the Legio II and was responsible for thirty battles, the subjection of two powerful tribes, the taking of the Isle of Wight and attacks on twenty British-Celtic hill forts. Cadbury may well have been among these last. Certainly Vespasian was operating in the right part of the country.

animated, boasted that over eighteen acres are defended in times of conflict and that as many as a thousand warriors would be called up to guard the heights in the event of a full-out Saxon attack. For our armies, of course, such numbers are relatively small. But we remembered the three hundred of the Gododdin or the small tribal armies of Dal Riada, and gasped. They also boasted that these platforms had been built and reinforced by masonry taken from wrecked villas nearby. Then, as we came to the base of the hill, they told us fantastic stories about Arthur and about spectral cavalry that battled in the sky above the fort on the darkest nights of the year.[1]

By the time we had reached the first gate on the lower reaches of the fort, our names and our mission had been checked several times by guards riding out to meet us. Under escort, we made our way up a broad track towards the principal gate and were surrounded stealthily by archers and warriors of other types, who could have annihilated us in moments if they had been so ordered. At the top of the hill road was a well-built wooden portal with towers – double doors and strong foundations hammered into stone – which could only be reached across a bridge and we milled there for some minutes before the order came to open, our breaths and that of the horses steaming around us. When the doormen finally let us in, we passed through into an impressive fort. All was built, as is typical of the British Celts, in wood. But, here within, we saw the same peculiar sight as had greeted us at Viriconium. These primitive buildings were clearly modelled on Roman archi-tecture, so much more striking than the plain, functional designs of the Saxons, while the central feasting hall resembled not so much the barns of the invaders as a slightly elongated villa from the south of Gaul.

After the stress of the journey, we confess that we fell asleep before we could even be brought to the lord of the place. But, as we were drifting off, a poet who was walking around the perimeter of our

---

1. *Translator's note:* Cadbury is one of several sites in the region connected by legend with Arthur. However, the earliest mention of this link, excepting the rather vague comment here, dates to the sixteenth century when the antiquarian Leland (*c.* 1540) claimed that the hill fort was no other than Camelot! As a 'fact' this was made much of in the excavations that took place there in the late 1960s, under the direction of Leslie Alcock, which uncovered the physical remains of some of the Dark Age structures described above.

lodgings was singing a song – a long, interminable, beautiful song – about a king called Geraint who died in battle against the Saxons. We were woken by geese in the morning, an hour ago. Couldn't write last night. Too saddle-sore and tired.

THE SOUTH COAST:
'THE ROAD HOME'

(I) WINCHESTER

Moving from out of the enclaves and into the southern Saxons' territory is never an easy business; and the traveller is well advised to hand over the task of negotiating passage to his hosts, who will have a long experience of bribing the enemies that plague their borders. Certainly, the embassy had a lengthy and tedious wait – and this, even though the Greeks had behind them the resources of the Fortress of War, the council of which rather naively believed that our party wanted to undertake a peace mission on their behalf. It is interesting and, we believe, instructive to report just how the preliminaries for negotiations were handled. As soon as the embassy had suggested that they speak on the natives' behalf, a treaty maker was sent out across the line of control. Nor was this, merely, a meeting with a nearby Saxon rogue and his drunken, laughing cohort. This British-Celtic representative was bundled off with specific instructions to speak only to 'the Chief Satan' himself, the king of Cant. The lord of this most south-easterly British kingdom was chosen, for just as Gwynedd is the mightiest of the British-Celtic kingdoms, and the Dal Riadans have a reputation among the Irish for military excellence, so among the Saxons it is the Cantian warriors who are the most feared. And, at least in the embassy's time, other Saxon kings called this ruler the Bretwalda or Britain-ruler, sometimes even giving him a half-hearted tribute in cows or begrudgingly sending warriors into battle with his forces.

The negotiator was handed from warlord to warlord, going eastwards. And after a month of this strange game of pass-the-messenger a reply snuck back: 'the Chief Satan' would indeed grant the Greeks an audience and looked forward to seeing the rich gifts that had been promised him. A bodyguard was also sent west to escort them and it was on a day in early October that the three remaining members of the embassy finally crossed one of those interminable fords where British-Celtic and Saxon warriors snarl at each other across the water. One can gauge their desperation, for Sophron, the log-writer, wondered in an adjunct to his work whether they might not perhaps be free of the Dark Isles before the first snows came.

The traveller is unlikely to have the luck to be accompanied by royal officers of the Bretwalda across the southern reaches of Britain. But he could do worse than follow the route that the embassy took towards Vintancaestir [Winchester] using what remains of the Roman road there. An old Celtic settlement this, it has, in the last years, been taken over by a Saxon warlord. And here we see once more that one might as well dress a goose in armour, as place one of these people in a town. We say this, for rather than clearing away the remains of ruined buildings and strengthening the collapsing defences, they have built their shacks in, of all places, the roads, doing this because the well-paved surfaces offer good drainage! Naturally, getting about has become all but impossible and passers-by must walk in the rubble, tripping through the dandelions and downed gutters.

To reach Vintancaestir, the traveller will be passing through a thoroughly unpleasant territory. In Roman times this region of British countryside was heavily populated and had, too, a good stock of farmers – even some Imperial estates were to be found there. But now the old villas have been left to slide into ruins and the melancholy explorer can walk through their doorless portals and examine halls with mosaics that the Saxon newcomers have made into hearths or improvised toilets. (Can there, we ask, be anything so heart-rending as to see a mosaic of the four seasons, done in the beautiful Romano-British style, covered in stools or fused black from the heat of bonfires?) In their shadow, meanwhile, local Saxons have set up their mud settlements, with poor imitations of Roman buildings and made the land their own in a wasteful and intemperate way: many of the original British-Celtic farmers have been driven out and much of the territory has been left to go fallow. In some areas, the ancient forests have even begun to encroach into what were, in the good old days, fine, ploughed fields kept black and level by sweating slaves.

The lack of Saxon organisation might go some way to explaining why the population here suffer so badly from famines. There was evidence everywhere, in the embassy's time, of lack of food and the three Greeks that remained were especially shocked at the distended stomachs of the Saxons' pale children. But this was not all. Women crouched in forests waiting for wild hens, rooks or even badgers for their pots,[1] while the escort recounted that many Saxons near the ocean, to preserve the rest of their community, had lined up on cliffs then, holding hands, jumped hundreds of feet to their deaths in the water below. Any traveller who gets this far, let us assure you, will have no fat left on his body. But whenever entering a famine area – and remember that all parts of Britain sooner or later become vulnerable to this scourge – never eat your food in public view. Instead, quote in a world-weary fashion one of the Saxons' favourite adages: 'What makes bitter food sweet? Hunger.'

Outsiders are rare and locals suspicious, be it in hungry season or full harvest. And if you travel off the main highway that leads towards Londinium, you must blow constantly on a horn to show your good intentions. We say this for the law of the region allows any south Saxon to slay or punish and ransom the traveller who does not make himself known in this way. If captured, then your exact fate will depend on how big your group is. If there are fewer than seven, then you will be classed as 'thieves'; if there are more than seven, but fewer than thirty-five, your group will be 'marauders'; if, though, you belong to a still larger group, then you will be 'raiders'. Thieves get off lightly here and have nothing more than their right foot or right arm amputated; but marauders and raiders are treated in a truly inhumane manner.

From these intimations the reader will already have understood that the southern Saxons are a savage people; and the descent into barbarism once you leave the enclaves is steep and unstoppable. Indeed, the log is peppered with accounts of their bestiality. We read, for example, of a

---

1. *Translator's note:* 'wild hens' are often mentioned in Anglo-Saxon sources and probably refer to pheasants or partidges. The reference to badgers, meanwhile, is in line with evidence from several early medieval sites in England, where archaeologists have found badger bones among the cooking refuse.

small community just outside Vintancaestir where the embassy were shocked to find the whole village had turned out to punish a girl whose 'crime' was to have been raped. The man had already been dealt with and the victim – the father, who had been dishonoured according to the Saxon laws – compensated. But now the waif of a girl, with her hands tied behind her back, was pushed and jeered by a mob into a ditch that was filled in with earth as her screams were smothered below. Her crime? The fact that she had become pregnant – the unborn child was interred with her – indicated that the rape had in some ways been desired.[1] This was the worst sight to greet the Greeks, but the Saxons of this region gave frequent proofs of their cruelty. For example, their king, in the little complex of huts he called his palace in Vintancaestir, outlined his latest genocidal plans for taking control of the nearby isle called Vectis [Isle of Wight]. He had, he explained, decided to invade and then put all the population, who had come from Cant, to the sword, bringing his own people to settle the territory instead.[2]

By now the reader will have understood that there are many dangers attached to moving through this region. But, be warned, these are not restricted to our fellow humans, as the last members of the embassy found to their cost. The Greeks were camping at a small Saxon settlement named the Valley of Broom [Bramdean, Hampshire], when Philippos, the party's chief negotiator, was bitten by one of the vipers that infest those places. Treated by one of the local wise women – she used soap, a mouldy apple and a sung spell to bring down the swelling[3] – he, of course, died that very day.

1. *Translator's note:* Pregnancy following on from rape was sometimes in the Middle Ages taken as proof of complicity. Note too that in the laws of Wessex the father or husband, not the raped woman, was the legal victim of the crime.
2. *Translator's note:* It seems unlikely that this infamous plan was carried out in the sixth century; certainly we have no evidence for it. But one of this warlord's descendants conquered Wight in just this way in the late seventh century, slaughtering the population, while sparing two young princes of Vectis just long enough to be baptized. For the full story see Bede's *Ecclesiastical History,* 4, 16.
3. *Translator's note:* Interestingly, one early Saxon charm against snake bit survives. We quote it here as it is very probably similar to that sung over Philippos: 'A worm came crawling, it bit a man/ Then Woden took nine glory-twigs/ And destroyed the adder so that it divided into nine/ Then poison was finished/ And came no more to the house.'

(II) PORTCHESTER

The escort had heard of recent skirmishing between the British-Celtic enclave of Londinium and the warriors of Cant, and, anxious to avoid enmeshing the two remaining Greeks in any fights along the south banks of the Thames, they instead headed to the coast to the Strong Port [Portchester]: a long route, but a sure one for their kingdom. After two days' riding, camping carefully on high unwooded ground, the party came to this place. What, the remaining Greeks asked themselves, would the Saxon version of a stronghold be; until now they had seen little evidence of defences among this people? But they were to be disappointed because, in fact, the defences that were, indeed, strong had nothing Saxon about them at all. The Strong Port was actually nothing more than a Roman shore fort that had been taken over by one of the Saxons' many robber barons. The impressive walls still stood as they had in Roman times.[1] But now, instead of ordered bunks and legionaries marching in time, there was the mess of a war party and their families spread out over the fortifications, some dwellings even being built outside the old bounds of the fort altogether.

The Strong Port is one of the main trading points on the south coast and the embassy described an almost constant stream of activity there. Royal boats put in from the Cantian ports on their way to Vectis, where a small Cantian colony has been set up. Frisians, the most famous trading race in the north, had stalls and spoke easily with the locals in a language very similar to their own. Frankish boats, too, docked with news from the Loire – indeed, the embassy had to resist the temptation to take up an offer of a trip back to civilisation. Then there were the Saxon boats that were setting out to raid and that would return, their hulls dripping with blood, crowded with bounties ripped out of Gaulish villas or stolen from Continental churches, not to mention a score of whimpering slaves.

But what the embassy most enjoyed about the fort was not its trading posts, but its impressive array of alcohol. The Saxons are enthusiastic

---

1. *Translator's note:* And much of the defences stand to this day... Indeed, Portchester was still being used until relatively recent times: in the early nineteenth century it served as a prisoner of war camp for French soldiers; and then, subsequently, its walls were incorporated into Britian's south-coast defences in the Second World War.

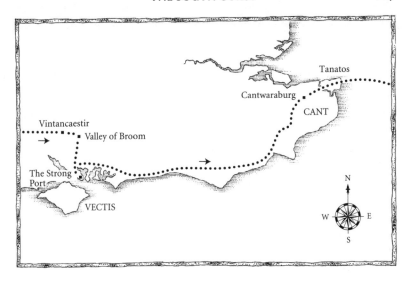

drinkers; indeed, they have the fame of being the most drunken of all the barbarians, which, considering the excesses of the Goths, is a truly extraordinary achievement. And at the Strong Port the embassy had the opportunity to see just how the locals produce the vast quantities that they imbue. The three main drinks of the Saxons are *beor* [beer], *ealu* [ale] and, rarest and most challenging of all, *win* [wine]. There are other drinks too: the cider that they lace with cherries, for example, or *med* imported from the British Celts – alcohol knows no border even in war. But it is these three that are responsible for most of the unconscious Saxons that you will find rolling about on the floor of halls long after decent folk have gone to bed.

By far the strongest of these beverages is *beor* which, the embassy estimated, was almost one-fifth alcohol. Pregnant women are advised never to drink this substance and those who cannot hold their drink should pass over it and stick either to *ealu* or *leoht beor* [light beer] as an alternative. We should warn the explorer that its potency is especially great in winter, for the hard British climate penetrates the casks where this liquid is kept and, freezing some of the water, leaves only alcohol behind so that sometimes cups are even flammable. Saxons enjoy this drink but also know its dangers. Before setting out on an evening of hard drinking, *overdrenc* they call it, you are advised to eat fried calf innards or drink water with green leaves mixed into it. The embassy followed these instructions with care, but still woke up with what the Saxons call 'hammers' in their heads.

Beor is usually sweet, hop-flavoured and mixed with herbs. *Ealu*, on the other hand, uses only malt and is far less strong. It is the most common drink and can be found in every settlement, where it is brewed in large containers. When a thirsty traveller arrives in a Saxon village, he should look out for a branch that is hung outside the alehouse. This branch, often taken from a birch, doubles both as a sign and as an instrument to stir the ale in the casks. We can safely recommend this excellent thirst-quencher and quote with approval a Saxon saying: 'When there is *ealu* I drink *ealu*, when there is no *ealu*, water.'

Unfortunately we cannot say the same for British wine. The reader will doubtless already have understood why. A weak sun and dull soils mean that there are not the conditions for grapes to grow there. And, though some Saxons continue to fight against the impossibilities of their sickly clime, the grapes they produce hardly deserve the name. The heavy red grape that we love never prospers; instead, they have to content themselves with not white, but yellow fruits that one year in two wither on the vine. When *win* is made it more often than not tastes acid and is always too dry: a fault that the clumsy Saxon winemakers try to correct by mixing honey into it.

Rarely an evening goes by when a Saxon warrior does not drink himself close to oblivion. However, note that 'close'. This people, strangely, hate drunkenness and speak badly of those who cannot hold their alcohol – 'like real men', as they would say. Indeed, a grave insult at a banquet is to scream 'you are drunk!' The British Celts forget the stupidities of alcohol: oaths, for example, are not valid if made while under the influence of a cask of *beor*. However, the Saxons take every insult and promise made while in the state as that of a sober man; another reason for never losing control while you are among them. The explorer will perhaps be thinking that he can easily resist even *beor* in frozen weather. Yet do not be so sure, for there are two terrible dangers in the alehouses. The first are the magic spells that they use to brew their various devilish mixtures. These are runes scratched on to and into the barrels that also help in the intoxication of the innocent traveller – secretly cross the beaker you are given before sipping from it. The second threat – and a far more serious one – are the cupbearers. The various Saxon women of the house are responsible for bringing drinks to the guest and if one takes a shine to the explorer, she will bring cup after cup to test his manliness; often the daughters of the owner take on this role and they cannot be refused.

The embassy had luckily been accompanied in their visit to the alehouse by one of the Frisian merchants, who knew the Saxons' ways and told them how to avoid embarrassment. If one is worried about being able to keep a bit of acid *win* down, then it is best to say that your local witch has insisted that you drink goat's milk for a month – the Saxons' most common medicine. Some of this beverage – usually sour and stained with charcoal – is always kept in reserve. Another solution, the one practised at Portchester, is to say that you are 'a pin man'. The Saxons have in their wooden cups a nail that is hammered in about halfway up. If you drink from one of these you can insist that the cup is not filled higher than its iron mark. This also excuses you from their idiotic drinking competitions, when they challenge each other to quaff an entire cup at a time. Certainly your manly prestige will suffer at the beginning of the evening, but at least you won't wake on the morrow with 'hammers' or a duel on your hands.

(III) CANTERBURY

From the Strong Port it is three or four days' walk to the bounds of Cant, home of the Cantware. This territory is famous, not only for the Weld or the Forestland [the Weald], but also for the local warriors who, for the last half-century, have pulsed out of its wooden heart, assuring the dominance of the Cantian king in the south of Britain. In another age it was within the bounds of this small kingdom that the armies of Caesar and Claudius the Stutterer first met the Britons in battle. And today this eastern peninsula is remembered reverently by its natives for another invasion, for this was also the place where, a century ago, post the Roman retreat, some of the first of the Saxon warlords, Horsa and Hengist, arrived in the island. Not that the reader should be surprised that it was the earliest of the British-Celtic provinces to be overrun; after all this is the part of Britain that is closest to the Continent. Indeed, setting out from one of the Cantian ports, you need little more than a day's sailing, or a feat of endurance rowing, to send your boat grinding against Frankish shores; while the eagle-eyed claim to be able to make out fires on the beaches of distant Gaul.

The explorer's first aim, once he has crossed the borders of this kingdom, should be to find his way to the region's capital – Cantwaraburg as the Saxons call it, or Doruvernia, the Fort of Alders, as it is known among the British Celts [Canterbury], for it is there that the king of Cant has his home. But though a Roman road is still intact in the region, travel is never simple among the Saxons. The Cantian territories are themselves divided into a series of what locals call *lathes*, with a *lathe*-lord ruling in each district on behalf of the king. It would be unwise to pass through any of these without express permission from the suitable authorities, and the journey across the kingdom can sometimes take as many as ten days, while riders are sent ahead to beg escorts and rights of way. The *lathe*-lords, incidentally, are picked from the best of the royal household. The king gives the *lathe*-lords land and a hall, while they in return serve him in war and in gratitude call him their loaf-giver.[1] *Lathe*-lords are generally very proud of their halls and, though you can be sniffy about the farmland or surrounding woods or even the peasant population that cultivate the region, take care not to say cruel words about these sheds, the centres of their world.

Worn out by the constant shocks to his civilised system, the traveller will tell himself that, after arriving in Cantwaraburg itself, he should search out the hall of the loaf-giver of Cant and abase himself beneath the feet of the mightiest of the kings of Britain. But not a bit of it! One of Britain's best-kept secrets, and one that it took the two remaining members of the embassy several days to learn, is that while Cant is the most powerful of the Saxon fiefdoms and, indeed, of any of the Dark Isles' kingdoms, it is not the king who controls the place. To find out who does, the traveller should walk to the front of the mortared building – it was once a church – where the king's guards play with Swedish blades and Jutish knives. Avoid the royal entrance, then turn

---

1. *Translator's note:* Loaf-giver (*hlaford*), or one who gives food to his clients, transmuted with the centuries into our word 'lord'. 'Lady', in Old English *hlafdige*, meant in its original form 'loaf-kneeder'.

sharp left down what remains of the Roman street until you find a queue of visitors waiting to talk to the power behind the throne. There petitioners from Dal Riada jostle with Deirans, humiliated in recent wars; Syrian merchants sent as go-betweens by the British Celts of the west chat to Londoners come down to negotiate a new truce; while Irish monks who got washed up on the wrong coast and now want to build a monastery in the environs try to push in front of Spanish traders who are hoping to sell their wares in one of the Cantian emporia.

And what is the power that attracts, like bees to flowers, these varied visitors? Enter the room and you will find the true sovereign of Cant, the ambassador of Frankia. For, though little known in our Mediterranean, the crowned heads of Frankia have long since called Cant their vassal, and all his kingdom from the Pale Cliffs that score the coast to its wooded interior pay rich tributes across the Channel. And while the Frankish kings of northern Gaul have never undertaken a full-scale invasion, they insist on the Cantian loaf-giver's obedience, and the Frankish ambassador takes a careful part in planning Cant's foreign relations, even those with the Hebrides and the wilder Irish kingdoms.

Despair, if you please, for poor Cant, for the humiliation of this foreign domination. But for yourself shed not a tear. The Franks have had far more contact with Roman ways and subsequently are more methodical and to-the-point in negotiations. Your meeting with the Frankish ambassador will be quick and there will be no need for special formulae or low bows. Then afterwards, your business over, you should go and make a polite visit to the king. And there, certainly, there will be the obeisances due to all monarchs. But a small man by the king's side will let the Cantian loaf-giver know Frankia's decision and whisper it carefully into his right ear. Indeed, if you get as far as this room, be assured that the answer to your question is 'yes'.

In the embassy's time, Frankia's representative in this reprehensible peninsula was a bishop. This careful and crafty individual had originally been sent to guard over a Parisian princess, an innocent who had been offered up to the king of Cant as a paramour. The excuse, it seems, was that she, as a Christian, needed a confessor in a heathenish land and that this holy man would serve her as a chaplain. But the bishop, in fact, proved obsessed by the power that he believed was his right. And

while in many ways the ideal ambassador, he – Liudhard, he was called –
went so far as to have coins minted with his name, the first to be made
in Britain since the Romans ceased hammering out their gold and
bronze into shining discs over a hundred years ago. Doubtless this
particular representative of the Frankish will has long since been buried
under a Cantian sod. But Frankish control, we are assured, continues
in Cant, and the first question the visitor should ask once he reaches
Cantwaraburg is the residence and rank of the new ambassador.

The explorer, however, now faces a further complication in the royal
city and it is one that we tell of between smiles and sighs. In the last
two years, rumours reached us that the Bishop of Rome [i.e. the Pope]
was planning a mission to bring the Saxons to the Cross and salvation!
The reader will naturally raise his eyebrows at this and, indeed, we
Britain experts had much merriment at His Holiness's expense. Converting the Saxons indeed: whatever will the Italians think of next! But
we have heard, almost by the last courier, that the mission, sent over
the Alps last autumn, arrived in Cant this spring. There, our ever-
optimistic Roman sources tell us, churches were built and miracles
worked on the heads of the blue-eyed Cantwine [men of Kent].

How long, we ask, before the inevitable apostasy? And in fact, even
the most enthusiastic at missionary control in Rome admit there has
also been a series of difficulties. The gravest has been the opposition of
the few British-Celtic Christians who remain in Cant and the south of
Britain. These are to be found either in the enclaves or dispersed around
the countryside in small settlements named *eccles* by the Saxons after
the churches that are found there.[1] And they, after all, have had a
longer and bitterer experience of the Saxons than has the Pope who,
incidentally, took a shine to that people while looking over some especially handsome Northumbrian slave boys. Consequently, these British
Celts have refused either to help the mission or to recognise its authority. One disastrous effect of this has been that it has no longer proved
possible, as Rome originally hoped, to have one archbishop in Londinium and another in Eoforwic [York]. Instead, a decree has been sent

---

1. *Translator's note: Eccles* place names derive from the Latin word *ecclesia* (church).
They seem to have been Saxon names for British-Celtic settlements with churches,
Christianity being a distinguishing feature in this epoch. The sole example known from
Kent is that of Eccles near modern Rochester.

out that their leader, a certain Augustine, will become archbishop of Cantwaraburg, a title that we are afraid will hardly have the same ring to it.[1]

The second problem, and an additional reason why the Roman church will fail in its efforts to convert this corner of Britain, is the locals' obsession not only with blood-dripping gods, but also their ancestors. The Saxons look forward constantly to the moment that they will die, preferably on the battlefield, and be carried aloft by ravens to the halls of paradise where their predecessors are said to live. Indeed, in their ignorance they see heaven as one long *beor*-fest with comely maidens bringing more cups, *scops* and lyres chiming in the background, while bearded grandfathers clap them on their backs, congratulating them on their martial deeds. When the king of Cant was asked whether he wanted to convert to Christianity, he actually proved quite willing until he heard that his ancestors would not be able to join him in heaven. At which point, storming out of the church, which had been built specially for the occasion, he was heard to shout 'I would rather spend eternity in hell with my own people, than sit alone in your gilded rooms!'

The missionaries have tried many sophisticated arguments to break down the resistance of the king and his nobles. But, despite the pressure of the Franks, they have had little success. The latest strategy involves a long, contorted paradox pointing out the impossibility of the heathen demons of the north – Tiw, Woden and all their damned fraternity – being born from nothing and an insistence that there must be something older and greater than even they. But the Saxons of Cant, who have not much time for philosophical abstraction, look on blankly and shake their heads when asked if they understand.

1. *Translator's note:* the original plan of Pope Gregory the Great had been, as our author suggests, to create one archbishopric for York and one for London. However, as the mission identified so closely with the kings of Kent, London was replaced by Canterbury.

(IV) THANET[1]

On the eastern bounds of Cant is the island of Tanatos [Thanet]: a word that in our own language means, of course, 'death'. And, suitably, everything on this miserable flat-topped isle seems to be concerned with dying; indeed, it even carries with it a kind of mortuary smell that revolts the nose and unsettles the stomach. The traveller will no doubt be smiling: 'Very well, I will miss the infernal hole, I am, anyway, near enough to Gaul and civilisation.' But few visitors to Cant manage to avoid those melancholy square miles for the very simple reason that it is from here that most ships pass over to the Continent. 'But surely', the same traveller will then reply, though now a little more nervously, 'our narrator exaggerates. Can really everything to do with the isle be concerned with death?' Well, the name of the place resolutely declares its allegiance; and it is hardly coincidence that the pagan Gauls claim that the spirits of the departed are rowed over to this block of British earth and, through all eternity, run and hide in the sand dunes there.[2] But the chief association with death – and the explorer might consider this, as exorbitant ferrymen punt him across the sound to the isle's haunted shores – is a massacre that took place on Tanatos a little less than a century ago and that still colours the land with its blood. Some of the first Saxons to arrive in Cant invited the local British Celts to a feast there and, at a preordained signal, pulled hidden knives out of their shoes and slaughtered all the natives, with the exception of their leader, who was ransomed off.

A visit to the island, then, is guaranteed to be unpleasant: the wind, the sea and the stench shock even its inhabitants. So, if you can leave Britain by another route, perhaps even a trip back to the Strong Port, for goodness sake do so. The two remaining Greeks of the embassy,

1. *Translator's note:* In the sixth century and, indeed, through all of the early Middle Ages Thanet was a genuine island – today it is a pseudo-island – being reached either by boat across the River Wantsum or over one of two fords. Slowly this channel silted up, creating the landscape that we now know, though it was still in use as late as the eleventh century.
2. *Translator's note:* The story of Frankish souls being rowed across to Britain is also mentioned by Procopius in his *History of the Wars*, 8, 20. There must be a suspicion that the very name Tanatos, meaning as our author explains 'death' in Greek, created the legend.

Manuel and Sophron, had, however, not the guile to steer clear of the place and were brought by insistent guides of the king to see several tourist attractions there.

They had said that the stone before us was dedicated to one of the original warlords, a certain Horsa who led the first Saxons on to the beaches of Tanatos. But we were sceptical as the script was Roman and this people are, with the exception of their runes, illiterate. We mused on this a while, until my companion pointed out that the clearly visible word HORS – there had never been an 'a' – was probably the end of the Latin word COHORS. Some foreigner had, presumably, played a joke on the locals, perhaps even breaking the stone at a strategic point, passing it off as a relic of the invasions. Both of us bent down and, now intrigued by the mystery, decided to turn the rock over to see if any other Latin letters appeared there to confirm our suspicions.

Our guides had wandered off while we worked on our puzzle. But we were woken from our injudicious study by one of them reappearing and shouting. On looking up, we saw that he was yelling not at us Greeks, but at three men who were standing over us with their short Saxon daggers drawn and who looked extremely unhappy with our stone-rolling escapades. The next moments were terrible and I will hardly bother to describe them. Sufficient to say that blood was drawn, and my last companion, Manuel the artist, bled his life and most of his guts away over the stone. Our guides managed to separate me from these three crude warriors before they could similarly spend my life-force. However, by the time the struggle was finished, and they had finally pulled me away from the dogs, one of my ears lay on the ground and there were injuries in my lower body. I was lain out half-conscious while the guides screamed at these malefactors, but our attackers were quite as angry. Even through the haze of my unconsciousness, their words showed that they were not random thugs, but that they had attacked us for a reason. It seems that this stone was a boundary point between their land and another portion of land and they had thought that in turning over the stone we had hoped to enlarge their neighbour's territory. On hearing, though, from the guides that we were guests of the king, their whole demeanour changed and they became apologetic, even desperate. But by then it was too late and my eyes were dragging down into sleep...

I awoke several hours later to find that I had been stretched out on a cart, in a barn of some type, and that around me a crowd of men had gathered, all of them bearded and moustached in a way that is typical of the Saxons. My rudimentary knowledge of their language – though Kentish is a rather different proposition from the tongue we had learnt in the north – informed me almost immediately that this was one of their courts and that our guides had taken on the role of witnesses against the farmers who had so excitedly tried to end my life. Next to me on the cart lay dead Manuel, who had mostly been covered with a white sheet. My head, meanwhile, had been bandaged and my middle parts wrapped around with dirty, gangrene-inducing linen. But despite these distractions I sat up and tried to look coolly at my attackers.

Their guilt they immediately admitted, though they claimed that we, in moving their boundary stone, had effectively been committing a theft. Countering this, our guides reminded them that we were under the king's protection and I noticed that this more than anything else terrified the three. At the end a compromise was hammered out between the elder of the court, a kind of judge, and the accused. They would drop the charge of shifting the boundary stone and I would be given a reduced status by the guides. I must admit to not having understood all the details, but it seems that as the king was our protector we had rights almost equal to his. These freeholders would have been bankrupted instantly in paying this and the result would have been a lifetime in slavery to settle their debts. So it was that the assembly began to examine my injuries. The bandage was peeled back from the ragged remains of my ear – the cold air stung – and the judge shouted: 'twenty shillings'. The bandages were also removed from my middle parts and after establishing that one testicle had been ripped away he shouted: 'sixty more shillings'. Then, looking at a large bruise on my face, he instructed: 'ten more shillings'. Grumbling, but not overly, for they in no way wanted to come into conflict with the king, the three began to undo pouches from their belt and summon other family members to help. Indeed, I lost consciousness listening to Frankish coins – the Cantwine have none of their own – being counted out on to the judge's table.

(V) LEAVING

What, then, about the traveller who has succeeded in not being gelded on Tanatos, bitten by vipers in the marches of Cant, rifled by disease at Corinium and, indeed, has escaped from the other 'thousand footfalls that death sets for man' in those places? For him, there is still the disagreeable task of taking his weary body over the stretch of water that separates barbarism from civilisation, the Saxon Channel. The crossing is normally made, as we have said, from Tanatos itself and there he will find a lively trade with northern Europe – there are sailors who fish at the mouth of the Rhine and even some who have seen the Baltic. Likewise, mariners from the south visit its shores, bringing everything from hops for Saxon *beor* to teeth-breaking grinding stones for querns.[1] Most of these ships return empty to the Continent and will be only too happy to give the weary traveller passage for a consideration, anything to offset their overheads.

Now we know that you have been for many months in dark places and that you want nothing more than to get out; but before rushing on to that boat, listen, we beg, to three last considerations that we believe fundamental for leaving Britain.

First, do not make the mistake of getting on a vessel owned by a rough northern merchant, thinking, as is possible in Ireland, that a nipple-suck will be enough. The more willing a Swedish captain is to take you without payment, the more likely it is that he is sizing you up for an unpleasant fate. Indeed, we have heard of several cases where travellers departing the terrible places of the Dark Isles have found themselves with a one-way ticket to the slave markets of northern Scythia.

Second danger: as you should avoid the northernmost routes, avoid too those that go south to Armorica. There you will find, in what was once the heart of the Roman province, a little Britain [Brittany] where British Celts and Saxons fight just as they do on the British side of the Channel, with that special insular ferocity of theirs. This second Britain was born in the times of disaster, when the Saxon invaders first came

---

1. *Translator's note:* these querns were used to grind wheat, corn and other crops. However, occasionally fragments broke off into the flour and threatened the teeth of those who accidentally bit on them.

to the island and many British Celts from the south coast fled to this place, believing that by so doing they would escape the savage conquerors. But, unfortunately for them, the Saxons also decided to colonise this part of the Continent, chasing the British Celts like dogs following cats, and in many parts of the coast they have established their own settlements.[1] So, rather than stepping again into this particular series of hornet nests, where a league of coastline can mean the difference between a Saxon and a British-Celtic port, we strongly advise taking a Spanish merchant ship going south of the Loire.

Now our third and final warning: once you come to land on the Frankish coast, shut up about your experiences in the Dark Isles! We say this, for it is borne out by the log-writer, Sophron, the last of the Greeks, that even on the safer stretches of Frankish coast, at points where you can see the south-eastern edge of Britain, the locals claim to know nothing of that strange world, swearing only to its barbarism and dangers. Pass fifty miles inland on one of the overland routes to the Mediterranean – we advise that towards Marseilles – and the fact that one has been to Britain will be laughed at with disbelief or taken as a challenge to the listener's credulity. Indeed, the further from the islands you travel, the more incredible become the stories the locals make up about them. (One acquaintance, for example, had an argument with a Frankish merchant who insisted that it was impossible for humans to breathe air on the northern side of Hadrian's Wall!) The explorer, of course, will know that these are nothing but the voices of those twins of rumour, 'arrant' and 'nonsense'. However, for those who spread these base tales, they often prove beliefs that are too strongly held to be shaken by anything so irritatingly simple as an eyewitness. Keep your horrors strictly to yourself, then, and allow Britain and Ireland to shrink from the horizon shrouded in nightmares, delirium and their neighbours' all-too pardonable ignorance.

---

1. *Translator's note:* Saxon settlements on the coast of what is today north-western France were, in fact, far fewer than those of the British Celts. However, they were numerous enough to leave traces behind them. The historian Edward James, in *Britain in the First Millennium* (Arnold, 2000), p. 110, gives the names of two towns in the Pas-de-Calais, Alincthun and Audincthun, 'which have an oddly English ring to them' and which are, in fact, Gallic equivalents of, respectively, Allington and Oddington, the product of Saxon (that is 'English') settlements in the region fifteen hundred years ago.

APPENDIX
BY SOTER, THE SECRETARY OF
THE MAP ROOM

I, Soter, was asked by my master, the author of the present volume, to add a short adjunct concerning his most important source: the small manuscript in which the mission of twenty years ago wrote its log. The volume is only three-quarters full – many of the pages remaining blank, four or five having even been cut from the binding for other purposes by unknown hands. The final page used by the embassy – almost immediately after the fight on Tanatos – is, in fact, covered with scrawlings in Greek, barely legible letters and numbers and additions that seem to have related to a doctor's bill. Then the script changes totally and the writing is that neat Latin of Gaul. In three short sentences, a local priest has recorded that Sophron, the last surviving member of the embassy, who had been responsible for almost all of the log entries on that party's long journey, passed away at Tours in central Gaul just before Christmas; the wounds he had received on his severed ear turned septic and spread across his face and into his brains. From this we can deduce that he did manage to cross to the Continent and even got halfway towards the Mediterranean. Poignantly his last jottings, difficult to read as they are, describe the pain involved in walking

What happened in those twenty years between Sophron's death and the day that the manuscript was brought to the Imperial court is a mystery. Some red stains on the lower edge of the book have been analysed and are likely derived from blood. But they could as easily have resulted from one of the embassy's early adventures as from a subsequent horror. Indeed, the only real clue we have is a series of numbers written on the inside cover, suggesting that the manuscript had been integrated into a library, and some words written over the first few pages that show a Latin writer had tried, unsuccessfully, to decipher the Greek. Are we to suppose that the priest who stayed with Sophron in his last hours appropriated the work for a nearby monastery? Nor do we know how the log found its way from this putative monastic library into the hands of the Syrian merchant who finally brought the codex to Constantinople.

We in the map room have speculated – idly – that one explanation might be the following. On the first page of the work was, as my master noted in his introduction, a short sentence written in Greek, Latin and Syriac stating that the Emperor would pay its weight in gold if the book were to be returned to him in Constantinople. In the codex's unfortunate encounters with water – it had clearly been wet and left to dry at one point – the Latin and Greek were blurred to the point that they are almost impossible to read. Is it not conceivable that a Latin abbot, noting this strange Syriac script but not being able to read the inscriptions, showed it to a passing Syrian merchant? This merchant, in turn realising the potential value of the work, then secreted it from the library and made his own way to our city. We will never know. But the merchant who was responsible for bringing it to the Emperor had clearly read his prize, and had frequently annotated it with Syriac, something that intensely annoyed my master while trying to decipher some of the less clear Greek passages and that may confuse later researchers.

The log has now been placed in the royal library. And only the seal of the Emperor will open the lock of the wooden casket in which it has been set. This small brown manuscript was no divine creation: it was the product of an embassy that, twenty years before our time, wasted their lives away in the British and Irish wildernesses. That party, as any who read the extracts quoted above will have understood, were not always wise in their decisions. Sometimes, indeed, their judgement proved reckless, sometimes ill-timed. But travel in Britain and its neighbour Ireland is a stressful, life-endangering business – this our master has taught us well – and whatever their moments of incompetence, the fact remains that our knowledge has been substantially increased by their trekking and frequent record-taking. It is only just that this work end, then, with a list of their names and their various fates, so that we can more easily pray for their souls.

(1) IGNATIOS, the translator: washed overboard on the crossing from Spain.

(2) STEPHANOS, the librarian: a fall in the Cambrian mountains.

(3) PETROS, the physician: throat slit by the Fenians in Ireland.

(4) SALLOS, bodyguard: blinded and left in the monastery of Clonmacnois after the Fenian attack.

(5) DOMITIANOS, scholar: frightened into the sea near Thule by beaked creatures.

(6) LAURENTIUS, the mapper: lost escaping from Catterick.

(7) SNEGDOULOS, the geologist: appendicitis on the northern banks of the Humber.

(8) LEONIDAS, the cook: stayed behind in Barleytun.

(9) ANDREAS, the book-carrier: struck down by plague.

(10) PHILIPPOS, the chief negotiator: bitten by a viper in the Valley of Broom.

(11) MANUEL, the artist: run through on Thanet.

(12) SOPHRON, log-writer: died of wounds in Tours.

NOTES AND SOURCES

What might be called 'the rules of engagement' for the reconstruction of sixth-century Britain and Ireland are as follows. I have used the date of AD 500 in the title to anchor the book. But, in fact, throughout I have taken events, individuals and institutions that date from the sixth century as a whole. For example, the monastery of Iona in the Hebrides discussed in Chapter Six was probably not founded till *circa* – all sixth-century dates are *circa* – 563. With customs I have, when basing myself on archaeology, only used material that is 'early medieval', i.e. 500–900. With customs described in written sources I have been more liberal. The bulk of material is from the early Middle Ages proper. However, sometimes we hear of a later local custom that we might suspect is of considerable antiquity and that was not recorded prior to that date simply because of a lack of surviving writing from the region. Take the case of Gerald of Wales, who wrote in the early twelfth century. Gerald records that some British men shaved their heads to move more easily in the forests. Is this a recent custom or one stretching back to Roman habits in the second and third centuries? We will never know. But sixth-century sources tell us that another group of British Celts, Bretons on the Continent, shaved their heads to fight. The correspondence is slight, perhaps irrelevant, but nevertheless makes one wonder.

Unavoidably for such a controversial period, I have strayed into territory that is hotly disputed. There is, for example, the violence ascribed to the Anglo-Saxon invaders. Most archaeologists would disagree here, claiming that at worst there was 'confusion and fusion' in those years of 'migration' (some even frown at the term 'invasion'). Most historians and place-name experts, meanwhile, would favour a more violent interpretation of Anglo-Saxon settlement. The format of what I have called 'fictionalised history' does not favour the expression of such academic doubts; though I have tried to note some of the most controversial cases in the notes that follow. Then there are also details in the narrative – especially in the log-entries, the pluperfect of the book – that are products of the fictional frame of *AD 500*. For example, no record or archaeological clue suggests that a Greek was killed by yobs on Thanet after turning over a boundary stone. But the stone they saw there is attested, the interpretation of the inscription – *horsa* for *cohors* – is credible and likewise the legal process the surivor was dragged through is in line with that found in the Kentish laws of the era.

To the reader who loses patience with the exoticising of Britain and Ireland – marshes described as swamps, constant references to 'natives' and in one case 'the bloody natives' – I apologise. However, in early drafts I decided it was necessary to emphasise the Greeks' perception of barbarity through the nearest thing in our language: the rhetoric of imperially-fuelled exploration and conquest. It is also worth saying that the author was predisposed to present the elements of sixth-century British and Irish life that have interested him over the years: there is a natural bias towards the curious, the exotic and the exuberant. I make no apology for this. But the absence of details on, say, Anglo-Saxon jewellery-making is not an absence of real knowledge, it is just that I find such details *intolerably* boring.

Finally, it should be noted that the works cited below are included for their content, not for their entertainment value. One of the tragedies of the study of this period is that so little that is both scientific and accessible has been published – the result of difficult sources and a host of 'maybes' and 'perhaps' that cloud the period. So before stepping into the citation quagmire, I include here some of the rare exceptions that can be recommended to the general reader: Charles Thomas, *Celtic Britain* (Thames and Hudson, 1991); or, by the same author, *Britain and Ireland in Early Christian Times AD 400–800* (Thames and Hudson, 1971); Samantha Glasswell, *The Earliest English: Living and Dying in Early Anglo-Saxon England* (Tempus, 2002); and Kathleen Hughes and Ann Hamlin, *The Modern Traveller in the Early Irish Church* (Four Courts Press, 1997). To these it is worth adding a very short list of Dark Age British and Irish works that the modern reader might enjoy: *Adomnan of Iona's Life of St Columba* (with an excellent introduction) by Richard Sharpe (Penguin, 1995); John Porter, *Anglo-Saxon Riddles* (Anglo-Saxon Books, 1995); Bede's *Ecclesiastical History*, available in various editions; J. G. Webb (tr.), *Lives of the Saints: The Voyage of St Brendan; Bede's Life of Cuthbert; Stephanus' Life of Wilfred* (Penguin, 1981) – all three texts above are used in this book. Then, last but not least, there is Procopius's *History of the Wars*, which tells the other side of the story: that of the sixth-century Byzantine re-conquest, and which appears in five Loeb volumes edited by H. B. Dewing (reprint 2000).

INTRODUCTION

(I) The Pretanic Isles is based on the ancient Celtic word for Britain. Britain and Ireland were often described as being at the end of the earth in antiquity; indeed, Britain was sometimes even described as 'another world'. 'The Tinny Isles' is based on Britain's reputation in the Mediterranean as a source of tin – see notes in Chapter Two for this. *Britannia et Hibernia* are, of course, the Latin names for the islands. 'Albion' is of considerable antiquity and is first encountered in Avienus, *Ora Maritima*: 'Ierne', meanwhile, is the ancient Irish name for Ireland found in Strabo, *The Geography*, 2,1. Avienus, *Ora Maritima* also speaks of Ireland though not Britain as the Sacred Isle. The Cannibals' Isles is based on a solitary report in Strabo, *Geographia*, 4, 5 that claims that the Irish ate human flesh. The Blessed Isles are first mentioned by Homer and are sometimes identified with Britain and Ireland. The evidence of a sixth-century Byzantine embassy to Britain is a line of Procopius, *The Secret History*, 29, 13 where we learn that the Emperor Justinian gave out gifts to the kings of Britain. Archaeology helps to flesh out contacts between the Byzantine state, Britain and even Ireland: for example, Anthea Harris, *Byzantium, Britain and the West: The Archaeology of Cultural Identity AD 400–650* (Tempus, 2003).

(II) The geographical and economical information given is based largely on Bede, *Ecclesiastical History*, 1, 1, while Britain as an isosceles triangle is to be found, instead, in Roman sources (see Barri Jones and David Mattingly, *An Atlas of Roman Britain* (Oxbow, 1990), pp. 17–18). For the *birrus* see Sheppard Frere, *Britannia: A History of Roman Britain* (BCA, 1967), p. 274. Today we would name the Picts as the original British people: they seem to have predated even the Celts. But *Gildas: The Ruin of Britain*, ed. and tr. Michael Winterbottom (Phillimore,

1978), pp. 21–5, in his description of the fifth-century invasions, envisaged the *Picti* as arriving from outside the border of Britain to steal British-Celtic land: Neil Wright, 'Gildas's Geographical Perspective: Some Problems', *Gildas: New Approaches*, ed. M. Lapidge and D. Dumville (Boydell Press, 1984) pp. 85–105. The contention that there are five languages spoken in Britain is one that is taken from Bede, *Ecclesiastical History*, 1, 1. However, it must be said that many believe that the Picts had, in fact, two languages. I have kept Bede's traditional numbering by assimilating one of these to British-Celtic. It is unsure that British-Celtic and Irish were close enough to be understood in the sixth century; certainly by the later part of the century they had drifted a long way apart. Perhaps we can assume some very modest inter-communicability – like modern German and English – in the late fifth and early sixth centuries.

(III) The 'two hundred or so kingdoms' depends very much on definition. It is likely that in the sixth century Britain had between twenty and thirty – though if one began to count sub-kings that number would grow very quickly. However, in Ireland the various *tuath* or tribes were considerably more numerous. The retreat of British Celts to ancient hill forts is attested at numerous archaeological sites, but also in *Gildas*, p. 28. The assertion that Pictish women had a special status 'not a on a par with, but closer to, that of a man' is controversial. No Pictish laws survive so we cannot check this statement and our only hint that it may have been the case is the special status granted to Pictish women in laws of descent (see the notes for Chapter Eight). It should be stressed that to keep the description of the *wergild* relevant to all four peoples it has been made *very* general and its meaning extended somewhat.

(V) The first route, that up the Rhine, is attested in archaeology of trade networks: Martin Welch, *Anglo-Saxon England* (BCA, 1992), pp. 116–17. The second route combines the Byzantines' preferred route to Marseilles with the road to the north undertaken in the very late sixth century and onwards by missionaries going to the Anglo-Saxon homelands and converts returning down these roads to Rome as pilgrims. The third route was taken by Byzantine ships, as the evidence of Byzantine remains on the western coasts of Britain make abundantly clear: Harris, *Byzantium, Britain and the West*, pp. 52–60. The British diaspora consisted of two major British-Celtic colonies that survive in our historical records: Brittany in France and Britonia in Galicia, in north-western Spain. It is not impossible that there were others that have escaped notice.

CHAPTER ONE

(I) 'One author' is the British-Celtic writer *Gildas: The Ruin of Britain*, ed. and tr. Michael Winterbottom (Phillimore, 1978), p. 16. For 'the British metal' see Roger D. Penhallurick, *Tin in Antiquity* (Institute of Metals, 1986), which concentrates overwhelmingly on the south-west of Britain. Sillina is described in Malcolm Todd, *The South West to AD 1000* (Longman, 1987), p. 11 and p. 217. The Priscillianists appear in the *Historia Sacra* of Sulpicius Severus 11, 51.

(II) For a general description of Tintagel and a bibliography see Christopher Snyder, *Sub Roman Britain (AD 400–600)* (BAR British Series 247, 1996), pp. 28–9. For other British alcoholic drinks see Chapter Fourteen and notes. The legend of a Dumnonian king (March) having donkey ears emerges in the Cornish tale Tristan and Isolde; the notion of the Dumnonian kings using a crown to hide their ears is a conceit spinning off that. Constantine was a sixth-century king of Dumnonia who was described by *Gildas*, pp. 29–30: the furious clergy-man uses Gildas's insults for Constantine, while the *Welsh Annals* date 'the conversion of Constantine to the Lord' to AD 589. St Ia is described in some detail in Nicholas Orme, *Saints of Cornwall* (OUP, 2000), p. 142.

(III) The low level of Latin among rural British Celts in the west of Britain is almost universally accepted by scholars: some would claim that even under the Empire, even in the south-east, a British-Celtic peasant would have spoken little of that language. The rounds, espe-cially that of Trethurgy, are described in Todd, *The South West*, p. 225. The heads pinned to the wall come from an ancient Greek writer describing the Celts, Diodorus Siculus, *Bibliotheke*, 5, 29: there is evi-dence that the British Celts also headhunted in the sixth century and, indeed, for many centuries to come. No coins were minted by the British Celts and archaeologists suggest that coins, when used, tended to be old issues: Ken Dark, *Britain and the End of the Roman Empire*

(Tempus, 2000), pp. 143–4; *The Life of St John the Almsgiver* describes Egyptian bronzes being exchanged for tin in the south-west of Britain. The pagan play is found in *The Life of St Samson of Dol*, Thomas Taylor (Llanerch, 1991: reprint), p. 49 and took place at Trigg in Cornwall. Arthur is often dated to the sixth century, though other possibilities including the fifth century or even a Roman commander in the third century have been credibly suggested; the author wanted to dwell on the legendary features of the once and future king here and so put the historical question to one side. Arthur's association with rocks in the wilds is taken up by Oliver Padel, 'The Nature of Arthur', *Cambrian Medieval Celtic Studies*, 27 (1994), pp. 1–31, though it should be noted that the first references are late (ninth-century). Arthur is linked repeatedly in British-Celtic legend with the Virgin, while the reference to the antipodes is found in E. K. Chambers, *Arthur of Britain: The story of King Arthur in History and Legend* (Sidgwick and Jackson, 1967), pp. 264–5 – contrary to what many of us today think, the ancients did speculate about the existence of islands on the other side of the world, seeing the world as a globe. The punch-up at Bodmin is based on the experiences of a later French party that came unstuck insulting Arthur: Chambers, *Arthur*, p. 249. For a general description of Exeter and bibliography see Snyder, *Sub Roman Britain*, p. 23. 'All roads' is invented but was likely a sentiment in sixth-century Devon.

(IV) The account of the visit to the Temple of Bacchus at Maiden Castle is based on Craig Cessford's reconstruction of certain archaeological finds there, including the two bodies that are buried in the narrative. See *Somerset and Dorset Notes and Queries*, 34 (1996–2000), pp. 46–9: a great deal of this is necessarily speculative and the late survival of British-Celtic paganism is unorthodox. 'Christian hoodlums' depends upon Ken Dark, *Civitas to Kingdom: British Political Continuity 300–800* (Leicester University Press, 1994), pp. 62–3. The Saxons' 'wide' faces, meanwhile, is based on the description of Sidonius Apollinaris, *Epistolas*, 8, 9.

CHAPTER TWO

(I) Successful Welsh exploits against the Romans in and immediately after their conquest of the peninsula are well attested: Sheppard Frere,

Britannia: A History of Roman Britain (BCA, 1967), pp. 76–87. The marvels on the Severn Estuary are both described in the *Historia Brittonum – Nennius: British History and the Welsh Annals*, ed. John Morris (Phillimore, 1989), pp. 81–3. The image of the Severn running red from source to sea is borrowed from a medieval Welsh tradition where it is associated with the battle of Digoll, for which Rachel Bromwich, *Trioedd Ynys: The Welsh Triads* (Cardiff, 2nd edition 1978), p. 182. Lundy's barbarous reputation under the Romans is attested in Solinus in his *Collectanea Rerum Memorabilium*, 20, 7. The hermits of Caldey are found in a seventh-century British-Celtic life, *The Life of St Samson of Dol*, tr. Thomas Taylor (Llanerch, 1991: reprint), pp. 26–30; and for Pyro's drunken fall see pp. 38–9, 'an unexpected thing' and one of the high points of insular hagiography. The appearance of the so-called Celtic tonsure still proves controversial. Two reasonable possibilities are the following: first, that described here, a semicircle at the front of the head with a complete cutting behind; second, a three-pointed or triangular tonsure. The paranoia about pollution from less strict Christians is well attested among the British Celts of this century; see, for example, *Gildas: The Ruin of Britain*, ed. and tr. Michael Winterbottom (Phillimore, 1978), pp. 80–82. The most striking seventh-century example relates precisely to this region and is found in a letter of Aldhelm to Geraint. This intolerance seems to have been the result of more archaic versions of Christianity surviving among the British Celts. The embassy's reference to Antioch, Alexandria, Rome and Constantinople is adapted from a phrase of the Irishman Cummian faced with similar insular intransigence: M. Walsh and D. Ó. Cróinín, *Cummian's Letter De Controversia Paschali and the De Ratione Conputandi* (PIMS, 1988), pp. 72–5.

(II) The Tenby poem is edited and translated by Ifor Williams, *The Beginnings of Welsh Poetry* (UWP, 1980), pp. 162–6. The Demetian bow is found in *Gerald of Wales: The Journey Through Wales/ The Description of Wales*, tr. Lewis Thorpe (Penguin, 1978), p. 113, likewise the girl with the harp, the eating and teeth-brushing habits of the Welsh, pp. 236–8, whereas the Welsh 'sing-song' is described on p. 242. British-Celtic hospitality, meanwhile, is referred to in *De proprietatibus gentium*, MGH, *Auctores antiquissimi* 11 (MGH, 1894), pp. 389–90. The seven bishops are described in Thomas Charles-Edwards, 'The Seven Bishop-

Houses of Dyfed', *Bulletin of the Board of Celtic Studies*, 24 (1971), pp. 247–62. Vortipor, his grey hair and incestuous habits, are found in *Gildas*, p. 31. A lord's visit is described in detail in the Welsh Laws and 'the feast' is found there: Ian F. Fletcher, *Latin Redaction A of the Law of Howel* (Pamphlets of Welsh Law, 1986), p. 46. The early material relating to David, Patron saint of Wales is set out by D. N. Dumville, *St David of Wales*, Kathleen Hughes Memorial Lectures on Mediaeval Welsh History, 1 (2000). The references to cold streams, virgins and nettles are all attested in early 'western' religious texts. The jackdaws of St David can be found in *Gerald of Wales*, p. 168. The legends of David's birth are discussed in Dumville, *St David*, p. 27. Finally, the educational techniques of southern Wales and especially the colloquy system of learning are set out by Michael Lapidge, 'Latin learning in Dark Age Wales: some *prolegomena*', *Proceedings of the Seventh International Congress of Celtic Studies* (Oxford, 1983), D. Ellis Evans et al., pp. 97–101.

(III) The British beaver is described in *Gerald of Wales*, p. 176 though at a date when it was almost extinct. For more on the beaver in early medieval times: James A. Spriggs, 'The British Beaver – Fur, Fact and Fantasy', *Leather and Fur: Aspects of Early Medieval Trade and Technology*, ed. Esther Cameron (Archetype, 1998), pp. 91–101. Powys is generally accepted to derive from the Latin *Paganus*, 'of the country'. The early history of Brycheiniog is frequently connected with the Irish in later Welsh texts and genealogies. However, the first artificial island (*crannog*) in this region – a peculiarly Irish or north British custom – seems to date from the ninth or tenth century: Christopher J. Arnold and Jeffrey L. Davies, *Roman and Early Medieval Wales* (Sutton Publishing, 2000), p. 164. The customs of the bards are described in the introduction of Patrick K. Ford, *Ystoria Taliesin* (University of Wales Press, 1992). The difficulty of their language is suggested in the Welsh tale, *The Dream of Rhonabwy*, found in Gwyn and Thomas Jones (tr.), *The Mabinogion* (Dent, 1986), p. 151. The sights to which Taliesin – an attested Dark Age poet – took the embassy are both found in the *Historia Brittonum*, pp. 81–3. The legend of the boar Oldwhite, meanwhile, is set out in the later Welsh tale *Culhwch ac Olwen*, in the previously cited collection, *The Mabinogion*.

CHAPTER THREE

(I) *Gerald of Wales: The Journey Through Wales/ The Description of Wales*, tr. Lewis Thorpe (Penguin, 1978) provides the phrase about Snowdonia's pasture, p. 230. Gerald is also responsible for the fearsome eagles that are mentioned in relation to Snowdonia, p. 195. A bibliography for Dinas Emrys is found in Christopher Snyder, *Sub Roman Britain (AD 400–600)* (BAR British Series 247, 1996), p. 34, including an account of the lake and the strange wooden foundations that have been found there. Both Vortigern and Ambrosius lived in the early or mid-fifth century – a period that is arguably even more obscure than the one described here – and *may* have been rivals. Vortigern was, in fact, a 'governor' for want of a better word, who ruled Britain sometime in the generation after Roman rule ceased *c.* 410. (The author 'discovering' letters from Vortigern in the archives of the Imperial *curia* is invention, but it is quite conceivable that Vortigern 'the proud tyrant' was in contact with what remained of the Roman Empire.) Ambrosius, meanwhile, was arguably – uncertainties abound – the British-Celtic general at the victory of the Siege of Badon Hill that *probably* took place later in the fifth century. The legendary passage concerning Ambrosius and Vortigern from 'the book market of Constantinople' is actually adapted from the *Historia Brittonum, Nennius: British History and the Welsh Annals*, ed. John Morris (Phillimore, 1989) pp. 70–72. The Great Prophecy and the British-Celtic 'national psychosis' lasted well into the later Middle Ages. It is given excellent coverage by Elissa Henken, *National Redeemer: Owain Glyndwr in Welsh Tradition* (University of Wales Press, 1996). 'The highest of the kingdoms' of Britain is based on a phrase used by *Gildas: The Ruin of Britain*, ed. and tr. Michael Winterbottom (Phillimore, 1978), p. 32.

(II) The eleven Cambrian trees are found in the Welsh law codes and discussed in Peter Fowler, *Farming in the First Millennium AD: British Agriculture between Julius Caesar and William the Conqueror* (CUP, 2002), p. 61. On wolves in Wales see J. E. Harting, *British Extinct Animals* (Trübner and co., 1880), pp. 125–30. The question of unenclosed settlements being of a lower class is discussed in Christopher J. Arnold and Jeffrey L. Davies, *Roman and Early Medieval Wales* (Sutton Publishing, 2000), pp. 164–5. Wales was both a-ceramic and without coinage in this period, whereas it had had both of these commodities in later Roman times. The Welsh obsession with family comes from *Gerald of Wales*, pp. 251–2, but can also be amply deduced from a host of earlier works. The details of the *sarhaed* for the king of Gwynedd appears in the Welsh Laws – Ian F. Fletcher, *Latin Redaction A of the Law of Howel* (Pamphlets of Welsh Law, 1986), p. 3 with even more exotic details; while a broader discussion of family, status and law (*cenedl* etc.) is to be found in Thomas Charles-Edwards, *Early Irish and Welsh Kinship* (OUP, 1993). Liberality in Welsh sexual *mores* is found in *Gerald of Wales*, p. 263, whereas the rules for divorce are found in Fletcher, *Latin Redaction*, pp. 62–3. 'The fairy husband' is not found in any ancient source, but the fairies are frequently described in medieval tales and the fairy's fear of iron is attested widely in folklore. Tacitus describes the druids of Mon in an atmospheric passage in his *Annals* 14, 30. Branwen's 'four-sided' grave is actually Neolithic and is found in Gwyn Jones and Thomas Jones (tr.), *The Mabinogion* (Dent, 1986), p. 38. The *Historia Brittonum* has the hill that turns around three times a year and the stone that walks by night (p. 83). Cybi and Seriol are described by Elissa Henken, *Traditions of the Welsh Saints* (D. S. Brewer, 1987), pp. 235–7. The chapel of the Blessed Virgin stood somewhere in northern Wales and the present author has guessed by placing it on Anglesey: Michael Lapidge, 'The *Vera Historia de Morte Arturi*: A New Edition', *Arthurian Literature*, 1 (1981), pp. 115–41 at p. 138.

(III) Magloconus is described in *Gildas*, pp. 32–4: the make-up of his court, meanwhile, is lifted from the Welsh Laws: Fletcher, *Latin Redaction*, p. 2. The fine horses of Powys are found in *Gerald of Wales*, p. 201. 'The game of the Irish monk' is inspired by a Latin text produced on Mon in the ninth century, edited by J. Loth, 'Un nouveau crypto-gramme', *Annales de Bretagne*, 8 (1892), pp. 289–93. 'They hide wisdom' is a nod at Charles Thomas's work on various Welsh inscriptions, but especially the Catamanus stone and that the interested reader should search out for him- or herself: *Christian Celts: Messages and Images* (Tempus, 2003).

(IV) Cunneda – history or legend? – is found in the *Historia Brittonum*, p. 14. His voyage from the inter-mural regions to northern Wales has been analysed in terms of Roman troop deployment or later Welsh myth-making. A synthetic account of the two Celtic languages at this date is given in Karl Horst Schmidt, 'Insular Celtic P- and Q- Celtic' in *The Celtic Languages*, ed. Martin J. Ball and James Fife (Routledge, 1993), pp. 64–98. The claim that Brittonic and Gaelic were still mutually comprehensible, meanwhile, has been discussed in the notes for the Introduction. *Ogam*, finally, is described in detail in D. McManus, *A Guide to Ogam* (Maynooth Monographs, 1991). It might be noted that almost all surviving *ogam* is found on stone inscriptions and that the scratching of sheep has sometimes been confused for this Irish script.

CHAPTER FOUR

(I) Drowned villages are attested in folklore up and down the Welsh coast; Gwyn Jones and Thomas Jones (tr.), *The Mabinogion* (Dent, 1986), p. 33 describes (a giant) wading across the Irish Sea in an earlier period; the idea of the sea being like a field of flowers is found in Dark Age Irish literature; while countless Irish and Welsh saints are credited with having gone for a stroll on the waves; see for example the year 806 in the *Annals of the Four Masters*. Ireland's lack of poisonous snakes is a fact and it was doubtless from this that its association with antidotes to poison comes; Bede discusses this in his *Ecclesiastical History*, 1, 1. St Mo Domnoc is said to have first brought honey bees to Ireland. Jerome's (short) account of the Attacotti, Irish – or just possibly northern British – warriors who served in the Roman army is found in *Adversus Iouinianum*, 2, 7, conveniently translated in *The Celtic Heroic Age: Literary Sources for Ancient Celtic Europe and Early Ireland and Wales*, ed. John T. Koch and John Carey (Celtic Studies Publications, 2003), p. 49. Palladius was the name of the deacon sent by Rome or proxies in Gaul to convert Ireland in 431. By the seventh century and perhaps already in the sixth some Irish churchmen referred to themselves as 'Roman', contrasting themselves with clergy who followed Irish Christian customs. The Irish belief in Egyptian descent is taken from their tales of origin found in their national history, the *Lebor Gabala*; it has even led to an entertaining (though unscientific) claim that Egyptians really arrived in prehistoric Ireland: Lorraine Evans, *Kingdom of the Ark: The startling story of how the ancient British race* [sic] *is descended from the Pharaohs* (Simon and Schuster, 2000). Irish units of value, for example the *cumal*, are discussed in Fergus Kelly, *Early Irish Farming* (Dublin School of Advanced Studies, 2000), pp. 587–99. For slaves, see T. M. Charles-Edwards, *Early Christian Ireland* (CUP, 2000), pp. 68–9 and Fergus Kelly, *A Guide to Early Irish Law* (Dublin School of Advanced Studies, 1988), pp. 95–7. The danger of Saxon slaves escaping is based on a passage of Bede, *Ecclesiastical History*, 4, 20. The geography of Ireland given in this chapter is not controversial, but some would put the number of *tuath* in Ireland much lower. The importance of Irish law may be exaggerated here; however, it did have many unusual features that set it apart from other European legal traditions (though it remained close to that of Wales). Auxilius – the name of one of St Patrick's companions in the Irish mission fields – is used several times in the following chapters: the experiences that he has related to the anonymous author are taken from St Patrick's *Confessio*. For the *ambue* see Kelly, *A Guide*, pp. 5–6 and the section there on outsiders. Nipple-sucking is referred to first in St Patrick's *Confessio*, 19. It is also attested in ancient Egypt and may have reached Ireland in a very distant epoch: Bernard Maier, 'Sugere mammellas: a Pagan Irish Custom and its Affinities' in *Celtic Connections: Proceedings of the 10th International Congress of Celtic Studies*, ed. Ronald Black (Tuckwell Press, 1999), pp. 152–61.

(II) The *Aes Dana* are described by Kelly, *A Guide*, pp. 39–67; the *briugu* likewise is found on pp. 36–8, as is the information on farters and jugglers, pp. 64–5. The account of Mac Dotha's hall and the fight between two war bands is based on the (eighth-century?) Irish tale *The Story of Mac Dotha's Pig*. However, here a Connaught war band has been replaced with a war band from Leinster.

(III) The relations between lord and client are found in Thomas Charles-Edwards, *Early Christian Ireland*, pp. 68–90; in reality, even clients had some cows of their own. The description of Kildare is based very loosely on the passage closing Cogitosus's *Life of Brigit*. The idea that Brigit had taken on aspects of an earlier pagan goddess, Brig, is widely canvassed; for example, Kim McCone, *Pagan Past and Christian Present* (Maynooth Monographs, 1992), pp. 161–2. The sex-change tale is medieval and was clearly written to explain a relationship between Drimnagh and its ecclesiastical neighbours. Finally, the passage describing the stench of bodies in a church was inspired by the opening of Michael Lapidge, 'The Saintly Life in Anglo-Saxon England'. in *The Cambridge Companion to Old English Literature*, ed. Malcolm Godden and Michael Lapidge (CUP, 1991), pp. 243–63.

CHAPTER FIVE

(I) Marriage and divorce in Ireland is covered by Fergus Kelly, *A Guide to Early Irish Law* (Dublin Institute for Advanced Studies, 1988), pp. 70–73. Cashel is described in T. M. Charles-Edwards, *Early Christian Ireland* (CUP, 2000), p. 146 and the Eoganachta, pp. 534–7, in the same work. Irish druids are described by Stuart Piggott, *The Druids* (Thames and Hudson, 1968), p. 45 and pp. 99–100; their ability to fly is suggested in a seventh-century Irish text, for which Marina Smyth, 'The Earliest Written Evidence for an Irish View of the World', *Cultural Identity and Cultural Integration: Ireland and Europe in the Early Middle Ages*, ed. Doris Edel (Four Courts Press, 1995), pp. 23–44 at p. 37. The last druids probably died out in the seventh century, though they could conceivably have survived to a later date. Skellig Michael, off the Kerry coast, was occupied in the early Middle Ages; however, our first evidence of the penitent's way is late.

(II) For the mythical geography of Ireland see Alwyn and Brinley Rees, *Celtic Heritage: Ancient Tradition in Ireland and Wales* (Thames and Hudson, 1961), pp. 118–39. The log entry is based on *Gerald of Wales: The History and Topography of Ireland*, tr. John O'Meara (Penguin, 1951), p. 110, an account that relates to kingship rituals not in Tara, but in a minor kingdom of the north in the twelfth century. Some have disputed this account as being Norman propaganda, but others have seen in it an ancient kingship ceremony preserving archaic Indo-European features. The kingship of Tara, meanwhile, is discussed in historical terms in Charles-Edwards, *Early Christian Ireland*, pp. 469–521 and in mythological terms in Rees, *Celtic Heritage*, pp. 146–72. The idea of marriage with sovereignty or the spirit of the land was certainly present in early medieval Ireland; and the chariot grating against the stone penis should probably be seen in this light. Ailill Molt was an early king of Tara whom the annals date towards the end of the fifth century. For *geis* see T. M. Charles-Edwards, 'Geis, Prophecy, omen, and oath', *Celtica*, 23 (1999), pp. 38–59. The claim that the western churches did not take bestiality as seriously as other sex crimes is suggested by some early penitentials: Ludwig Bieler, *The Irish Penitentials* (Dublin, 1975), pp. 112–15.

(III) Cruachain and the Ciarraigie nAi are described by Charles-Edwards in *Early Christian Ireland*, pp. 39–40; the *oenach* being found in the same work at pp. 556–9. The two legal cases mentioned are based on accounts in Fergus Kelly, *Early Irish Farming* (Dublin School of Advanced Studies, 2000), pp. 120–21 (dogs) and p. 180 (pigs). A description of Irish fasting is found in Daniel Binchy, 'A pre-Christian survival in mediaeval Irish hagiography' in *Ireland in Early Mediaeval Europe*, ed. D. Whitelock et al. (CUP, 1982), pp. 165–78. The game of the faminators is based on duelling rhymes found in M. Herren, *Hisperica Famina I: The A-Text* (PIMS, 1974): the passages included are written in the hisperic style though invented. The Fenians are described in Kim McCone, 'Werewolves, Cyclopes, Díberga, and Fíanna: Juvenile Delinquency in Early Ireland', *Cambridge Medieval Celtic Studies*, 12 (1986), pp. 1–22.

(IV) Clonmacnois and its traditions of wonders, especially the floating ships, are described in an article by John Carey, 'Aerial Ships and Underwater Monasteries: the Evolution of a Monastic Marvel', *Proceedings of the Harvard Celtic Colloquium*, 12 (1995), pp. 16–28. The locust as a flying mole is taken from the Welsh annals, David E. Thornton, 'Locusts in Ireland? A Problem in the Welsh and Frankish Annals', *Cambrian Medieval Celtic Studies*, 31 (1996), pp. 37–53 at p. 38. The astronomical achievements of early Irish monks, meanwhile, are found in Daniel McCarthy and Aidan Breen, 'Astronomical observations in the Irish Annals and their Motivations', *Peritia*, 11 (1997), pp. 1–43. The *aurora borealis* really was described as flying dragons in early medieval Ireland.

CHAPTER SIX

(I) The Dal Riadans were an Ulster people based in north Antrim, who set up colonies in northern Britain. They at no time referred to themselves as an empire: this is rather the perception of the Greeks faced with a series of territories stretching (unusually) across the two islands. In fact, in their homelands the Dal Riada were a minor people and their share of the high-kingship of Ulster was actually fairly infrequent. It is speculation to say that the Attacotti came from Ulster, though that people was very probably Gaelic: see the notes for Chapter Four for references. The claim of descent from a man-dog is a reference to the Irish hero Cu Chulainn, who, in fact, was an ancestor of the Cruthni, the neighbours of the Dal Riada. The numbers of the Dal Riadan army are loosely based on an early Irish text, the *Senchus fer n-Alban* found in J. Bannerman, *Studies in the History of Dal Riada* (Scottish Academic Press, 1974); the colonies in northern Britain may actually have provided as many as 2,000 warriors. Ample background and bibliography to St Patrick and Armagh can be found in David N. Dumville et al., *Saint Patrick: AD 493–1993* (Boydell Press, 1993); the text of St Patrick's *Confessio*, where the saint outlines his life story, appears in many editions including A. B. E. Hood, *St Patrick: His Writings and Muirchu's Life* (Phillimore, 1978). The vision of Christ on the cross is implied by *Confessio*, 20; Patrick's fast against God is found in *The Tripartite Life of St Patrick and other Documents relating to that Saint* (1887, 2 vols), I, pp. 112–20 – this is legendary and is unlikely to relate to events in Patrick's life; the idea that Patrick was the last of the prophets, meanwhile, is to be found at several points in the *Confessio* and certainly reflects Patrick's own perception of events. Armagh's 'forgery' was actually a technique undertaken by many different Irish churches in this period to justify ownership such that early Irish saints' lives have been called 'title-deed boxes'. The early Irish annals have several references to monastic houses meeting each other in war. For the malefic psalms see Dan M. Wiley, 'The Maledictory Psalms', *Peritia*, 15 (2001), pp. 261–79.

(II) The wars for Man in the sixth century are noted laconically in the *Annals of Ulster*, 577 and 578; the expedition to Orkney is recorded in the same for 580. Dal Riadan dominance in these two regions did not last long, if it were, in fact, ever established. Early records – Bede, Orosius, inscribed stones – give us conflicting reports about whether Man was populated by the British Celts, the Irish or both. For this reason I have chosen to talk of a hybrid language. The fairies of Man are documented in W. Y. Evans Wentz, *The Fairy Faith in Celtic Countries* (Humanities Press, 1977: reprint). The idea of pilgrims going to the White House ('the Luminous House') in Galloway may be suggested by an unusual collection of graffiti at Maughold: R. A. S. Macalister, *Corpus Inscriptionum Insularum Celticarum* (Gov't Print, 1949), II, p. 191. The tale of Maccuil is found in Murchiu's *Life of St Patrick*, Hood, *St Patrick*, pp. 72–4.

(III) For Dunadd see now *Dunadd: An early Dalriadic Capital*, Alan Lane and Ewan Campbell (Oxbow, 2001). The various episodes relating to life on Iona are found in Adomnan's *Life of St Columba:* Naples 1, 28; the ivory sword 2, 39; the exhausted crane 1, 48. Examples of Colum Cille's 'second sight', meanwhile, are found throughout this book. The simplest translation to procure (with an excellent introduction) is that of Richard Sharpe (Penguin, 1995). Animals serving saints are taken from the corpus of medieval Irish saints' lives: St Ciaran had a stag as his bookstand, while the bluebottle bookmark was of St Mochua. Colum Cille's scars are ascribed to an angel having beaten him. However, Alfred Smyth, *Warlords and Holy Men: AD 80–1000* (EUP, 1984), pp. 97–8 suggests that this was a later legend created to explain away an embarrassing proof of earlier martial endeavour: the hypothesis cannot be proved but is pleasing.

CHAPTER SEVEN

(I) This chapter is largely concerned with the hints that the inhabitants of Britain and Ireland knew of lands beyond them in the northern seas. In the course of the early Middle Ages we can be quite certain that visits were made to the Shetlands, Faeroes and Iceland. However, any contact with Greenland, North America or even more daringly the Caribbean is unproven and speculative – certainly none of these entered the geographical traditions of the early Irish. The customs of the 'desert seekers' are discussed in a recent collection of essays, Jonathon Wooding ed., *The Otherworld Voyage in Early Irish Literature* (Four Courts Press, 2004). For other details: the legend of the whale appears in the *Voyage of St Brendan* (an early Irish text describing the miraculous travels of St Brendan in the ocean); the Irish off the coast of Africa is a reference to St Alba, who is found by St Brendan on an island sometimes identified with the Canaries or Madeiras; Cormac and the beasts appear in Adomnan's *Life of St Columba*, 2, 42. The various data on early exploration of the northern Atlantic is most enjoyably set out in a volume edited by Geoffrey Ashe, *The Quest for America* (Praeger Publishers, 1971) where volcanoes, Eskimos, Chronos (pp. 19–20), coral seas and icebergs are all looked at in detail. The reference to the midnight sun appears in J. J. Tierney and L. Bieler (eds), *Dicuil: Liber de Mensura Orbis Terrae* (Scriptores Latini Hiberniae, 1967), pp. 74–5.

(II) 'Pict' as a swear word is found in St Patrick's *Epistola*, 2, 12 and 15. Note *Scotti* (Irish raiders) in these passages are equally offensive. *Gildas: The Ruin of Britain*, ed. and tr. Michael Winterbottom (Phillimore, 1978) describes the Picts attacking Romans – the reference is actually to citizens (*cives*) – on the wall (p. 23); and it is Gildas who provides the image of Picts as worms coming out in the sun (p. 23), a reference to their raiding once the weather clears up in the spring and a compliment that he also extends to the Irish. The reference to the Orkney Islanders submitting prematurely to Claudius is found in Eutropius, see Sheppard Frere, *Britannia. A History of Roman Britain* (BCA, 1967), p. 66. Columba sends a messenger north to save Cormac in *Life of St Columba*, 2, 42. The nature of the Pictish language is a debated point; I favour Kenneth Jackson's view that there were two Pictish tongues, one Celtic and one pre-Indo-European, 'The Pictish Language', *The Problem of the Picts*, ed. F. T. Wainwright (Nelson, 1955), pp. 129–66. But these are very uncertain matters. For descriptions of archaeological finds on Orkney in this period see Jane Downes and Anna Ritchie (eds), *Sea Change: Orkney and Northern Europe in the Later Iron Age, AD 300–800* (Pinkfoot Press, 2003). Brochs are described in Ian Armit, *Towers in the North: The Brochs of Scotland* (Tempus, 2003). Most were built deep in prehistory, but some were still being used in the early Middle Ages. The 'underground siesta stations' that archaeologists term souterrains is a nod at a late Viking text that records 'the Picts barely exceeded pigmies in stature. They did marvels, in the morning and in the evening, in building strongholds, but at noon they entirely lost all their strength, and lurked through fear in little underground houses.' This was written long after the Pictish civilisation had been destroyed and we see here the later Norse inhabitants of the Orkneys coming to their own conclusions about the curious sub-terranean chambers that they had found.

CHAPTER EIGHT

(I) The account of the 'Loch Ness monster' found here is taken, as I hint in a footnote on that page, from Adomnán's *Life of St Columba*, 2, 27; the body of water being described seems, though, to be the River Ness rather than the loch proper. The original miracle worker was Columba, who in this version is changed into 'a Gaelic priest, one of Columba's men'. The 'monster' rule that posits the predominance of water beasts in the north and Ireland and land beasts in the south of Britain was formulated, many years ago, by the Irish scholar James Carney; our sources bear him out.

(II) The name Alba and the Albans is a controversial one for which see D. Broun, 'The origin of Scottish identity' in *Nations, Nationalism and Patriotism in the European Past*, ed. C. Bjorn and A. Grant and K. J. Stringer (Copenhagen, Academic Press, 1994), pp. 35–55. Matrilineal descent among the Picts is also controversial and is based – largely – on a passage in Bede's *Ecclesiastical History*, 1, 1 that says the Picts sometimes used female descent for royal heirs. Some claim that this system never, in fact, existed; and, even if it did, the claim that women would have had more power under this system is highly debatable. *Pett* seems to have been a Pictish word to describe a unit of land and survives in several modern place names in north-east Scotland: Pitlochry, Pittenweem etc. Kenneth Jackson usefully sets these out on a map in 'The Pictish Language', *The Problem of the Picts*, ed. F. T. Wainwright (Nelson, 1955), pp. 129–66 at p. 147. It has even been suggested that the word Pict may mean 'the people of the Pett', though most prefer 'the painted ones'. Burghead, the Fortress of the Bulls, as I have called it for its cult associations, is described in Anna Ritchie, *Picts: An introduction to the life of the Picts and the carved stones in the care of the secretary of state for Scotland* (HMSO, 1989), pp. 12–15. The phrase 'milking a bull' is inspired by Adomnan's *Life of St Columba*, 2, 17. The drowning room is consistent with Pictish customs and suggested by Ritchie. The cave of the beheadings was inspired, instead, by descriptions of Covesea, for which Lloyd and Jenny Laing, *The Picts and the Scots* (Alan Sutton, 1993), pp. 107–8.

(III) Aberlemno, the most important centre of Pictish 'hieroglyph stones' or, as they are known to modern historians, 'symbol stones', is described in Ritchie, *Picts*, pp. 22–7. The symbols themselves have never been satisfactorily decoded. However, for this book I leant – very slightly – on W. A. Cummins, *The Picts and their Symbols* (Sutton, 1999), a work that does, though, present problems.

(IV) The description of Pictish warriors is taken from various symbol stones such as will be found in Laing, *The Picts and the Scots*. For the silver discs see ibid., p. 117 and for the silver necklaces see Ritchie, *Picts*, p. 7. St Andrews is unlikely to have been built as early as the sixth century, but the connection between Andrew and Asia (Scythia) is a valuable one, made by Ursula Hall, *St Andrew and Scotland* (University of St Andrews, 1994). The final section on converting the Picts is based on Ian Wood, *The Missionary Life: Saints and Evangelisation of Europe 400–1050* (Longman, 2001). Note though that the examples are drawn from similar pagan communities across Europe, not from the conversion of the Picts, about which we actually know very little.

CHAPTER NINE

(I) The two walls were both built in the second century, though, in fact, Antonine's Wall was quickly abandoned. Hadrian's Wall seems to have been abandoned at the end of Roman rule, but was then reoccupied – 'the half-hearted attempts' described here – in the fifth century by a British-Celtic successor government – Ken Dark, 'A Sub-Roman Re-Defence of Hadrian's Wall?', *Britannia*, 23 (1992), pp. 111–20. Estimates for the number of soldiers on the walls are, of course, approximate; in fact, Hadrian's Wall when first built may have had even more. The *Pictae* ships are to be found in Vegetius, *De Re Militari*, 4, 37. The shore forts are described in Andrew Pearson, *The Roman Shore Forts: Coastal Defences of Southern Britain* (Tempus, 2002). The shore forts are to be found on the southern coasts, but some signal stations were found on the north coast. The Syrians on the Tyne (at South Shields) are described in D. C. A. Shotter, 'Numeri Barcariorum: A Note on *RIB* 601', *Britannia*, 4 (1973), pp. 206–10. Arthur and his oven are found in K. A. Steer, 'Arthur's O'on: A Lost Shrine of Roman Britain', *Archaeological Journal*, 115 (1958), pp. 99–110. The theatre in the Roman style relates to Yeavering, Christopher Snyder, *Sub Roman Britain (AD 400–600)* (BAR British Series 247, 1996), p. 51.

(II) The Rock of the Clyde is described ibid., pp. 46–7. Gildas is said to have been born in the territory of the Damnonii near Strathclyde: Hugh Williams (tr.), *Two Lives of Gildas by a monk of Ruys and Caradoc of Llancarfan* (Llanerch, 1990: reprint) – an uncertain tradition. Gildas's love poems do not survive – they may be nothing more than a ghost in a library catalogue – see A. Smith, 'Gildas the Poet', *Arthurian Literature*, 10 (1990), pp. 1–11. Gildas's views on penitential matters are found in *Gildas: The Ruin of Britain*, ed. and tr. Michael Winterbottom (Phillimore, 1978), pp. 84–6. The insults that Gildas uses for the Saxons are lifted from the anti-English prophetic poem *Armes Prydein*, ed. Ifor Williams (Dublin Institute for Advanced Studies, 1982).

(III) The Gododdin and the description of their defeat at Catraeth is based on the surviving text of the poem of the same name, A. O. H. Jarman, *Aneirin: The Gododdin, Britain's Oldest Heroic Poem* (Gomer Press, 1990). This remains one of the most controversial Dark Age texts; some date it to the sixth century contemporary with the battle, others to later, perhaps as late as the ninth century. The description of British cavalry tactics owes a good deal to Jenny Rowland, 'Warfare and Horses in the Gododdin and the Problem of Catraeth', *Cambrian Medieval Celtic Studies*, 30 (1995), pp. 13–40 at pp. 27–8. There is (late) Gaelic material for composing poems in the dark, see Patrick K. Ford, *Ystoria Taliesin* (University of Wales Press, 1992), pp. 15–16, and several verses in *The Gododdin* that may describe Aneirin's imprisonment can also be read as the poet left underground to prepare his masterpiece. The cowardly members of the Gododdin are based on Bede, *Ecclesiastical History*, 2, 2 where a British-Celtic noble, Brocmail, fled from the battlefield and into eternal disgrace.

CHAPTER TEN

(I) The mongrel nature of the Saxons is the reason we commonly, when referring to the invasion period, refer to 'Angles, Saxons and Jutes' though, in fact, there were even more peoples involved. An excellent introduction – concentrating on the archaeological evidence – is Catherine Hills', *Origins of the English* (Duckworth, 2003). The Aquitanian

writer Sidonius Apollinaris, *Epistolas*, 8, 6, describes the Saxons cruci-
fying captives before returning home with their booty; it is not impossible that these were Saxons operating out of the south of Britain. The
account of the siege of Lindisfarne is to be found in *Historia Brittonum,
Nennius: British History and the Welsh Annals*, ed. John Morris
(Phillimore, 1989) p. 79. This incident may be legendary.

(II) Blowing on horns is found in Ine's Lawcode, translated in
The Laws of the Earliest English Kings, ed. F. L. Attenborough
(Llanerch, 2000: reprint), p. 43, while the wayside springs are found
in Bede's *Ecclesiastical History*, 2, 16. The chasing-out of the older
British-Celtic population with swords and spears is an echo of *The
Life of Bishop Wilfrid by Eddius Stephanus*, ed. and tr. Bertram
Colgrave (CUP, 1927), Chapter 17. The word *wealh*, meaning both
British Celt and slave, is discussed in A. E. David Pelteret, *Slavery in
early Medieval England* (Woodbridge, 1995) and in M. L. Faull, 'The
Semantic Development of Old English *wealh*', *Leeds Studies in English*,
new ser., 8 (1975), pp. 20–44; and K. Cameron, 'The Meaning and
Significance of Old English Wealh in English Place-Names', *Journal
of English Place Names*, 12 (1979–1980), pp. 1–53. It should be noted
that Wealh place-names, of which there are many in modern England,
are frequently associated with eccles place-names, see the notes to
Chapter Fifteen. The mysterious kingdom of Elmet did, in the south
Pennines, survive the fall of its British-Celtic neighbours and it is
described by Bede, the *Ecclesiastical History*, 4, 23; its final extinction
came in the early seventh century. The poems of Taliesin describe
the fallen court of Urien of Reget, a kingdom that has never been
satisfactorily placed on the map, Ifor Williams (ed.), *The Poems of
Taliesin* (University of Wales Press, 1987). The description of Carlisle
is based on a passage in the *Vita Sancti Cuthberti*, Chapter 4; see also
Christopher Snyder, *Sub Roman Britain (AD 400–600)* (BAR British
Series 247, 1996), pp. 45–6.

(III) Goodmunddingham is found in Bede's *Ecclesiastical History*,
2, 13. For various pagan customs described here see David Wilson,
Anglo-Saxon Paganism (Routledge, 1992), especially pp. 35–6 (months).
See also John D. Niles, 'Pagan survivals and popular belief', *The Cam-
bridge Companion to Old English Literature*, ed. Malcolm Godden and
Michael Lapidge (CUP, 1991), pp. 126–41. For Anglo-Saxon food see

Peter Fowler, *Farming in the First Millennium AD: British Agriculture between Julius Caesar and William the Conqueror* (CUP, 2002), p. 251. The *scop* depends on the essay by Lewis Flint Anderson, *The Anglo-Saxon Scop* (University of Toronto, 1973). The passage on wisdom was quarried from Paul Cavill, *Maxims in Old English Poetry* (D. S. Brewer, 1999), while the final speech of the high priest is an adaptation of Bede, *Ecclesiastical History*, 4, 23 with a bit of Peig Sayers mixed in.

CHAPTER ELEVEN

(I) The material for this section is taken overwhelmingly from Gail Drinkall and Martin Foreman, *The Anglo-Saxon Cemetery at Castledyke South, Barton-on-Humber* (1998), and their analysis of skeletal remains and grave goods there; note especially demography (p. 222), squatting facets – the proof that Anglo-Saxon workers squatted often (p. 227), dental health (p. 235), trepanation (p. 236), birds placed with bodies (pp. 238–9, p. 358), veils (p. 270), hippopotamus tusk (p. 272), women's clothes generally (p. 272, and pp. 276–9), suspended objects and amulets (pp. 286–7, 290–91), contacts with the Rhine e.g. (p. 311), branches in graves (p. 361). Castledyke has been taken here as a standard Saxon village and information from various other books has been added including Gale R. Owen-Crocker, *Dress in Anglo-Saxon England* (MUP, 1985); Sam Lucy, *The Anglo-Saxon Way of Death* (Sutton, 2000); and David Wilson, *Anglo-Saxon Paganism* (Routledge, 1992). The role of Anglo-Saxon women in law is found in A. L. Klinck, 'Anglo-Saxon Women and the Law', *Journal of Medieval History*, 8 (1982), pp. 107–21 and M. A. Meyer, 'Land Charters and the Legal Position of Anglo-Saxon Women', *The Women of England*, ed. B. Kanner (Hamden, 1980), pp. 57–82. The description of the Anglo-Saxon language is speculative. Our earliest written versions of the tongue show surprising uniformity, with only fairly small differences of dialect. However, the many tribes involved in the migration might point to an early period of linguistic chaos. For more see Orrin W. Robinson, *Old English and its Closest Relatives: A Survey of the Early Germanic Languages* (Routledge, 1992). The reference to the bishop of York is invented, but it is the kind of detail that we would expect if there was continuity between British-Celtic and Saxon communities, as many archaeologists and historians suggest. The political affiliations of the village have not been touched on here. They are generally believed to have been with Lindsey, covered in section three of this chapter.

(II) Nicholas Brooks, 'The Formation of the Mercian Kingdom' in *The Origins of Anglo-Saxon Kingdoms* (Leicester University Press, 1989), pp. 159–70 for Mercia. The border on the river or the fight at the ford with the English is attested in British-Celtic poetry, Jenny Rowland, *Early Welsh Saga Poetry* (D. S. Brewer, 1990), pp. 468–76. An early medieval text on customs of the border between the Anglo-Saxons and the British Celts is published by Frank Noble, *Offa's Dyke Reviewed* (BAR, 1983), pp. 104–9. A useful bibliography for work on Wroxeter is Christopher Snyder, *Sub Roman Britain (AD 400–600)* (BAR British Series 247, 1996), pp. 43–4, but see also now Roger White, 'Wroxeter and the transformation of the late-Roman urbanism', *Towns in Decline AD 100–1600*, ed. T. P. Slater (Ashgate, 2000), pp. 96–119. The word *cumbrogi* is sometimes interpreted as 'fellow citizen'; the present interpretation depends, instead, upon Thomas Charles-Edwards, 'Language and Society among the Insular Celts', *The Celtic World*, ed. Miranda Green (Routledge, 1995), pp. 703–36 at pp. 710–16. A terrible plague seems to have swept through Ireland and Britain in the mid-sixth century, as well as one in the fifth century: Clare Stancliffe, 'The thirteen sermons attributed to Columbanus and the question of their authorship', *Columbanus: Studies on the Latin Writing*, ed. Michael Lapidge (Boydell, 1997), pp. 93–202 at pp. 180–81; and also for a later bout of plague in the islands, J. R. Maddicott, 'Plague in Seventh-Century England', *Past and Present* 156 (1997), pp. 7–54.

(III) The idea of an 'island' of Lincolnshire is a possibility, but is controversial. Details on the archaeology of Lincoln itself and the surrounding area can be found in Snyder, *Sub Roman Britain*, pp. 48–9. Shared pottery is discussed in Ken Dark, 'Pottery and Local Production at the end of Roman Britain', *External Contacts and the Economy of Late Roman Britain and Post-Roman Britain* (Boydell, 1996), pp. 53–66 at pp. 58–9. The idea that Anglo-Saxons and British Celts got on unusually well in Lincolnshire is often suggested in the secondary literature. Riddling is well attested among the Anglo-Saxons: all the riddles are mauled and curtailed adaptations of surviving examples. One easily available collection is John Porter, *Anglo-Saxon Riddles*

(Anglo-Saxon Books, 1995), see especially p. 17 (the shield), p. 37 (the onion) and p. 62 (the key).

CHAPTER TWELVE

(I) The Fens are covered briefly in David Hill, *An Atlas of Anglo-Saxon England* (Blackwell, 1981), pp. 11–13. Hallucinogenic rye is a modern guess based on Bertram Colgrave (tr. and ed.), *Felix's Life of Saint Guthlac* (CUP, 1956), pp. 86–9; Guthlac lived in the fens and had many visions and it has been suggested that these visions depended on fungi that grew in his over-damp bread. British Celts surviving in the Fens are found in the same work, pp. 108–11. (These devilish Britons, however, are sometimes said to be simple visions.) The *thyrs* are a race of goblins feared by the Anglo-Saxons and the fen-dwelling Grendel in the poem *Beowulf* is at one point described as being a *thyrs*. A description of some mythical Anglo-Saxon creatures can be found in John D. Niles, 'Pagan survivals and popular belief' in *The Cambridge Companion to Old English Literature*, ed. Malcolm Godden and Michael Lapidge (1991), pp. 126–41.

(II) The phrase 'shoot the arrow first' is invented in the style of the Anglo-Saxon adages quoted previously. The Swedish connections of the East Anglian dynasty have been set out in many places, but see especially John Hines, 'The Scandinavian Character of Anglian England: an update' in Martin Carver (ed.), *The Age of Sutton Hoo* (Boydell, 1992), pp. 315–29. The connections with the Beowulf legend are set out in Sam Newton, *The Origins of Beowulf and the Pre-Viking Kingdom of East Anglia* (D. S. Brewer, 1993), see especially pp. 143–4 for the Shuck; though these remain controversial. The house described is the *grubenhaus* of archaeologists: see Martin Welch, *Anglo-Saxon England* (BCA, 1992), pp. 21–3. There is much doubt as to how exactly these were built; here I have followed the plank-floor solution. Another possibility is that the family actually stepped down into their quarters. The composition of a typical Anglo-Saxon warrior band is found in John Hines, 'The Military Context of the adventus Saxonum: some Continental Evidence' in *Weapons and Warfare in Anglo-Saxon England*, ed. Sonia Chadwick Hawkes (Oxbow, 1989), pp. 25–48; and Stephen Pollington, *The English Warrior from Earliest Times till 1066*

(Anglo-Saxon Books, 2002). The ritual deposition of weapons in bogs is found in the Anglo-Saxons' homeland but has not so far been evinced in Britain: an accident of archaeology or did the custom fail to cross the Channel with them? The military tactics of the East Anglians, refusing to retreat from a downed lord, are those suggested by such poems as *The Battle of Maldon* and are paralleled elsewhere in the barbarian world.

(III) Sutton Hoo is examined from many different perspectives in Carver, *The Age of Sutton Hoo*. 'Bretwalda' is a controversial word found in Bede's *Ecclesiastical History*, 2, 5: the real meaning of this 'office', if that is not too strong a word, is unknown, but it seems to have depended on hegemony among the Anglo-Saxons. The long description of a boat burial is taken from a Germanic ship burial in what is today Russia that seems, in many ways, similar to that which we glimpse archaeologically at Sutton Hoo; the text itself can conveniently be read in G. N. Garmonsway and J. Simpson, *Beowulf and its Analogues* (Dent, 1968), pp. 341–5. Cremation customs are set out in Sam Lucy, *The Anglo-Saxon Way of Death* (Sutton, 2000), pp. 104–22.

(IV) For Colchester there is Christopher Snyder, *Sub Roman Britain (AD 400–600)* (BAR British Series, 247 (1996), pp. 15–16, including a description of the attack on the city that depends on the problematic findings of Victorian archaeology. (The dislike of Roman cities is well attested among the barbarian peoples.) The curious fact that the genealogies of the East Angles have Caesar in them has never been satisfactorily explained – a British-Celtic substratum? The reference to Julius as a name among the East Angles is, anyway, a playful nod to this fact.

CHAPTER THIRTEEN

(I) The story of the end of Roman Britain has been set out many times. See, for example, Christopher A. Snyder, *An Age of Tyrants: Britain and the Britons AD 400–600* (Sutton, 1998), pp. 17–25. The most controversial issue is that of whether Britain unilaterally declared independence or whether the decision was, as is suggested here, a decision of the Roman government. *Gildas: The Ruin of Britain*, ed. and tr. Michael Winterbottom (Phillimore, 1978), p. 27. The idea of enclaves in the south-east is debatable; this passage depends upon some very important research in Ken Dark, *Britain and the End of the Roman Empire* (Tempus, 2000), pp. 97–103. It should be noted that this remains highly controversial and the case for the eastern enclaves is based on suggestive, but nevertheless negative, evidence – essentially the striking lack of Anglo-Saxon archaeological remains from these areas. For Londinium see Christopher Snyder, *Sub Roman Britain (AD 400–600)* (BAR British Series 247, 1996), pp. 16–17. Bonus is the only British-Celtic poet from Roman times whose name has come down to us – though none of his work survives. The tavern next to the temple of Isis is mentioned in John Morris, *Londinium: London in the Roman Empire* (Phoenix, 1999), p. 233 while the southern side of the river is generally thought to have been wilder, standing outside official control. The origins of the marble of Roman London are conveniently set out in Barri Jones and David Mattingly, *An Atlas of Roman Britain* (Oxbow, 1990), p. 220. London Cathedral is discussed briefly in Ken Dark, *Britain*, p. 51 The hexameter, which probably dates from the mid- or late fifth century, is found not in an inscription but in *Gildas*, pp. 23–4. The idea of a senate, as opposed to kings or tyrants, for the enclaves is taken from Dark, *Britain*, pp. 144–9 – it is intriguing but not demonstrable. The gifts of the council include the famous *Vergilius Romanus* manuscript that is sometimes said to be British-Celtic. The Germanic warriors protecting British-Celtic London – an old idea revived by Dark, ibid., p. 100.

(II) The shrine of Alban is detailed in Rosalind Niblett, *Verulamium: The Roman City of St Albans* (Tempus, 2001), pp. 136–40. The waterworks, ibid., pp. 132–3. The repaired crockery takes up and localises a theme touched upon by Dark, *Britain*, p. 135. Calleva Atrebatum is described in Snyder, *Sub Roman Britain*, pp. 41–2; Circencester, ibid., pp. 39–40; Bath, ibid., p. 19 – it is questionable whether curse stones were still being made this late, though there is some evidence that Christians also wrote out their hates; Glastonbury, ibid., pp. 23–4. Oxford as holy centre is found in John T. Koch, 'A Welsh Window on the Iron Age: Manawydan, Mandubracios', *Cambridge Medieval Celtic Studies*, 14 (1987), pp. 17–52 at pp. 47–9.

(III) South Cadbury is described in Snyder, *Sub Roman Britain*, pp. 27–8. The poem of Geraint is translated in John T. Koch and John

Carey, *The Celtic Heroic Age: Literary Sources for Ancient Celtic Europe and Early Ireland and Wales* (Celtic Studies Publications, 2003), p. 308. The archaeologist Ian Burrows estimated that a minimum of 870 warriors would have been needed to defend the ramparts there.

CHAPTER FOURTEEN

(I) Kent seems to have become the dominant kingdom among the Saxons in the second half of the sixth century. At this time it was certainly capable of arranging diplomacy with the British Celts at a distance as, for example, see the Conference of Augustine's Oak, Bede, *Ecclesiastical History*, 2, 2. For ancient Winchester see Christopher Snyder, *Sub Roman Britain (AD 400–600)* (BAR British Series 247, 1996), p. 30. For the villas in south-central and south-western Britain see Keith Branigan, *The Roman Villa in South-West England* (Moonraker, 1976). For famines and scavenging food see Ann Hagen, *A First Handbook of Anglo-Saxon Food and Drink: Production and Distribution* (Anglo-Saxon Books, 1994), pp. 101–10, whereas the description of cliff-jumpers is found in Bede, *Ecclesiastical History*, 4, 13. On roads see the article of F. M. Stenton, 'The Road System of Medieval England', in *Preparatory to Anglo-Saxon England, being the Collected Papers of Frank Merry Stenton*, ed. D. M. Stenton (Clarendon Press, 1970), pp. 234–52 which refers though, predominantly, to a later date. The description of punishments for those who leave the highways refer to the laws of ancient Wessex, *The Laws of the Earliest English Kings*, ed. F. L. Attenborough (Llanerch, 2000: reprint), p. 41, p. 43 and p. 49. The raped girl is based on the (controversial) examination of a dead body found in Worthy Park, Hampshire; for an overview see Sam Lucy, *The Anglo-Saxon Way of Death* (Sutton, 2000), pp. 70–72.

(II) Portchester is described in Snyder, *Sub Roman Britain*, p. 17. The description of Frisians is based on Dirk Jellema, 'Frisian Trade in the Dark Ages', *Speculum*, 30 (1955), pp. 15–35. The final section on alcohol is based on an excellent chapter in Ann Hagen, *A Second Handbook of Anglo-Saxon Food and Drink: Processing and Consumption* (Anglo-Saxon Books, 1995), pp. 204–50, though with more scepticism as to the quantity and quality of wine grapes in Britain.

(III) The legend of Horsa and Hengist is set out in Bede, *Eccle-*

siastical History, 1, 15. Snyder, *Sub Roman Britain*, describes Canterbury, p. 14. The domination of Franks in the sixth century has been set out in many articles by Ian Wood. See, for example, his 'Frankish Hegemony in England', *The Age of Sutton Hoo*, ed. Martin Carver, (Boydell, 1992), pp. 235–42. It remains, however, controversial. There was certainly a Frankish bishop in the royal court of Kent in the later sixth century, Bede, *Ecclesiastical History*, 1, 25. The nod to a Roman mission looks forward to Augustine's mission at the very end of the sixth century, planned by Pope Gregory the Great: outlined in book one and two of Bede, *The Ecclesiastical History* – it was an enormous success. A description of *eccles* settlements can be found in 'Eccles in English Place Names', *Christianity in Britain 300–700*, M. W. Barley and R. P. C. Hanson (Leicester University Press, 1968); however, recent doubts have also been expressed for the etymology for this word. The phrase where the Kentish king refuses Christianity is based on comparative Germanic material on fears of losing contact with ancestors in the afterlife. The arguments about the genealogy of the gods, meanwhile, is adapted from Bishop Daniel of Winchester's letter to Boniface in the eighth century: *Epistola* 23.

(IV) The incredible story of souls arriving in Britain is found in Procopius's *History of the Wars*, 8, 20. It is discussed by E. A. Thompson in 'Procopius on Brittia and Brittania', *Classical Quarterly*, 20 (1980), pp. 498–507. The legends of the massacre on Thanet are set out in the *Historia Brittonum*, see *Nennius: British History and the Welsh Annals*, ed. John Morris (Phillimore, 1989), pp. 68–9. The stone of Horsa is found in Bede, *Ecclesiastical History*, 1, 15 'in eastern parts of Kent'. The court case is based on the conventions found in ancient Kentish law: Attenborough (ed.), *The Laws of the Earliest English Kings*, pp. 4–17.

(V) For grinding querns, often volcanic in origin, see Martin Welch, *Anglo-Saxon England* (BCA, 1992) p. 108. A recent description of the settlement of Brittany in English is Pierre-Roland Giot, Philippe Guigon and Bernard Merdrignac, *The British Settlement of Brittany: the First Bretons in Armorica* (Tempus, 2003).

GLOSSARY

The reader will find here a list of the non-modern place names used in this work as well as a selection of relevant Dark Age vocabulary coming from Old Welsh, Old Irish, Anglo-Saxon and Pictish. I have tended to anglicise plurals, except in Latin where an English form would grate. Also it should be noted that the following list can make no claim to being consistently reconstructed 'sixth-century' forms. They are, in fact, a pot-pourri of names and terms taken from across the early Middle Ages.

Aberfrau: Aberffraw on the southern coast of Anglesey, ancient 'head court' of Gwynedd.

Aberlemno: hill-top site in Angus with numerous Pictish symbol stones.

Aes Dana: 'the People of the Craft', Irish term for those who belong to professions depending on skill and knowledge including smith, poet and lawyer.

Alau: the River Alaw, a river in northern Anglesey.

Albani: Pictish word for the Picts.

Alltud: 'foreigner' or 'outsider' in Middle Welsh.

Ambue: Irish, a 'non-person' or 'an outsider'.

Ard Macha: Armagh in County Armagh.

Armorica: the Latin name for the region of Gaul that included the area that is today Brittany.

Attacotti: a mysterious people that served in the Roman army and that came either from among the Picts or the Gaels.

Barleytun: Barton-on-Humber; the element 'bar' derives from Old English *bere* (barley).

Beor: beer.

Blai: no violence or use of weapons, used in times of assembly or truce.

Botmenei: Bodmin, 'The House of the Monks'.

Bretwalda: a word of uncertain meaning used of an especially powerful Saxon king. Perhaps 'Britain ruler'.

Briugu: 'host' in Irish, individual who owns a hostel and serves and puts up travellers at his expense and who is classed among the *Aes Dana*.

Brycheiniog: Brecon in southern Wales.

Calleva: Silchester.

Cambria: Latin name for Wales.

Camulodunum: Colchester.

Cant: Kent.

Cantref: British-Celtic administrative unit, into which most British-Celtic kingdoms were divided.

Cantwaraburg: Canterbury.

Cantware: the men of Kent.

Cantwine: men of Kent.

Catraeth: probably modern Catterick in North Yorkshire.

Cell Dara: Kildare in Ireland.

Cenedl: clan or extended family in Middle Welsh.

Civitas (civitates plural): 'county', the basic unit of territory in the Roman administration, each with its own council and government.

Coiced: 'fifth' in Irish, term used for 'province' of which there were five: Leinster, Munster, Meath, Ulster and Connaught.

Corinium: Circencester

Corn Gafallt: hill near Rhayader in central Wales with several pre-historic cairns dotted around its shoulders. Often the medieval inhabitants of Britain and Ireland explained prehistoric tombs and monuments through legend.

Cracca: British-Celtic word for the lyre.

Croagh Patrick: mountain in County Mayo where St Patrick is said to have fasted against God.

Cumal: 'pound' or 'dollar', the main unit of Irish currency, actually meaning a female slave.

Cumbrogi: the British Celts' own name for themselves, meaning 'men of the border' or 'fellow citizens'.

Curragh: boat with a wickerwork structure, covered in leather.

Dal Riada: an Ulster people who by the sixth century had taken control of much of the north of the Irish Sea and above all the Inner Hebrides and Argyll.

Deira: the Saxons that later became one half of the kingdom of Northumbria.

Demetia: Dyfed in Latin.

Din Etin: a northern fortress, probably modern Edinburgh.

Dinas Emrys: hill fort on the southern edge of Snowdonia that marked one of the main paths through the range.

Doruvernia: Latinised British-Celtic name for Canterbury.

Draca: dragon

Dumnonia: the south-western peninsula of Britain, including modern Devon and Cornwall.

Dunadd: capital of the British Dal Riada, a stronghold on the Argyll Peninsula.

Ealu: ale.

Eboracum *see* Eoforwic

Eccles: place names, indicating British-Celtic settlement, based on Latin *ecclesia* (church).

Eg: island.

Elmet: British-Celtic kingdom in the south Pennines.

Emain Macha: Navan Fort, a few miles to the west of Armagh in County Armagh.

Eoforwic: Saxon name for York. (York arrived only later, the result of Viking mispronunciation of the Saxon mispronunciation of the original Latin name Eboracum.)

Eoganachta: chief people of Munster in south-western Ireland.

Eorl: lord.

Ercing: Archenfield in Herefordshire.

Eryri: Snowdonia in Middle Welsh.

Etin: Edinburgh.

Fenian: groups of young hoodlums, who work their way through the Irish countryside hunting and robbing.

Fidach: Pictish province, today Moray.

Fidchell: Irish board game.

Fide: Pictish province in what is today Fife.

Ford of the Oxen: Oxford.

Fortress of the Bulls: Burghead near Inverness; archaeologists have found many Pictish designs of bulls at this sight, suggesting a bull cult.

Fortress of Loile: Carlisle.

Fortress of War: South Cadbury, hill fort in Somerset; *cad* in British Celtic means war.

Galanas: the Middle Welsh word both for feud resulting from death and the resulting payment to satisfy the family of the deceased.

Garmani: Bede in his *Ecclesiastical History*, 5, 9 tells us that this was the name that the British Celts used to describe the Saxons. The word is clearly related to our word 'German'.

Gaul: Latin word for France.

Geis: restriction or taboo in Irish preventing an individual from a certain course of action.

Godmunddingaham: Goodmanham.

Gronte: Cambridge.

Hafren: the River Severn.

Hearp: harp.

Helmingham: lost place name in Norfolk.

Hill of the Dead: Spong Hill, one of the largest cremation cemeteries in Britain.

Hill of the Temple of Bacchus: Maiden Castle in Dorset. The name is based on the presence of a pagan shrine there, possibly to Bacchus.

Hoo: Sutton Hoo in Suffolk.

Hot Waters: Bath.

Isca: Exeter, Roman capital of the Dumnonians.

Isles of the Sheep: the Shetlands and the Faeroes.

Land of the Cats: Caithness.

Lindsey: Lincolnshire.

Lindum: Lincoln.

Little Pigs: the Orkneys, likely Celtic etymology of the Orcades as they were called in Latin.

Loidis: Leeds.

Londinium: London in Latin.

Luminous House: The White House (a church dedicated to St Martin) in Whithorn (Galloway) named for its white stone.

Lys **(Cornish) or** *llys* **(Welsh):** court in British Celtic. Head court is the *penlys*.

Maccuil: Maughold on the Isle of Man.

Manu: the Isle of Man.

Med: mead, preferred drink of sixth-century British-Celtic warriors, sweet with a bitter aftertaste.

Metcauld: Lindisfarne in British Celtic.

Mon: the Welsh name for Anglesey.

Oenach: Irish assembly held once yearly in the *tuath*.

Ogam: Irish writing system where letters are represented by horizontal strokes down an edge of stone or wood.

Orcades *see* Little Pigs

Pen: head in Welsh.

Peninsula of the Men of Leinster: the Lleyn Peninsula in Gwynedd.

Penlys see *Lys*

Pett: Pictish word meaning 'piece', perhaps predominantly 'piece of land'.

Pictae ships: Vegetius, a late Roman writer, discusses these ships, the sails of which are dyed green to blend in with the sea, that are used to attack pirates.

Pyro's Isle: the island of Caldey off the southern coast of Wales.

Pyro was the sixth-century monk who founded a monastery there.

Rath: stronghold in Irish.

Reget: a British-Celtic kingdom of the north, location unknown, sometimes, though uncertainly, associated with Cumbria.

Rosy Valley: Glyn Rhosyn.

Runes: ancient Germanic symbols used for writing and magic.

Sarhaed: 'insult' in Middle Welsh legal terminology and the compensation price fixed for this insult.

Scop: bard. The word means literally and suggestively 'one who shapes'.

Scythia: Scandinavia, though also some confusion with Scythia in Asia.

Seax: the Saxons' characteristic weapon, for which they were named: a kind of machete.

Sid: Irish word for the fairy people who dwelt under the hills and mounds of that land.

Sillina: antique name for the Scilly Isles. Note that at this date the archipelago was, in fact, a single island. Only in subsequent centuries did the sea create the chain of islands that we know today.

Silura: ancient name of Lundy.

Strong Port: Portchester, (Hampshire).

Syrians: some western Europeans referred to easterners of whatever nationality in this way in the sixth century.

Tanatos: Isle of Thanet in Kent, a real island in this period.

Tara: Tara, County Meath in Ireland.

Tenby of the Fishes: modern Tenby in southern Wales, 'of the Fishes' to distinguish it from another Tenby in the north.

Thule: Iceland.

Thyrs: a goblin beast.

Tref: settlement in Middle Welsh.

Tuath: tribe or kingdom in Irish.

Ulaid: the Men of Ulster.

Usa: the River Ouse.

Vale of Citheinn: unidentified site on Anglesey.

Valley of Broom: Bramdean, Hampshire.

Vectis: the Isle of Wight.

Verulamium: St Albans.

Vintancaestir: Winchester.

Viriconium: Wroxeter.

Wealh: 'slave' or 'British Celt'. From this word derive Wales and Cornwall.

Wergild: In Saxon 'man-gold', the amount each man or woman's life was valued at for legal purposes.

Win: Wine.

INDEX